My Childhood

MAXIM GORKY

SANAGE PUBLISHING HOUSE

Paperback: 978-939131621-1

Any references to historical events, real people, or real places are used fictitiously. Names, characters, and places are products of the author's imagination.

Printed by:

Sanage Publishing House LLP
Mumbai, India

sanagepublishing@gmail.com

Maxim Gorky was born Alexei Maximovich Peshkov in 1868. He spent his youth as a nomadic labourer. In 1898 his collection of Stories and Sketches was published and proved an immediate success. His plays include The Lower Depths (1902), Summerfolk (1904), Children of the Sun (1905), Barbarians and Enemies (1906) and Yegor Bulichev (1932). His other books include Childhood and My Universities and the novel The Mother. A socialist from his early days, he never joined the Communist Party. He offered qualified support to the Soviet state after 1918, living abroad from 1924 to 1932. In 1934 he became head of the Writers' Union but his work showed an increasing awareness that something had gone wrong with the revolution.

CONTENTS

I

On the floor beneath the window of a small, dusky room lay my father, remarkably long and all dressed in white; the toes of his bare feet were strangely widespread, and the fingers of his gentle hands, now quietly crossed on his breast, were likewise distorted. The dark discs of copper coins closed his laughing eyes, his kind face had become livid, and I was terrified by the glint of his set teeth.

My mother, in a red skirt but little else, was kneeling beside him, combing back his soft hair with the black comb I had used as a saw to cut through the rind of watermelons. She kept muttering something in a deep, hoarse voice; her grey eyes were swollen and seemed melting into large tears.

My hand was being held by my grandmother—a roundish woman with a large head, enormous eyes, and a funny, fleshy nose. She was all soft and dark and fascinating. She too was weeping, but in a peculiar way that formed a pleasant accompaniment to my mother. She trembled all over and kept pushing me towards my father, but I hung back, hiding behind her skirts. I was afraid and uncomfortable.

I had never before seen grownups cry and did not understand the words my grandmother kept saying to me:

"Go take your leave of your daddy. You'll never see him again. He's died, my darling, before his time, before his hour...."

I had just recovered from a serious illness, during which my father—I remember that very well—had come and played with me merrily. But suddenly he disappeared and his place was taken by this strange woman who was my grandmother.

"Did you have to walk far to get here?" asked her.

"I didn't walk, I rode. You don't walk on the water, you fig," she answered. "I came down from the Lower,* higher up."

---

* The Lower" is the English translation "of "Nizhni" -short form of "Nizhni-Novgorod." -*Trans.*

This sounded very funny and mixed up: higher up in our house lived some bearded, painted Persians, while in the cellar lived an old yellow-skinned Kalmyk who sold sheepskins. You could descend by sliding down the banister, or by somersaulting if you fell off—I knew this well enough. But where did the water come in? She was all wrong and crazily mixed up.

"Why do you call me a fig?"

"Because you're so big," was her laughing retort.

She had a kind, bright, lilting manner of speech. From the very first day she and I became great friends, and now 1 was anxious that we both get out of this room.

My mother upset me. Her tears and wailing filled me with unwonted alarms. I had never seen her like this before: ordinarily she was a stern woman, who wasted no words. She was clean and smooth and large as a mare; she had a firm body and exceedingly strong hands. But now she was unpleasantly swollen and dishevelled. Her clothes were torn, and her hair, usually piled into such a neat, bright cap on top of her head, was flowing over her bare shoulders and into her eyes, with one braid swinging into my father's sleeping face. I had been standing in the room for some time, but not once had she so much as glanced at me, absorbed as she was in combing my father's hair and weeping.

The soldier who was on duty glanced into the room, along with some dark-faced muzhiks.

"Hurry and lay him out," cried the soldier irritably.

The window was hung with a dark shawl which blew out like a sail. Once when my father had taken me for a ride in a sailboat there had come an unexpected crash of thunder. My father had laughed, pressed me between his knees, and cried:

"That's all right, don't be afraid, son!"

Suddenly my mother sprang up heavily, then fell on her back, her hair streaming over the floor, her sightless face livid, her teeth clenched like those of my father.

"Lock the door—take Alexei out," she gasped in an awful voice.

My grandmother pushed me aside as she rushed toward the door.

"Don't be afraid, good people,!" she cried. "Don't touch her! Go away, for the love of Christ! It's not the cholera! It's the birth pains beginning! Take pity, good people!"

I hid behind a trunk in a dark corner, from where I could watch my mother writhing on the floor, moaning and grinding her teeth, while my grandmother crawled about, murmuring tenderly and happily:

"In the name of the Father and the Son! Try to bear it, Varyusha!* Holy Mother of God, merciful patron. . . ."

I was terrified. They kept moving about on the floor near my father, groaning and crying and bumping into him, but he lay there motionless, seeming to laugh at them. This kept up for a long time. Several times my mother struggled to her feet, only to fall back again; my grandmother bounced in and out of the room like a great black ball; suddenly a baby cried in the darkness.

"Thank God," breathed my grandmother. "A boy!"

She lighted a candle.

I must have fallen asleep in the corner, for I remember nothing else.

My next vivid recollection is of a deserter spot in a cemetery on a rainy day; I was standing on a slippery mound of earth gazing down the hole into which they were lowering my father's coffin. The bottom of the hole was filled with water and frogs— two of them had jumped onto the yellow lid of the coffin.

The only people at the grave were the dripping guard on duty, two grumpy muzhiks with spades, my grandmother and I. All of us were bathed in a fine spray of rain.

"Dig it in," said the guard, moving away.

My grandmother wept, covering her face with the ends of her shawl. The muzhiks bent over and threw the first spadefuls of dirt into the hole. The water splashed and the frogs began to leap against the walls of the grave, but the clumps of earth beat them back.

---

* The suffixes -sha, -yusha, -oshka, -ochka, added to proper names, convey a feeling of intimacy and affection, e.g., Varya—Varyusha, Alexei—Alyosha.— Trans.

"Get away, Alyosha," said my grandmother, taking me by the shoulder. I slipped out of her grasp, because I did not want to go away.

"Oh Lord," she sighed, in a tone which left some doubt as to whether she was complaining about me or the Lord. For a long time she stood there silent, with lowered head; even when the grave was entirely filled in she kept on standing there.

The muzhiks packed the earth with the backs of their spades; a wind rose and drove the rain away. Grandmother took me by thehand and led me to a distant church standing among a forest of dark crosses.

"Why don't you cry?" she asked me when we were outside the cemetery. "You ought to cry."

"I don't feel like it," I said.

"Well, if you don't feel like it, you needn't," she answered quietly.

It was most surprising that she should have told me to cry. I rarely cried, and then only when my feelings were hurt—never from bodily pain. My father had always laughed at my tears, but my mother had shouted:

"Don't dare cry!"

After that we rode in a droshky down a wide, muddy street between dark red houses.

"Won't the frogs get out?" I asked.

"No they won't, God bless them," she answered."

Neither my mother nor father had ever spoken the name of God so frequently and with such familiarity.

A few days later my mother and grandmother and I were riding in the small cabin of a boat. My infant brother Maxim had died and was lying on the table in the corner wrapped in white tied with red tape.

1 sat on top of our trunks and bundles, looking out of the bulging window that reminded me of the eye of a horse. Murky, foaming water kept running down the glass. Sometimes it would wash completely over it. Then I would involuntarily jump down to the floor.

"Don't be afraid," said my grandmother, lifting me up in her soft arms and putting me back on the bundles.

A moist grey fog hung over the water; every once in a while a dark strip of land somewhere in the distance would emerge from the fog, only to dissolve again. Everything about us was shaking. Only my mother stood firm and motionless, leaning against the wall with her hands behind her head, her eyes tightly closed. Her face was dark and grim and sightless. She never spoke a word, and seemed somehow new and different. Even the dress she was wearing was unfamiliar to me.

Every once in a while my grandmother would say to her softly:

"If you'd only be having a bite to eat, Varyusha—just a wee bite . . ."

But my mother remained silent and motionless.

Grandmother spoke to me in a whisper; she spoke a bit louder to my mother, but timidly and cautiously, and very rarely. It seemed to me that she was afraid of my mother. I could understand this, and it drew me all the closer to my grandmother.

"Saratov," said my mother in an unexpectedly loud, harsh voice. "Where's the sailor?"

Even her words were strange and unfamiliar—"Saratov," "the sailor"....

Into the cabin came a broad-shouldered, grey-haired man dressed in blue and carrying a little box. Grandmother took it from him and began to place the body of my brother in it. When she had finished she carried it to the door on outstretched arms, but she was so fat she could not get through without turning sidewise, so she stood there nonplussed, looking very funny.

"Oh, mother!" cried my own mother impatiently, taking the coffin out of her hands. Then they both disappeared and I remained in the cabin with the man in blue.

"So your brother's gone and left us," he said, bending over me.

"Who are you?"

"A sailor."

"And who's Saratov?"

"A city. Look out the window. There it is."

The land was moving past the window, dark and lumpy and wreathed in mist, reminding me of a large hunk of bread just cut from the loaf.

"Where did grandmother go?"

"To bury her grandson."

"Will they put him in the ground?"

"Of course they will."

I told the sailor how they had dug in live frogs when they buried my father. He lifted me in his arms, hugged me tight and kissed me.

"Ah, sonny, it's not much you understand yet!" he said. "It's not the frogs are to be pitied—the devil with them—it's your mother. Just look what grief's done to her!"

There was suddenly a great shrieking and blowing-up above, but I knew it was the steamboat and was not afraid. The sailor put me down hurriedly and rushed out, saying as he went:

"Have to be off!"

I also wanted to *be* off. I went out of the cabin. There was nobody in the dark, narrow passage. Not far from the door I could see the glitter of brass on the stairs. I looked up and caught sight of people with baggage and bundles in their hands. It was clear that everyone was leaving the boat, which meant that I too must leave.

But when I reached the deck in the midst of all the muzhiks at the gangplank, people began shouting at me:

"Who are you? Who do you belong to?"

"I don't know."

For a long time they pushed me and shoved me and felt me. At last the grey-haired sailor appeared and said:

"He's from Astrakhan—came put of his cabin,. . . ."

He picked me up and ran back to the cabin, where he put me up on the bundles and shook his finger at me.

"I'll give it to you!" he threatened as he went out.

Gradually the bustle overhead quieted down, the steamer stopped trembling, the splashing of the water ceased. A wet wall blocked the window of the cabin; it became dark and stuffy, and the bundles seemed to swell up and crowd me out. What if they left me here on this empty steamer for good?

I went to the door. It was shut tight and I was unable to turn the brass knob. I took a bottle of milk and swung it at the knob with all my force. The bottle smashed and the milk flowed over my feet and into my boots.

Crushed by my failure, I lay down on the bundles aad cried myself to sleep.

When I woke up the steamer was once more trembling, the water splashing, and the window of the cabin was shining like the sun. My grandmother was sitting beside me combing her hair and frowning as she muttered something to herself. She had an amazing quantity of blue-black hair which fell thickly over her shoulders, breast and knees, sweeping down to the floor. With one hand she lifted it off the floor and held it tight, while with the other she forced a coarse wooden comb through the heavy strands; her mouth was I screwed up, her dark eyes flashed with anger, and her face looked little and amusing in that mass of hair.

She seemed in a bad mood today, but when I asked her why she had such long hair, her voice was as soft and friendly as it had been the day before.

"Most likely a visitation from the Lord— 'Here, spend your days combing this accursed mane!' In my youth I vaunted it; in my age I curse it. But get back to sleep, child. It's early yet—the sun's scarce up."

"I don't want to sleep any more."

"Well don't, if you're not wanting to," she agreed, braiding her hair and glancing at the couch where my mother lay on her back straight as an arrow. "How did you be breaking that bottle yesterday? Speak soft."

She had a peculiar way of singing her words that made it easy for me to remember them—words as vivid and luscious as flowers. When she smiled, the irises of her dark eyes expanded and shone with an inexpressible light; her smile revealed strong white teeth, and in spite of the numerous wrinkles on her swarthy cheeks, her whole face seemed young and bright. It was spoiled only by her fleshy, red-tipped nose with its flaring nostrils. She took snuff from a black, silver-embossed box. Everything about her was dark, but through her eyes one glimpsed the warm, cheerful, unquenchable light which illumined her from within. She was stout, and so bent as to be almost hunchbacked, but she moved about with the ease and agility of a large cat. And she was just as soft as that affectionate animal.

It seemed that until her arrival I had been sleeping, hidden away in the darkness. But she came and woke me up and led me out into the light. She spun all my surroundings into a single, unbroken thread, then wove it into multicoloured lace; she immediately became my friend for life, the one who was nearest and dearest to me, and the one I most understood. Her selfless love of life enriched me and gave me the strength to cope with my hard future.

Steamboats moved slowly forty years ago. It took us a long time to reach Nizhni-Novgorod, and I well remember those first days, drenched with beauty.

The weather was fine, and from morning to night I was up on deck with my grandmother, floating there beneath the bright sky, between the banks of the Volga embroidered with the golden silk of autumn. The rust-coloured boat with a barge in tow moved lazily against the current, nosing its way with a gentle slapping of paddles through the grey-blue water. The barge was grey and resembled a water bug. The sun stole imperceptibly above the Volga; every hour brought something new—everything about us changed. The green hills were folds in the rich raiment of the earth. Towns and villages seemed made of gingerbread as they passed in the distance; golden autumn leaves floated on the water.

"Just see how wonderful it is!" my grandmother kept exclaiming as she moved from one side of the deck to the other, her face radiant, her eyes dilated with joy.

Often she would stand looking at the shore quite oblivious of my presence, her hands crossed on her breast, her lips curved in a smile, her eyes filled with tears. Then I would tug at her dark, flowered skirt.

"Eh?" she would say, pulling herself together. "Like as if I was asleep and having a dream."

"What are you crying about?"

"That's from happiness, my lad, from feebleness, my darling," she would say with a smile. "It's an old one I am now, with more than threescore summers behind…"

Then she would take a pinch of snuff and begin to tell me fantastic stories about saints and animals and kind robbers and dark powers.

She told her tales in a quiet, mysterious voice, her face close to mine, gazing into my eyes with dilated pupils as though she were pouring into my heart a stream of strength to support me. She sang rather than spoke, and the further she went, the more rhythmic became her style. It was an inexpressible joy to listen to her, and when she had finished a tale I would cry:

"Go on!"

"And then it was like this: under the stove sat the hearth goblin, a splinter of noodle in his paw. Rocking he sat, and moaning: 'Oh, little mice, little mice! Oh, I shall die, little mice!' "

She grabbed up her own foot and sat rocking back and forth with her face all screwed up as though she were the sufferer.

Sailors gathered round—good-natured, bearded men— and they laughed as they listened, and praised her and also asked for more.

"Go on, granny, tell us another!"

And then they would say:

"Come along and have supper with us."

At supper they would treat her to vodka and me to watermelon and cantaloupe; that was all done on the sly, for there was a man on board who forbade the eating of fruit. If he caught anyone with fruit he would grab it away and toss it into the river. He was dressed like a guard, with brass buttons down his uniform, and was always drunk. People hid from him.

My mother rarely came up on deck and in general avoided us. She remained as silent as ever. To this day I remember her tall, handsome figure, her grim, dark face crowned by fair braids—all of her powerfulness and her hardness, seen as though through a fog or a bright cloud. And across the years comes the unfriendly gleam of her grey eyes, as enormous as those of my grandmother.

One day she said sternly:

"You make a laughingstock of yourself, ma."

"Let the folks be laughing, if they like," replied my grandmother good-naturedly. "It's a world of good it'll be doing them!"

I remember my grandmother's childlike joy on catching sight of Nizhni. "Look, look how fine it is!" she cried as she grabbed me by the hand and pushed me toward the rail. "There's your Nizhni for you! What a beauty! Look at the domes of the churches—as if they was flying!" She turned to my mother almost in tears. "Take a look, Varyusha! You've most forgot it, I reckon. Drink in the joy of it!"

Mother smiled gloomily.

The steamer came to a halt opposite the lovely city. It stopped in the middle of the river, which was crowded with ships and bristling with hundreds of masts. A large boat filled with people approached our steamer and hooked on to the lowered gangplank, up which the people climbed to our deck. At the head of them rushed a lean little old man in a long black coat. He had green eyes, a hooked nose, and a beard red as gold.

"Father!" called my mother in a loud voice, throwing herself into his arms. He seized her head in his little red hands and began stroking her cheeks and squealing excitedly:

"Eh, eh, you silly! Ha! So here you are! Ah-h, tck, tck, tck!"

Grandmother hugged and kissed everybody all at once, whirling about like a propeller.

"Here, quick," she said, pushing me toward the people. "This is Uncle Mikhailo; this is Yakov; here's Aunt Natalya; and these boys are cousins—both named Sasha; and cousin Katerina; all our tribe—just look how many!"

"How are you, mother?" my grandfather asked her.

They kissed each other three times.

Then my grandfather snatched me out of the crowd and said, with his hand on my head:

"And who might you be?"

"I'm from Astrakhan, out of the cabin."

"What's that he's saying?" asked my grandfather, turning to my mother. But then he pushed me along without waiting for an answer. "Got his father's cheekbones," he observed. "Get down into the boat."

We rode to shore and climbed up the cobbled road between two high embankments covered with yellow, trampled grass.

My grandfather walked up ahead with my mother. He came only to her shoulder and took quick little steps, while she glanced down on him from above and seemed to float through the air. Behind them walked my uncles without speaking: Mikhail, with black, straight hair and a body as thin as my grandfather's; Yakov, with blond, curly hair. Then came some fat women in bright-coloured dresses, and about six children, all of them older than me and very quiet. I walked with my grandmother and little Aunt Natalya. She was pale and blue-eyed and had an enormous belly. Every once in a while she would stop to catch her breath and murmur:

"Oh, I can't go another step."

"Why did they have to bring you along?" muttered my grandmother angrily. "A stupid tribe!"

I did not like either the children or the grownups and felt like a stranger among them. Even my grandmother seemed to have faded and become distant.

I especially disliked my grandfather, immediately sensing an enemy. He roused in me a wary curiosity, and I paid him particular attention.

We reached the end of the climb. Built against the right embankment at the very top stood a low, one-storied house from which the street took its beginning. It was painted a dirty pink and had bulging windows with the roof pulled down low over them. It seemed large when I viewed it from outside, but inside the rooms were little and dark and crowded. Irritable people kept milling through them, like on the steamer just before docking; children flocked about like thievish sparrows, and the entire house was permeated with an acrid, unfamiliar odour.

I found myself out in the yard, which was no more pleasant. Vats filled with thick, coloured water stood about everywhere, while huge cloths were strung up on lines to dry. From a low, ramshackle shed in one corner came the glow of a wood fire in a stove; something was boiling and bubbling and an invisible person was pronouncing strange words in a loud voice:

"Santalin—magenta—sulphuric acid. . . ."

II

This was the beginning of a swift, eventful, and inexpressibly strange life. I remember it like a sombre tale told by a good genius who was yet painfully realistic. Now, as I recall the past, I sometimes have difficulty in believing that it was really like that; I am inclined to refute and protest many of the facts, so dark and cruel was the life of this "stupid tribe."

But the truth is beyond all commiseration, and it is not about myself I am writing, but about the stifling and horrifying surroundings in which the ordinary Russian lived and still lives.

My grandfather's house was filled with hot vapours of hostility—the hostility of each toward all. The older people were completely poisoned by it, and even the children were contaminated. Later I learned from my grandmother's stories that my mother had arrived just at a time when her brothers were demanding that their father divide his property among them. The unexpected return of my mother made this demand more urgent. They were afraid she would ask for the dowry which my grandfather had withheld because she had married "self-willed," without his approval. My uncles claimed that this dowry should be divided between them. For some time they had been carrying on a bitter argument as to which of them should open up a shop in the city, and which in the settlement of Kunavino, on the other side of the Oka River.

Soon after our arrival a quarrel broke out in the kitchen while we were having dinner. My uncles suddenly jumped up and leaned across the table, yelling and shouting in my grandfather's face, baring their teeth and shaking themselves like dogs. My grandfather struck the table with his spoon, turned red in the face, and shrieked hoarsely:

"I'll turn you out to beg in the streets!"

With a painful grimace, my grandmother said:

"Give them everything, father. Go ahead and give it them, and have some peace."

"Tut, you conniver!" he cried with flashing eyes. It seemed strange that anyone as small as he could shout so deafeningly.

My mother rose and walked slowly to the window, where she stood with her back to all of them.

Suddenly Uncle Mikhail gave his brother a smashing blow in the face. The latter let out a howl, grabbed his brother, and the two of them went rolling across the floor, panting and grunting and swearing.

The children began to cry; my pregnant Aunt Natalya let out a despairing wail; mother seized her in both arms and led her away; Yevgenia, the jolly, pock-marked nanny, chased the children out of the kitchen; chairs crashed; apprentice Tsiganok straddled Uncle Mikhail's back, while Grigori Ivanovich, a mangy, bearded master-workman in dark; glasses, calmly tied his hands with a towel.

My uncle scraped his thin black beard across the floor and let out horrible hoarse sounds.

"Brothers, ha! Blood brothers' Phooh, what people!" cried my grandfather as he ran around the table.

At the very beginning of the argument I had been frightened up onto the stove, from where I watched my grandmother wash the blood from Uncle Yakov's battered face. He wept and stamped his feet, while she said despairingly:

"Come to your senses, you accursed ones! What a wild tribe!"

My grandfather shouted at her as he pulled at his torn shirt:

"So these are the brutes you brought into the world, you old witch!"

When Uncle Yakoy went out, she cowered into a corner.

"Holy Mother of God," she wailed, "please do give my children some sense!"

My grandfather stood with his eyes glued to the table where everything was spilled and overturned.

"Better keep your eye on those sons of yours, mother," he said quietly, "or they'll be doing away with Varvara. . . ."

"God knows what you're saying! Here, take off your shirt so's I can be mending it." She took his face in her hands and kissed him on the forehead, while he, so much shorter, buried his head on her shoulder.

"Looks like I better divide up, mother."

"Yes, father."

They spoke together for a long time. At first their conversation was amiable, but soon grandfather began pawing the floor like a cock before a fight and shaking his finger at my grandmother.

"I know you all right; you think more of them than you do of me," he complained in a loud whisper. "But that Mikhail of yours is a hypocrite, and that Yakov an infidel! They'll squander all I own—they'll swill it all down!"

With a clumsy movement of my shoulder, I knocked down a flatiron which went clattering off the stove and landed in the slop bucket. My grandfather sprang up, yanked me towards him, and stared into my face as though he were seeing me for the first time.

"Who put you up there on the stove? Your mother?"

"I climbed up myself."

"You're lying."

"No I'm not. I was scared."

He pushed me and gave me a whack over the forehead.

"The image of your father! Get out!"

I was only too glad to get out of that kitchen.

I could see very well that my grandfather kept following me with his sharp green eyes, and I was afraid of him. I remember that I was always trying to hide from those searing eyes. It seemed to me that he was mean; he addressed everyone in a tone that was offensive and sarcastic, taking delight in teasing and provoking people.

"Phooh, what people!" he was fond of saying, and the sound of that long-drawn-out "oo" always made me feel chilled and forlorn.

During the tea hour in the evening, when my grandfather and uncles and the workmen left the shop and came wearily into the kitchen, their hands stained with dye and raw with acid, their hair tied back with tape, making them resemble the dark icons in the corner of the kitchen—during that dangerous hour my grandfather sat opposite me and made his other grandchildren envious by speaking to me more often than to them. There was something very right about him, very smooth and neatly chiselled. In spite of the fact that his embroidered satin vest was old and worn, his cotton shirt wrinkled, his pants patched at the knees, he gave the impression of being cleaner, better dressed and better looking than his sons, who wore suit coats, starched cuffs, and silk neckerchiefs.

A few days after our arrival he set me to learning my prayers. All the other children were older and had already been taught to read and write by the deacon of the Uspen-sky Cathedral, a church whose golden domes could be seen from the windows of our house.

I was taught by my quiet, timorous Aunt Natalya, who had the face of a child and such transparent eyes that it seemed possible to look straight through them to the back of her head.

I loved to sit and stare at her without blinking. This made her uneasy, and she would narrow her eyes, twist her head, and ask in a voice that was almost a whisper:

"Do say this, please, 'Our father who art....'"

"What does it mean, 'who art'?"

"Don't ask," she would reply, glancing furtively about. "It only makes it worse if you ask. Simply repeat after me, 'Our father. .. .' Well?"

I Could not understand why asking would only make it worse. The words "who art" took on a secret meaning, and I purposely distorted them:

"Who heart," "Whose heart. . . ."

But my white-faced aunt, who seemed to be slowly melting away, would patiently correct me.

"No, just say it simply, like this—'who art. . . .' '

But neither she herself nor the words she spoke were simple. This annoyed me and made it difficult to remember the prayer.

One day my grandfather checked up on my activities.

"Well, Alexei," he said. "What you been doing today? Playing? See that from the lump on your forehead. Don't have to be very smart to get a lump on your forehead, but what about learning 'Our Father'?"

"He has a bad memory," whispered my aunt.

My grandfather laughed and raised his red eyebrows.

"If that's the case, have to give him a licking. Your father ever lick you?" he asked, turning to me.

I did not understand what he was talking about, so I remained silent.

"Maxim never beat the child and forbade me to," answered my mother.

"How's that?"

"He said that beatings never taught anybody anything."

"He was a fool, that Maxim, may his soul rest in peace!" answered my grandfather testily.

His words offended me, and he noticed this.

"What you pouting about? Better watch your step! Sasha's going to get a nice little ripping up on Saturday on account of that thimble," he said, smoothing back his red and silver hair.

"How will you do it?" I asked.

Everybody laughed, and my grandfather replied:

"Just wait and you'll find out."

I hid in the corner and began to figure it out: to rip meant to take apart the clothes brought to be dyed, but to lick and to beat apparently meant the same thing. People beat horses and dogs and cats, and in Astrakhan the soldiers beat the Persians—I had seen that with my own eyes. But I had never seen anyone beat little children. To be sure, my uncles sometimes gave their children a whack over the forehead or the back of the head, but the victims seemed not to mind, simply rubbing the sore spot a bit and then forgetting it. Sometimes I would ask them if it hurt.

"Not the least little," they would answer bravely.

I knew about the famous incident with the thimble. Between teatime and supper, my uncles and the master-workman would sew together pieces of dyed cloth into one length and attach the cardboard tags. As a joke on the half-blind Grigori, Uncle Mikhail told his nine-year-old nephew to heat the workman's thimble over the candle. Sasha held the thimble over the flame with a pair of tongs until it was red hot, then he placed it near Grigori and hid behind the stove. But at that moment my grandfather came in, sat down to work, and picked up the hot thimble.

I remember running into the kitchen to see what all the noise was about and finding my grandfather jumping comically about, holding his ear with his burnt fingers and shouting:

"Who did this, you harum-scarums?"

Uncle Mikhail was bending over the table pushing the thimble about with his finger and blowing on it; Grigori was sewing imperturbably, the shadows licking across his huge bald pate; Uncle Yakov came running in and slipped behind the stove to hide his laughter; my grandmother began to grate a raw potato for a poultice.

"It's Yakov's Sasha did it," said Uncle Mikhail all of a sudden.

"That's a lie," cried Yakov, jumping out from behind the stove.

From somewhere in the corner his son began to bawl.

"Don't believe him, papa!" he called. "He told me to do it!"

My uncles began to quarrel. Immediately my grandfather calmed down, placed the poultice on his finger, and went out without a word, taking me with him.

Everyone said that Uncle Mikhail was to blame. It was only natural that during tea I should ask if he was to be ripped and beaten.

"He ought to be," muttered my grandfather, glancing askance at me.

Uncle Mikhail pounded the table with his hand and shouted at my mother:

"If you don't take that puppy of yours in hand, Varvara, I'll screw his head off!"

"You just try laying a finger on him!" answered my mother.

Everyone was silent.

She had the knack of throwing people back with a few short words that were utterly squelching.

I could see that everyone was afraid of my mother; even my grandfather addressed her in a different tone—quieter than the one he used with others. This pleased me.

"My mother's the strongest of all!" I would boast to my cousins.

They never denied it.

But what happened on the next Saturday shook my opinion of my mother.

By Saturday I too had managed to get into trouble.

I was fascinated by the way the grownups changed the colour of cloth. They would take something yellow, dip it in black water, and the material would come out dark blue—"indigo." Or they would rinse something grey in reddish water and it would come out dark red—"mulberry." All very simple, but incomprehensible.

I nursed a secret longing to try my hand at dyeing, and I confided this to Yakov's Sasha, a polite, serious boy who was always trailing the grownups, offering them his services. Everyone but my grandfather praised him for being smart and obliging.

"Phooh, the little toady!" the old man would say, glancing contemptuously at the boy.

Yakov's Sasha was dark and skinny, with bulging eyes, like a crab. He spoke in a hushed, hurried voice, half swallowing his words and glancing furtively about as though he were planning to run off and hide. Usually his brown eyes were immobile, but when he was excited the very eyeballs seemed to tremble.

I did not like him. I liked Mikhails Sasha much better, in spite of the fact that he was inconspicuous and something of a dolt. He was quiet and had his mother's sad eyes and winning smile. His teeth were very ugly—they protruded from his mouth and grew in a double row in his upper jaw. This kept him busy: he had his fingers constantly in his mouth trying to loosen and yank out the teeth in the back row; he meekly permitted anyone who wished to feel them. But I could find nothing else of interest about him. He was always alone in the overcrowded house, sitting off by himself in some dark corner or spending his evenings at the window. It was pleasant to say nothing when you were with him—to sit close beside him at the window and say nothing for a whole hour, watching the daws wheel and plane about the Uspensky Cathedral, whose golden domes stood out in fine relief against the red glow of the sunset. The birds would soar and plunge, then suddenly spread a black net across the fading sky and disappear, leaving a vast emptiness behind them. When you

watch something like this you have no desire to speak, for your
breast is full of an aching pleasure.

Uncle Yakov's Sasha, on the other hand, could speak at length
and impressively about anything, like a grownup. When he found
out that I was anxious to learn the dyeing trade, he advised me to
take the Sunday tablecloth out of the sideboard and dye it dark
blue.

"White things take the colour better than any others, I'm
sure of that," he said very seriously.

I dragged out the heavy tablecloth and ran into the yard with
it, but scarcely had I dipped one end of it into the vat containing
"indigo" when Tsiganok threw himself upon me, grabbed the
tablecloth out of my hands, wrung it in his enormous paws, and
shouted to my cousin who was watching from the shed:

"Run for your grandmother!"

He turned to me and shook his tousled head ominously.

"You'll get it for this all right," he said.

My grandmother hurried out. She gasped when she saw the
mischief, and even wept a few tears as she scolded me in her
funny way:

"Oh, you Permyak, you, with your cabbage ears! You ought
to get picked up and flopped down somewheres on the other
side!"

Then she began to plead with Tsiganok:

"Don't you be telling his grandfather, Vanya! I'll hide it away
and maybe it'll pass over somehow. ..."

"You needn't worry about me, but you better see that Sasha
don't go squealing," replied Vanya anxiously, wiping his wet
hands on his stained apron.

"I'll give him a coin to close his mouth," said my
grandmother as she led me into the house.

On Saturday, just before vespers, somebody took me into
the kitchen. It was dark and quiet there. I remember that the doors
into the entranceway and the other rooms were tightly closed,
that the autumn evening lurked grey and misty beyond the
windows where the rain was murmuring. On a bench in front of
the black mouth of the stove sat Tsiganok, unwontedly sullen;

my grandfather was standing at a tub in the corner pulling long birch wands out of the water, measuring them, stacking them together, and flicking them through the air with a great swish. My grandmother was standing somewhere in the shadow, loudly sniffing tobacco and muttering:

"Enjoys it, the brute. . . ."

Yakov's Sasha wàs sitting on a chair in the middle of the kitchen digging his fists into his eyes and wailing like an old beggarman:

"Forgive me, for the love of Christ. . . ."

Uncle Mikhail's Sasha and his sister stood behind the table, stiff as posts.

"I'll forgive you after you've had your deserts," answered my grandfather, running a long, wet wand through his fist. "Well, take down your pants."

He spoke calmly, and neither the sound of his voice, nor the movements of the boy on the squeaking chair, nor the shuffling of my grandmother's feet, violated the unforgettable silence of that shadowy kitchen beneath the low, smoke-grimed ceiling.

Sasha got up, unfastened his pants, dropped them to his knees, and stumbled toward the bench, all bent over. It was awful to watch him—my own knees started trembling.

But it was even worse when he meekly lay face down on the bench and Vanya tied him under the armpits and around the neck with a long towel, then bent over and held him by the ankles.

"Alexei!" called my grandfather. "Come closer! Well, who am I talking to? This is what is meant by a ripping—have a good look! One! . . ."

With a short swing of his arm he brought the wand down on Sasha's bare body. The boy yelped.

"Don't pretend," said my grandfather. "That didn't hurt! But this one will!"

He gave him a lash that immediately brought a flush to the skin and left a nasty red welt. My cousin gave a long howl.

"Don't like it?" asked my grandfather, rhythmically moving his arm up and down. "Not to your taste? Here's your thimble for you!"

Whenever he raised his arm something inside my breast was lifted along with it, and whenever he dropped his arm it was as if I too had fallen.

Sasha wailed in a high, thin voice that was horrid to hear.

"I won't do it again. Didn't I tell you about the tablecloth? It was me who told. ... ."

"Telling tales won't clear you. The tattle-tale gets the first lashing. Now it's your turn for the tablecloth!"

My grandmother threw herself at me and snatched me up.

"You'll not be touching Alexei! I'll not let you, you brute!"

She began to kick at the door.

"Varvara! Varvara!" she shouted.

My grandfather rushed over, knocked her off her feet, grabbed me and hauled me to the bench. I struggled in his arms, pulled his red beard, and bit his finger. He roared and squeezed me and finally threw me down on the bench so that I struck my face. I remember him crying wildly:

"Tie him down! I'll kill him!"

And I remember my mother's white face and her enormous eyes. She kept running back and forth in front of the bench.

"Stop it, father! Let him go!" she gasped.

My grandfather beat me until I lost consciousness. For several days after that I was ill and lay face down on a wide, hot bed in a little room with one window in it and a little red light which was kept constantly burning in the icon corner.

The days of my illness were important days of my life. During that time I seemed to suddenly grow older and develop a new quality—that of being deeply concerned about all people. It was as though the skin had been torn off my heart, making it unbearably sensitive to every injury, my own or another's.

First of all, I was shocked by the quarrel which took place between my mother and grandmother. In this tiny room my big, black grandmother swooped down upon my mother, forcing her into the icon corner and hissing:

"Why didn't you snatch him away, eh?"

"I was frightened."

"A big creature like you! For shame, Varvara! Old as I be, I had no fear! For very shame!"

"Leave me alone, ma! I'm sick of it!"

"You're not a-loving of him! Not a-pitying of the poor little orphan!"

"I'm an orphan myself—for all my life!" said my mother in a loud, pained voice.

Then they both began to cry, sitting on the trunk in the corner.

"If it wasn't for Alexei I'd go away—somewhere far away!" said my mother. "I can't go on living in this hell. I can't, ma! I haven't the strength!"

"Ah, child of my flesh, my own heart!" whispered my grandmother.

Now I knew: my mother was not strong after all; she, like all the others, was afraid of my grandfather. And I was responsible for keeping her here in this house where she could not bear to live. This thought was depressing. Actually my mother disappeared soon after that. She went visiting somewhere.

One day my grandfather came to see me, all of a sudden, as though he had dropped down from the ceiling. He sat on the edge of the bed and felt my head with fingers cold as ice.

"How do you do, young man. ... Go ahead and answer me— don't hold a grudge. Well, what?"

I felt like kicking him, but it hurt to move. His hair seemed redder than ever; he kept nodding his head uneasily while his bright eyes roved over the walls. Out of his pocket he took a gingerbread goat, two candy trumpets, an apple, and some raisins, and placed them on the pillow next to my nose.

"See, I've brought you some presents."

He bent down and kissed me on the forehead; then he began talking, stroking my forehead the while with his rough little hand stained a bright yellow, especially around his crooked, bird-like nails.

"Gave you a little more than your share this time, sonny. I was so mad—you bit me and scratched me and—well, I just lost my temper. But it's not so bad that you got an overdose this time— we'll count it to your credit next time. You just remember one

thing—when your own folks do the beating, it's no offence—
just a good lesson! But don't let others touch you—only your
own folks—they don't count. Think I didn't take my share in my
day? In your worst dreams you couldn't imagine the way they
beat me, Alyosha! They beat me so hard it must have made the
Lord God weep to watch them. And what came of it? Just look at
me now—me, the orphan, son of a beggarwoman—head of a
whole workshop, ordering people around."

He pressed toward me with his lean, well-built body, and
began to tell me about his childhood, skilfully piling his hard
words one on top of the other.

His green eyes flashed and his hair bristled with gold as he
trumpeted into my face:

"You came here on a steamer. The steam brought you here,
but when I was young it was my own strength I pitted against the
Volga, pulling the barges. The barge in the water—me on the
bank, barefoot, over the sharp stones and the boulders, keeping
it up from sunrise to nightfall, the sun streaming down till it made
your head feel like an iron pot with something boiling inside,
and you all bent over like a hairpin—your bones creaking—going
on and on, not seeing where, the sweat streaming into your eyes,
your heart moaning, your lips groaning—ah yes, Alyosha, you
have nothing to complain about! On and on you go until you fall
out of the harness, your face buried in the earth and you glad of
it, for at least it means the strength has passed clean out of you,
to the last drop. And there you lay 'til it's time to pass on or pass
out, and little difference it makes which. That's how we lived in
the eyes of God, in the eyes of our blessed Lord Christ Jesus! . .

Three times I measured the length of Mother Volga in such
wise: from Simbirsk to Rybinsk, from Saratov to here, and from
Astrakhan to Makaryev, to the fair—trails covering many
thousands of versts! But in the fourth year I was promoted to
bailer—the boss could see I was more, than the ordinary run!"

As he spoke, he seemed to grow before my eyes like a cloud,
changing from a lean little old man into a hero of fabulous
strength—one who singlehanded hauled a huge grey barge against
the current of the great river.

Sometimes he would jump off the bed and demonstrate how the *burlaks** walked in their harness and how they bailed out the water; he would sing unfamiliar songs in a bass voice, then once more spring youthfully back onto the bed, a wondrous creature who went on talking in a Voice which grew ever deeper and more convincing.

"But in spite of it all, Alexei, when we'd come to a halt on a summer's evening, in Zhiguli, and build a campfire at the foot of a green hill—oh, those were the times, Alexei! While the porridge was boiling, some *burlak* would start up a soulful song for his heart's ease, and the rest of us would join in—oh, but it'd make your very flesh creep to hear us, and the Volga herself seemed to gather speed, like a horse, rearing and charging to the very heavens! Then all our troubles were swept away like dust before the wind; in our singing we'd forget even the porridge until it went sizzling over into the fire, and then it was a beating over the head the cook would get—'have your song, but don't forget your job!' "

Several times people came to the door and called him, but I would always plead:

"Don't go yet!"

He would laugh and wave his hand.

"Let them wait," he would call.

He went on telling me tales until evening, and when he bid me an affectionate farewell and left, I knew that grandfather was neither mean nor terrifying. It was painful to remember that it was he who had beaten me so cruelly, yet I could not forget it.

My grandfather's visit opened the door to everyone else, and from morning to night someone was sitting at my bedside, trying in every way to amuse me. I remember that these attempts were not always successful. My grandmother came more often than anyone else; she even slept with me. But the one who left the deepest impression on my mind was Tsiganok. He came in the evening—a stocky, broad-shouldered fellow with a huge head covered with dark, curly hair. He was all dressed up in his Sunday

---

* Haulers of barges.—*Trans.*

clothes, consisting of a honey-coloured silk shirt, wide plush trousers, and squeaky boots that wrinkled about his ankles like an accordion. His hair shone, his slanting eyes flashed merrily from under heavy brows, his white teeth gleamed from under the black line of his young moustache, and his shirt glowed, softly reflecting the red light of the icon lamp.

"Take a look," he said, pulling up the sleeve of his shirt to reveal a network of red scars on his bare arm. "See how swollen it is? But it was even worse; they've almost healed.

"I could see your grandad was crazy with fury, like to beat you to death, so I put my arm under the whip in the hope it would break. Then your grandad would have to get a new one, giving your granny or your mother a chance to snatch you away. But it didn't break—too well soaked. But still I spared you some of the lashes—you can see for yourself how many. I'm a slick one, I am!"

He gave a soft, silky laugh.

"I felt so sorry for you I couldn't breathe," he added, glancing once more at his swollen arm. "I could see it would turn out bad, but there he kept on, swinging away. ..."

He snorted like a horse and tossed his head and began to pass remarks about my grandfather with a childlike simplicity that immediately won my sympathy.

I told him that I loved him very much, and he answered with this same unforgettable simplicity:

"I love you too. That's why I took this pain on myself—for love of you. Think I'd have done it for anyone else? Spit on them—that's what!"

Then, with many furtive glances at the door, he began to teach me a lesson.

"Next time they give you a licking," he said, "see you don't tighten up, hear? It hurts twice as bad when you tighten up. Let your body go free, so's to be soft, like jelly! And don't hold your breath. Breathe for all you're worth and yell at the top of your lungs. You just remember this!"

"Why, will they beat me again?" I asked.

"What do you think?" answered Tsiganok calmly. "Of course they will! You'll get it lots of times yet!"

"What for?"

"Your grandfather will find what for, all right!"

And once more he began to teach me, with the greatest concern:

"If he begins striking straight, just swishing down and that's all, you can lie there soft, without moving. But if he brings it down and then draws it across your body to pull the skin off, then roll toward him, in the direction of the wand, hear? That makes it easier!"

He winked a dark, slanting eye at me and said:

"When it comes to beatings, I know more than a policeman. You could make a pair of pants out of all the skin's been licked off me!"

As I looked into his merry face, I recalled the tales my grandmother had told me about Ivan-the-Prince, and Ivanushka-the-Fool.

III

When I got well, it became clear to me that Tsiganok occupied a privileged position in our household. My grandfather did not shout at him as often and as roughly as he did at his sons, and when he spoke of him in his absence he would narrow his eyes and shake his head.

"Golden fingers that Ivan's got, devil take him! Mark my words, it's no mean fellow growing up along of us!"

My uncles were also friendly with Tsiganok and never played tricks on him, as they did on the master-workman Grigori. Almost every evening they thought up some mean joke to play on the latter—they would heat the handles of his scissors, or put a tack on his chair, or place materials of different colours in the pile he was stitching, so that in his blindness he would sew them together into one length and be upbraided for it by my grandfather.

One evening after dinner, when Grigori had fallen asleep on the bunk in the kitchen, they painted his face magenta, and for a long time he went about looking comical and terrifying: his long red nose hung down like a tongue between the two dark discs of his spectacles, which gleamed dully against the background of his grey beard.

My uncles were inexhaustible in thinking up such tricks, but the workman took them without a word, only muttering to himself and taking the precaution of spitting copiously on his fingers before picking up the scissors, the iron, the tongs, or his thimble. This became a habit with him, so that even at the dinner table he would wet his fingers before touching a knife or a fork, to the vast amusement of the children. When he was hurt, a wave of wrinkles would pass over his large face, strangely mounting to his forehead, lifting his brows, and disappearing somewhere on his bald pate.

I do not know what my grandfather thought of his sons' sport, but my grandmother would shake her fist at them and shout:

"You shameless devils; you fiends, you!"

Behind Tsiganok's back, my uncles would speak maliciously and sarcastically of him, criticizing his work and calling him a thief and a sluggard.

I asked my grandmother why this was.

"It's because each of them wants Vanya to be working for him when he has his own workshop," she answered. "So each belittles him afore the other, sly ones they be! But both are afraid Vanya will choose to stay here with your grandfather 'stead of going with them. And your grandfather has his own lights—he's like to go and open up a third workshop along of Vanya. That'd be bad for the uncles, see?"

She laughed quietly.

"Set God hisself a-laughing, the way they go on! And your grandfather sees their cunning, and teases them a-purpose: 'I'll be buying Vanya a recruit certificate,' says he, 'so's they won't take him to the army. Can't be sparing of him.' Now doesn't that make them mad, though! They don't want that, and grudge the money—the certificate costs a lot."

Once more I was living with my grandmother, as I had on the steamer. And every evening before I went to sleep she would tell me fairy tales, or stories from her own life which were as good as fairy tales. But when she spoke about the practical affairs of the family—about dividing up my grandfather's property, or about my grandfather's intention of buying a new house for himself— she spoke ironically and with detachment, as though she were a neighbour, and not the second eldest in the household.

From her I learned that Tsiganok was a foundling. On a rainy night in the early spring they had found him on the bench beside the gate of our house.

"There he lay wrapped up in a sheet," she said thoughtfully and mysteriously. "So frozen he couldn't make a peep."

"Why do people give their babies away?"

"When a mother has no milk and nothing to feed her babe, she finds out where a wee one has just been born and died, and takes her own and leaves it there."

There was a moment's pause while she combed her hair.

"It's all on account of poverty, Alyosha," she went on, sighing and looking up at the ceiling. "Some people do be so poor there's no words for it! And it's counted a disgrace should an unmarried girl have a baby! Your grandfather was for taking Vanya to the police, but I talked him out of it: let's keep him, says I, it's God as has sent him 'stead of our dead ones. Eighteen souls I brought into this world. A whole streetful if they had lived— eighteen houses! You see they married me off afore I was fourteen years old, and my first baby came afore I was fifteen. But God had a love for the offspring of my flesh—one after another He took them to be His angels. And hurtful it was, and joyful!"

As she sat there on the edge of the bed in her nightgown, all covered with black hair, a huge shaggy figure, she resembled the she-bear which a bearded muzhik from the forests of Sergach had recently brought into our yard.

'Took the best ones. He did, and left me the worst," she chuckled, crossing her snow-white breast and shaking all over. "I was happy to get Vanya—it's such a love I have for wee ones like you! So I took him in and had him christened, and here he's lived and grown into a fine lad. First I called him the Beetle— account of his buzzing—he used to go crawling around, buzzing like a beetle. Love him, Alexei, he's a simple soul."

I did love Ivan, and was struck dumb by the wonder of him.

On Saturdays, when grandfather left for vespers after having thrashed the children who had sinned during the week, a life began in the kitchen that was indescribably amusing: Tsiganok would catch some black roaches from behind the stove, make a harness of thread, a paper sleigh, and drive the four black steeds up and down the table, which had been scraped a shining yellow.

"They've gone to fetch the archbishop!" he would cry excitedly as he steered them with a tiny stick.

He would stick a piece of paper to the back of another roach and send it scurrying after the sleigh, explaining:

"They forgot their bag, so here's a monk taking it to them."

Then he would tie the legs of still another roach, so that it stumbled along, pushing itself with its head.

"The deacon leaving the saloon for vespers!" Vanya
announced, clapping his hands in glee.

He would demonstrate his trained mice for us, making them
stand and walk on their hind legs, with their long tails trailing
behind them and their beady eyes blinking comically. He was
very gentle with his mice, carrying them inside his coat, feeding
them sugar from his own mouth, kissing them, and saying
convincingly:

"The mouse is a very wise neighbour and very affectionate.
The house goblin is fond of mice and is easy on anyone who
feeds them."

Tsiganok could do tricks with cards and money. He would
shout louder than any of the children, and indeed could scarcely
be distinguished from them. One day in a card game with the
children, he was left the "pig" several times running. He was
very much offended, pouted and dropped out of the game. Later
he complained to me snifflingly:

"It was all put up, I know! They winked at each other and
passed cards under the table! Call that playing? I can cheat as
well as them!"

He was nineteen years old, and bigger than the four of us
put together.

I have an especially vivid impression of him on holiday
evenings when my grandfather and Uncle Mikhail went visiting.
Uncle Yakov, curly-headed and dishevelled, would bring his guitar
into the kitchen and grandmother would arrange refreshments.
There was always an abundance of food, and vodka was poured
from a green decanter with red flowers skilfully blown into the
glass. Tsiganok whirled like a top in his Sunday clothes. Grigori
would come sidling quietly in, his spectacles flashing darkly.
Yevgenia would be there, our pock-marked, red-faced nanny, fat
as a jug, with cunning little eyes and a deep bass voice. Sometimes
the hairy deacon from the Uspensky Cathedral would come, in
addition to some other dark, slimy people who resembled pikes
and pickerels.

Everybody ate a lot and drank a lot and gave deep sighs.
The children were treated to their share (which included a

wineglass of sweet liqueur), and gradually a strange, wild hilarity developed.

Uncle Yakov lovingly tuned his guitar, and when this was done, invariably said one and the same thing:

"Well, I'm beginning!"

Shaking back his curls, he would bend over the instrument and stretch his neck like a goose. His round, carefree face assumed a dreamy expression, and an oily film dimmed his lively eyes as he softly plucked at the strings, playing a tune that drew you irresistibly to your feet.

His music demanded utter silence; it rushed like a rivulet from somewhere far away, seeping through walls and floors and rousing in the heart a sad, restless feeling. It made you feel sorry for yourself and everyone else. The grownups seemed to become children, and everyone sat motionless, in pensive silence.

Mikhail's Sasha listened with particular concentration. He would lean toward his uncle with his whole body, his eyes glued to the guitar, his mouth open, with saliva drooling from the corners. Sometimes he would become so absorbed that he slipped off his chair, and on such occasions he remained where he fell, on all fours, his eyes retaining the same fixed stare.

Everyone sat breathless under the charm of the music; only the samovar went on humming quietly, without disturbing us. The two small windows gazed out into the darkness of the autumn night; occasionally someone would knock softly on the panes. On the table quivered two yellow flames of candlelight, sharp as lances.

Uncle Yakov fell deeper and deeper into a trance; it seemed that he was fast asleep, with his teeth clenched. But his hands kept on living a life apart; the curved fingers of his right hand fluttered like a bird at the opening of the soundboard, while the fingers of his left rushed up and down the finger board.

When he had had a drink or two, he would begin to wail an endless song in an unpleasantly sibilant voice:

If Yakov was a little pup
His howls would wake the neighbours Up—

O-o-o-o Dear Lord!
O-o-o-o I'm bored!
A nun comes walking down the street,
A crow goes cawing at her feet,
O-o-o-o I'm bored!
A cricket chirps behind the stove,
A frog is croaking in the grove,
O-o-o-o I'm bored!
A beggar hung up his pants to dry,
Another stole them, passing by—
O-o-o-o I'm bored!
So bored, oh Lord!

I could not bear this song, and when my uncle sang about the beggars, I wept in inconsolable grief.

Tsiganok listened to the music as attentively as anyone else, running his fingers through his mop of curly hair, staring into the corner and breathing noisily. Sometimes he would exclaim plaintively:

"Oh, if only I had a voice! Wouldn't I sing though!"

"Enough of tearing your heart out, Yakov!" my grandmother would say with a sigh. "Give us a dance, Vanya!"

Not always did they comply with her request, but sometimes the musician would press against the strings for a second, then clench his fist, and with a wide gesture, thrust something soundless and invisible onto the floor, shouting like a hoodlum:

"Enough of this dreariness! Onto your feet, Vanya!"

Vanya would get up, preen himself, straighten his yellow shirt, and mince into the centre of the room as though he were walking on glass.

"Make it faster, Yakov Vasilyevich," he would modestly request, blushing in embarrassment.

The guitar broke into a wild rhythm, heels began to beat time, dishes rattled on shelves and table, while Tsiganok whirled in the centre of the room, swooping like a bird, waving his wing-like arms, moving his feet so swiftly that the eye could not follow them. With a whoop he sat on his haunches and whirled like a golden top, lighting everything with the shine of silk, which glowed and flamed in its shiver and flow.

Tsiganok danced inexhaustibly, with utter self-oblivion, and it seemed that if the door were opened, he would dance out into the street, through the city, and away to some unknown land. . .

"Cut across!" shouted Uncle Yakov, beating time with his foot.

He gave a piercing whistle and shouted a couplet in his irritating voice:

> *If it wasn't for spoiling my shoes on the way,*
> *I'd run from my wife this very day!*

The people at the table caught the spirit. Sometimes they would shout or squeal as though seared by hot iron; the bearded master-workman kept tapping out the time on his bald head and muttering under his breath. Once he leaned toward me, his soft beard sweeping my shoulder, and whispered in my ear as though I were a grownup:

"If only your father was here, Alexei Maximovich! He'd light a different flame! A jolly fellow he was! Remember him?"

"No."

"Ha! Used to be he and your grandmother. . . . Here, wait a minute!"

Grigori rose to his feet—tall, emaciated, resembling the image of a saint—bowed to my grandmother, and said in an unusually deep voice:

"Akulina Ivanovna, be so good as to do a dance for us. Remember how you used to with Maxim Sawateyevich? Now do us the favour!"

"Goodness Sakes, what are you saying, Grigori Ivanovich? Oh, my!" laughed my grandmother, shrinking away. "Me dance? Just to make people laugh, is that it? . . ."

But everyone began to urge her, and suddenly she got up like a young girl, adjusted her skirt, straightened her spine, threw back her heavy head, and glided off, crying:

"Let them laugh as wants to! Come on there, Yakov! Tune up!"

My uncle threw himself back and stretched his legs, half closing his eyes and playing a slower tune. Tsiganok stopped for a moment, then jumped up and began leaping about my grandmother as she glided silently over the floor as though floating in air, gracefully moving her arms, her brows raised and her dark eyes gazing into the distance. I thought she looked funny, and let out a snort, but Grigori shook his finger at me and all the grownups glanced at me in displeasure.

"Get away, Ivan!" called out Grigori with a laugh, and Tsiganok obediently moved off to one side and sat down, while nanny Yevgenia stuck out her Adam's apple and began to sing in a fine deep voice:

'Til Saturday the whole week through, The maiden worked at making lace, Weak and thin her fingers grew, Ah, how pale and wan her face!

My grandmother seemed more to be telling a story than dancing. Now she would move slowly, thoughtfully, swaying from side to side and glancing about from under her raised arm, hesitating in her movements as she carefully felt her way. Then she would stop as though suddenly frightened, her face frowning and quivering. Suddenly her features would light up with a kind, friendly smile, and she would jump to one side as though making way for someone to pass, pushing others aside. Then she would stand listening with lowered head, a happy smile slowly lighting her face. All of a sudden she would burst into a dance, whirling about taller and straighter than she had ever been before, and so wildly attractive in this moment of resurrected youth that it was impossible to take one's eyes off her.

And all the while nanny Yevgenia kept blowing like a horn:

They danced from early mass on Sunday To the breaking of the dawn. All too soon the day was Monday— And the holiday was gone.

When the dance was over, my grandmother took her place at the samovar. Everyone praised her, but she modestly protested.

"Enough, enough! You've never seen a real dancer," she said, as she arranged her disordered hair. "There was a girl, now, where I lived in Balakhna—I've forgot her name and whose she was—

never would she dance but some would cry with the joy of
watching her! A heart's holiday it was just to look at her; you
couldn't want for anything else! How I envied her, sinner that I
was!"

"Singers and dancers are the salt of the earth," observed
nanny Yevgenia severely, and began to sing something about King
David.

"You ought to get a job dancing in a saloon," said Uncle
Yakov to Tsiganok, as he threw his arm over his shoulder. "You'd
give people a treat all right!"

"I want to sing," complained Tsiganok. "If God would give
me a voice, I'd sing without stopping for ten years, and then it
wouldn't matter what happened to me—even if I became a monk!"

Everyone drank vodka, especially Grigori.

"Watch out, Grigori, or you'll go completely blind," warned
my grandmother as she poured him glass after glass.

"What of it?" he answered. "I don't need eyes any more.
I've seen everything."

He did not get drunk, but became more and more voluble,
talking to me all the time about my father.

"He had a big heart, he did, my good friend Maxim
Sawateyevich. ..."

Grandmother sighed and agreed with him:

"Ah yes, child of God that he was. . . ."

I found all this vastly interesting and was held in a state of
tense excitement. The atmosphere gave rise to a kind of quiet,
untiring gloom, and the gloom and the joy lived together in the
hearts of the people, inseparable, the one supplanting the other
with an elusive, inexplicable swiftness.

Once Uncle Yakov, who was not particularly drunk, began
to rip his shirt, tear at his curly hair and colourless moustache, at
his nose and protruding lip.

"Why, oh why?" he wailed, the tears flowing. "Why should
it be so?"

He struck himself on the cheek, on the brow, on the breast,
sobbing the while.

"I'm wicked and worthless, a lost soul!"

"Aha! That's it!" roared Grigori.

"Enough, Yakov! The good Lord knows what to teach us," said my grandmother, also a bit tipsy, as she caught at her son's hands.

She became even better after having something to drink. Her smiling dark eyes poured a warm light over everyone, and she would say in a singsong voice as she fanned her flushed face with her handkerchief:

"Oh Lord, oh Lord, how good it all is! Just look how good it all is!"

That was her heart's cry, her life's slogan.

I was amazed by the tears and cries of my carefree uncle. I asked my grandmother why he wept and struck himself.

"You have to know everything!" she grumbled reluctantly, not at all in her usual manner. "Wait a while—it's too soon for you to be sticking your nose into such things."

That only whetted my curiosity. I went into the workshop and began questioning Ivan, but he also avoided answering me, only laughing quietly, glancing at the master-workman out of the corner of his eye and pushing me out of the shop.

"Enough! Get out of here, before I let you down into one of those vats and dye you a bright green," he shouted.

The master-workman was standing before a low, broad stove with three vats built into it. He was stirring the contents of one of them with a long black stick with which he would then lift up the cloth and watch the coloured water drain off. The bright fire was reflected in his leather apron, as varicoloured as the brocaded vestments of a priest. The dye water bubbled in the vats and a cloud of acrid smoke streamed through the door and across the wintry yard.

The master-workman glanced at me from under his glasses with red and filmy eyes; then he turned to Ivan.

"Can't you see I need some wood?" he said gruffly.

When Tsiganok ran out into the yard, Grigori sat down on a sack of santalin and beckoned me to him.

"Come here," he said.

He sat me on his knee, swept my cheek with his warm, soft beard, and told me things I shall never forget.

"Your uncle beat his wife to death, and his conscience gives him no peace, understand? It's right you should know every-thing—keep your eyes open or you'll have a hard time of it."

It was easy to talk to Grigori, like to my grandmother, but it was frightening. It seemed as though he could see through everything when he glanced out from under his dark glasses.

"And how did he beat her to death?" he went on unhurriedly. "Here's how—he'd get in bed with her, cover her with the quilt, head and all, thump and pound her night after night until she died. What for? Couldn't tell you himself."

Ivan came in with a load of wood and squatted in front of the fire to warm his hands, but Grigori went on impressively without paying any attention to him.

"Maybe he beat her because she was better than him and he envied her. The Kashirins can't stand anything good, sonny. They envy it, but they can't take it to themselves, so they wipe it out. You ask your granny how they squeezed your father out of this life. She'll tell you everything—she can't stand lies—can't understand them. She's a kind of saint, your granny, even if she does take a drop now and then and likes her snuff. Kind of a holy woman. You keep in with her, sonny . . ."

He pushed me away and I went out into the yard stunned and horrified. Vanya overtook me when I reached the entranceway.

"Don't be afraid of him, he's a good sort," he whispered in my ear, his hand on my head. "Look him straight in the eye—he likes people who do that."

Everything was strangely upsetting. I knew no other life, but I had a vague recollection that my mother and father had not lived like that; they had spoken other words, known other amusements, and had always sat and walked alongside of each other, close together. In the evenings they had sat at the window singing songs, laughing loud and long, so that the neighbours would gather to listen. I remember that the upraised faces of these neighbours had always reminded me of dirty dinner plates. Here, on the contrary, people rarely laughed, and when they did you could not be sure what they were laughing at. They were always shouting at each other, threatening each other, and whispering off in the corner. The children were silent and inconspicuous, beaten to earth like dust in the rain. I felt like a stranger in this house, and the life about me pricked me with a thousand needles, rousing my suspicions and forcing me to watch everything with strained attention.

My friendship with Ivan grew. From sunrise 'til late at night my grandmother was busy about the house, so I spent most of the day trotting at the heels of Tsiganok. He continued to protect me with his arm whenever my grandfather flogged me, and would show me his swollen fingers the next day with the complaint:

"No point in it. Don't help *you* any, and look what / get! That's the last time—hereafter you take what's coming to you!"

But the next time he would take the unearned punishment all over again.

"You said you wouldn't do it any more."

"Saying and doing are two different things—don't know myself how it happened."

Soon I learned something about Tsiganok that increased my interest and devotion.

Every Friday Tsiganok would hitch the sorrel gelding Sharap (a mischievous beast with a sweet tooth—my grandmother's favourite) to the broad sledge, dress himself in an enormous cap and a short sheepskin tightly girdled with a green sash, and go to market to buy the week's supply of food. Sometimes he would be gone for a long time. Then everyone would become nervous, and keep going to the window, breathing on the frosted glass to get a glimpse into the street.

"Coming yet?"

"Not yet."

My grandmother would worry the most:

"Ah me!" she would say to her sons and husband. "You'll be the death of a good man and a good horse! It's a conscience you want, you shameless creatures! Never satisfied with what you've got! A stupid tribe, a greedy lot! The Lord'll punish you yet!"

My grandfather would frown and mutter;

"Oh, all right. This is the last time . . . "

Sometimes Tsiganok would return only at noon; then my grandfather and uncles would rush into the yard to meet him, while behind them would come my grandmother, furiously sniffing her snuff and waddling like a bear—for some reason she was always clumsy at such times. The children would come running out, and then would begin the joy of unloading the sledge, packed with fresh game, whole pigs, fish, and cuts of meat of every variety.

"Bought everything we ordered?" asked my grandfather eyeing the sledge with his sharp little eyes.

"Everything, just as ordered," answered Ivan merrily, jumping about the yard and rubbing his mittened hands to warm up.

"Stop rubbing your mittens like that—they cost money," shouted my grandfather sternly. "Bring back any change?"

"No."

My grandfather slowly walked about the sledge, muttering as he went:

"Looks like you've brought back an awful lot of stuff again. Sure you haven't bought some of it without money? See that don't happen in my house, hear?"

And he would hurry away with his face all screwed up.

Then my uncles would merrily make for the sledge and start guessing the weight of the fowls, fish, giblets, legs of veal, and chunks of meat.

"You made a fine choice, all right!" they would say, whistling and shouting in approbation.

My Uncle Mikhail went into particular ecstasies. He would hop around the sledge as though he were on springs, sniffing with the nose of a woodpecker, smacking his lips and blissfully narrowing his restless eyes. He was as lean as my grandfather, and resembled him, except that he was taller, and dark as a gypsy. He would thrust his frozen hands up his sleeves and ask:

"How much money did the old man give you?"

"Five rubles."

"And here's at least fifteen rubles' worth. How much did you spend?"

"Four rubles ten."

"In other words, ninety kopeks in your pocket, eh? Hear that, Yakov? That's one way to make money."

Uncle Yakov laughed softly as he stood there in the cold in his shirt sleeves, blinking at the frosty blue sky.

"How about standing us each to a half pint, Vanya?" he would drawl.

My grandmother unharnessed the horse.

"What is it, my love? What is it, my kitten?" she would murmur as she worked. "Wanting to play a bit? Go ahead. Go right ahead—the Lord don't object to a little playfulness."

The huge Sharap would toss his mane and scratch at her shoulder with his white teeth, snatching off her silk kerchief, glancing into her face with merry eyes, and neighing softly as he shook the hoarfrost off his lashes.

"Is it a piece of bread you're wanting?" she would ask as she thrust a great hunk, well salted, between his teeth, holding her apron under his mouth and watching him chew.

"He's a beauty, that gelding, granny," Tsiganok would say, as playful as a young colt himself. "He's so smart!"

"Get away! Stop wagging your tail around here!" cried my grandmother with a stamp of her foot. "You know I have no use for you on such days!"

She explained to me that when Tsiganok went to market, he did less buying than he did stealing.

"Grandad gives him a fiver; he spends three—and steals ten rubles' worth," she said sullenly. "He loves to steal, the rascal! Tried It once—it worked—everybody here at home laughed and praised him, so he made a habit of it. Your grandad got so fed up on poverty when he was young, it has made him tight in his old age. He thinks more of money than of his own children. Only too glad to get something for nothing. As for Mikhail and Yakov—

She dismissed them with a wave of her hand and became silent for a moment.

"It's a tangled lacemaking, Alyosha," she continued, glancing into her snuffbox, "done by a blind old hag as got the pattern twisted. Little wonder you and me can't make head or tail out of it. But once they catch Vanya for stealing, they'll beat him to death. . . ."

Again she was silent for a brief space, and when she went on, her voice was very soft.

"Ah me! Lots of rules we've got, but no truth to base them on. . . ."

The next day I begged Tsiganok not to steal any more.

"They'll beat you to death. . . ."

"They won't catch me—I'll get away: I'm a clever one, and my horse is a fast one," he said with a laugh which was soon eclipsed by a frown. "Oh I know it's all wrong to steal, and dangerous. I do it just for the fun of it. And I don't save up any money; those uncles of yours get it all out of me in the course of a week. But I don't care—let them have it. I get enough to eat."

Suddenly he picked me up and shook me gently.

"You're thin and light, but you got good bones. You'll grow up into a strong fellow. Listen, learn to play the guitar—ask your Uncle Yakov to teach you—no fooling! Only you're too young yet, that's the trouble! A little chap, but got a temper! I don't think you like that grandad of yours, do you?"

"I don't know."

"I don't like any of these Kashirins except granny. Only the devil could like them!"

"And me?"

"You're not a Kashirin. You're a Peshkov. That's different blood, a different tribe."

Suddenly he squeezed me tightly and said with almost a groan:

"God, if only I could sing! Wouldn't I wring the hearts though! Well, get along, brother. Got to start working."

He let me down on the floor, put a handful of nails into his mouth, and began tacking some wet black material to a large square board.

Soon after that he was killed.

It happened like this: leaning against the fence of our yard, near the gate, lay a huge oaken cross ending in a thick pedestal. It had lain there for a long time. I remember noticing it when I first came to live in that house. At that time it was new and yellow; now it had become darkened by autumn rains and gave off the pungent odour of seasoned oak. It was badly in the way in our small, littered yard.

Uncle Yakov had bought it to place on his wife's grave, swearing to carry it to the cemetery on his own shoulders on the first anniversary of her death.

The anniversary fell on Saturday, at the beginning of winter.

It was cold and windy and snow came flying off the roofs. My grandmother and grandfather and the other three grandchildren rode ahead to the cemetery for the ceremony. Everyone else went out into the yard. I was left at home as a punishment for some crime I had committed.

My uncles, Mikhail and Yakov, dressed in identical black coats, lifted the head of the cross and placed its arms on their shoulders. With difficulty Grigori and a strange man lifted the heavy pedestal and placed it on Tsiganok's broad shoulders; he swayed and placed his feet wide apart to brace himself.

"Can you manage?" asked Grigori.

"Don't know. Pretty heavy."

"Open the gate, you blind devil," roared Uncle Mikhail.

"Shame on you, Vanya," said my Uncle Yakov. "We're both lighter than you."

But Grigori turned to Vanya as he opened the gate and admonished sternly:

"Take care not to strain yourself! Well, God be with you!"

"You mangy old fool!" shouted Uncle Mikhail from the street.

Everybody in the yard laughed and started talking in loud voices, as though pleased that the cross had been removed.

Grigori took me by the hand and led me into the workshop.

"Maybe your grandfather won't flog you today," he said. "Seems like he's in a good humour."

He sat me on top of a pile of wool ready to be dyed, gently wrapped it around me, and began to speak to me thoughtfully as he sniffed the steam coming from the vats:

"I've known your grandfather for thirty-seven years, sonny," he said. "I saw the beginning of this business, and now I'm witnessing the end of it. We used to be good friends—went into business together, thought it up together. He's a smart one, your grandfather! See, he made himself bogs here—I wasn't able. But the Lord's smarter than any of us: one smile of His, and the wisest is left standing there blinking his eyes like a fool. You don't know the how and the why of things yet, but it's right you should know everything. The life of an orphan's not easy. Your father, Maxim Sawateyevich, was a trump if there ever was one— he understood everything. That's why your grandfather didn't like him and wouldn't have a thing to do with him. . . ."

It was pleasant to sit and listen to his kind words and watch the red and gold fire playing in the stove, the milky cloud of steam rising from the vats and settling to freeze on the planks of the slanting ceiling. Through a ragged crack I glimpsed a blue ribbon of sky. The wind had died down, the sun was shining, and the yard seemed to have been sprinkled with ground glass. From the street came the crunching of sleigh runners; blue smoke curled from the chimneys of the houses, and light shadows flitted over the snow as though they too were telling their story.

The tall, bony Grigori, with his long beard and large ears, looked like a kind wizard as he stood there hatless, stirring the boiling dyes and giving me instructions:

"Always look people straight in the eye; even a dog that's after you will stop in his tracks if you do that...."

His heavy glasses pressed on the bridge of his nose, causing the end to turn blue, like my grandmother's.

"What's that?" he said, stopping suddenly. He listened for a second, closed the draft in the stove with his foot, and bounded across the yard. I followed at his heels.

Tsiganok lay on his back in the middle of the kitchen floor; from the window streamed two broad shafts of light, one of which fell on his head and breast, the other on his feet. His forehead shone with a strange light; his brows were raised; his slanting eyes stared at the sooty ceiling; his dark lips twitched and emitted a pink froth; thin streams of blood oozed out of the corners of his mouth, down his neck and onto the floor, while blood ran freely from underneath him. Ivan's legs lay limp, and from the way his wide pants clung to the floor, it was clear that they were soaked. The floor had been scrubbed with sand until it shone bright in the sun. Rivulets of blood ran toward the doorway, lighted vividly where they crossed the shafts of sunlight.

Tsiganok lay motionless except for the fingers of his outstretched arms, which kept scratching at the floor, causing his dye-stained nails to glisten in the sunlight.

Nanny Yevgenia crouched beside Ivan to place a candle in his hand, but he could not grasp it; the candle fell, and its flame was extinguished in blood. The nurse picked it up, wiped it off, and once more tried to place it in his restless fingers. The kitchen seethed with suppressed excitement which blew me like a wind off the doorsill, but I clung tight to the jamb.

"He stumbled," said Uncle Yakov in a colourless voice, jerking his head. He himself had become faded and wrinkled, and he kept blinking his colourless eyes.

"He fell, and if crushed him—struck him in the back. It'd have smashed us too if we hadn't let go in time."

"Then it was you that smashed him," said Grigori hoarsely.

"Well, what do you think we. . ."

"You!"

The blood kept flowing; near the door it had already formed a pool which darkened and seemed to be rising. Tsiganok lay there making noises as though in his sleep, while the pink froth kept coming out of his mouth and his body kept melting away, growing flatter and natter, levelling down to the floor as though merging with it.

"Mikhail took a horse and went to the church to fetch pa," whispered Uncle Yakov. "I dumped him in a droshky and hurried back here with him. ... A good thing I didn't carry the pedestal myself, or look where I'd be now. . . ."

Once more the nurse fixed the candle in Tsiganok's hand, dripping wax and tears into his palm.

"Stick the candle to the floor at his head, clumsy!" cried Grigori roughly.

"That's right."

"Take off his hat!"

The nurse pulled off his hat, and Ivan's head struck the floor with a dull thud. Now his head was turned, so that the blood flowed more freely from his mouth, but only from one corner. This went on for a frightfully long time. At first I had expected Tsiganok to have a rest, then sit up, spit disgustedly, and say in his usual manner:

"Phooh! This heat!"

That was what he always said on awaking from his after-dinner nap on Sundays. But instead of sitting up, he kept lying there and melting away. The sun had withdrawn; the shafts had shortened and now lay only on the window sills. His face and hands had grown dark, his fingers no longer moved, and the froth had stopped bubbling from his mouth. Three candles had been placed about his head, their golden flames lighting the blue-black mass of his hair, the pinched tip of his nose, and his bloodstained teeth, and throwing wavering patches of light over his swarthy cheeks.

Nanny knelt weeping beside him.

"Ah, you poor little pigeon! Such a joy you were!" she whispered.

It was cold and terrifying. I climbed under the table and hid there. Then my grandfather came lumbering into the kitchen in his racoon coat, followed by my grandmother in her greatcoat with little tails about the collar. With them came Uncle Mikhail, the children, and many strangers.

My grandfather threw his coat on the floor and shouted:

"The bastards! To do in a chap like this! Why, in five years he'd have been worth his weight in gold!"

The clothes on the floor cut off my view of Ivan, and in crawling to a better position I got in my grandfather's way; he kicked me aside as he shook his little red fist at my uncles.

"Wolves, that's what you are!"

Then he sank down on a bench, grasping it tightly with his fingers as he whimpered and muttered in a squeaky voice:

"Oh I know—you couldn't stomach him. Ah, Vanya, foolish boy! What can we do now? What can we do, I say? The horse is old, the harness sold. . . . Well, mother, looks like the Lord's had it in for us these last few years, eh? What do you say, mother?"

My grandmother had thrown herself down on the floor beside Ivan and was feeling his face, his head, his breast, breathing into his eyes, picking up his hands and rubbing them, knocking over all the candles. At last she rose heavily to her feet, a vast black figure, her black dress shining, her black eyes rolling fearfully as she said in a low voice:

"Out of here, you accursed ones!"

Everyone except my grandfather disappeared.

Tsiganok was buried unnoticeably, unobtrusively.

IV

I lay on a wide bed, with a heavy quilt folded round and round me, listening to my grandmother praying. She was on her knees, pressing her breast with one hand while with the other she occasionally crossed herself unhurriedly.

I could hear the crackling of the frost beyond the window. Greenish moonlight glanced through the lacy pattern of the frozen pane, illuminating with its phosphorescent light the kind face with its prominent nose and dark eyes. The silken headdress covering my grandmother's hair shone like metal, while her dark dress streamed from her shoulders in shifting folds that piled upon the floor about her.

When she had finished praying, she silently undressed, placing her clothes neatly on the trunk in the corner. Then she came to bed, and I pretended to be sound asleep.

"Stop making believe, you little rascal. You're not asleep," she said softly. "You're not now, are you, pigeon-widgeon? Here, let's have a bit of that quilt."

Sensing what was to follow, I could not resist a smile; then she shouted:

"Aha! So it's sport you want to make of your old grandmother, is it?"

She took hold of the edge of the quilt and yanked it with such force and such skill that I went sky-rocketing into the air, whirling around and landing back in the feather bed while she roared with laughter.

"Take that, you little pixy! Guess that'll hold you!"

Sometimes she would pray for such a long time that I would fall asleep and not hear her come to bed.

Days of trouble, quarrels and fighting always ended in these long prayers; it was most interesting to listen to my grandmother giving the Lord all the details of what had happened. There she knelt, a mountainous form, beginning her prayers in a quick, unintelligible whisper which grew into a deep grumbler:

"You know yourself, Lord, it's only natural everyone should want to better himself. Mikhail, now, being the oldest, is the one as should stay here in town—it's an offence to send him over the river to a new place as nobody's tried before and there's no telling how it'll turn out. But father has a preference for Yakov. Is it right for a father to love his children unequal? He's a stubborn one, the old man is. You'd do well to give him a drop of sense, Lord."

She would glance at the dark icons with her huge, shining eyes as she went on giving advice to that God of hers.

"Send him a good dream, Lord, showing him how to divide with his sons."

She would cross herself and bow until her broad brow struck against the carpet, then, straightening up, go on speaking convincingly:

"And why not send a drop of joy to Varvara? What's she done to get in your bad graces. Lord? Why is she worse than the others? Who ever heard of such a young, strong woman living in such misery? And then Grigori, Lord—mind his eyes—getting worse every day. Once he's blind, what's left for him but to go begging his bread, and would that be right?—him as has poured out all his strength in grandad's business. . . . But the old man'll give him no help. . . . Ah, Lord, dear Lord. . . ."

For a long time she would remain silent, with drooping head and hanging arms as though she had fallen asleep.

"What else?" she would say at last, wrinkling her brows. "Be merciful to all the faithful; and forgive me, accursed fool that I am, as you know only too well; it's a foolish mind leads me to sin and not a wicked heart."

Then she would give a deep sigh and say with loving satisfaction:

"But there's nothing you don't know, dear Lord; nothing you don't understand, blessed Father."

I was very fond of my grandmother's God, he seemed so near and dear to her. Often I would say:

"Tell me about God."

She had a special manner for speaking about Him; she would always sit down and close her eyes and speak in a soft voice, strangely drawing out her words; I can still remember how she would draw herself up, take a seat, throw a kerchief over her head, and begin to weave her fancies until I fell asleep:

"There the Lord sits on a hill, surrounded by the meadows of paradise; sits on a sapphire throne under the silver lindens, lindens that bloom all the year round, for there is no winter in paradise, and no autumn, so that the flowers bloom from year's end to year's end, bringing joy to the saints of heaven. And all around the Lord fly a multitude of angels—thick as snow, or a swarm of bees—or like a flock of white doves flying from heaven to earth and back again, telling the Lord about us creatures here below. And each of us has his own angel—yours and mine and grandad's—for the Lord is the same to all His creatures. Here, now, comes your angel and says to the Lord: 'Alexei went and stuck his tongue out at his grandfather.' So the Lord gives His orders: 'Let the old man give him a beating,' says he. And so it is with everybody and everything, each rewarded according to his deserts—grief to some, joy to others. And it's all so fine that the angels mutter their wings in joy and keep singing, 'Praised be the Lord, the Lord on high!' While He just looks on with a smile, as much as to say, 'Well, go ahead my pretties, once it pleases you!'"

And my grandmother herself would smile and nod her head.

"Have you seen all that?"

"I haven't seen it, but I know it," she answered musingly.

Whenever she spoke about God and paradise and the angels, she became small and meek, her face lost the scars of age, and her moist eyes radiated a particularly warm light. I wound her heavy satiny braids around my neck and sat motionless, charmed by these tales which I could never get enough of.

"It's not given to mortals to look on the face of God—blind them it would. Only the saints can behold Him with wide-open eyes. But angels I've seen. They become visible when your heart's been purged. Once I stood in the church at early mass, and there at the altar I could see two of them—like fog they were—see right through them, and bright as bright, with wings to the floor, all lacy and gauzy. They kept moving about the throne, helping old Father Ilya: when he'd raise his feeble old arms to pray there they'd be, a-holding up his elbows. So old and blind he was that he kept bumping into everything, and soon after that he died. I was so happy to see them I nearly fainted with joy; my heart ached nigh to bursting and the tears came streaming from my eyes—ah, what a delight it was! How splendid everything is with God up in heaven, Alyosha, my pigeon-widgeon! And hoy splendid it is down here on earth!"

"Even here in our house?"

"Yes, everywhere, praised be the Holy Virgin," said my grand mother, crossing herself.

This was puzzling: certainly it was hard to agree that everything was well in our house, where relations were becoming more strained every day.

I remember once passing the open door of Uncle Mikhail's room and catching a glimpse of Aunt Natalya all in white, rushing about the room with her hands pressed to her breast, crying in a dreadful, low voice:

"O God, take me away from here, let me go. ..."

I understood her prayer, and I understood Grigori when he kept muttering:

"Soon as I'm blind I'll go off begging, and that'll be better than this!"

I hoped he would hurry and go blind so that I could become his guide and go off with him, to wander through the world begging our bread. I once spoke of this to him. He laughed into his beard and said:

"All right, we'll go together. And I'll cry through the streets so's all shall hear, 'This is the grandson of Vasili Kashirin, owner of the dye works!' That'll be funny, all right!"

I had noticed that often my Aunt Natalya's lips were swollen and there were black-and-blue marks on her yellow face.

"Does uncle beat her?" I asked my grandmother.

"On the sly, curse him!" she answered with a sigh. "Your grandfather doesn't allow it, so he does it at night. He's a mean one and she's got no backbone."

Then she would go on, warming to her story:

"But they don't beat nowadays the way they used to! Oh, sometimes they'll give it to you in the teeth or the ear or yank at your braid for a minute or two, but it used to be they'd torture you for hours! Once your grandfather beat me on the first day of Easter week from early mass to sundown—beat me—take a rest— then start all over again. With the horse reins or anything else at hand."

"What for?"

"Can't remember now. Once he beat me 'til I was half dead and then gave me nothing to eat for five days—I hardly managed to pull through that time. Or again...."

I was struck dumb by such facts: my grandmother was twice the size of my grandfather, and I could not imagine his getting the better of her.

"Is he so much stronger than you?"

"Not stronger, but older. Besides which, he's my husband. It's him God's put in charge of me, and ordered me to bear it."

I used to love to watch her dust the icons and clean their mountings. Our icons were very elaborate: set with pearls and precious stones and inlaid with silver. She would handle them with deft fingers.

"What a sweet face!" she would murmur as she crossed herself and kissed them.

"All covered with dust and soot! Blessed Mother of God, omnipotent, shedding joy unspeakable! Just look here, how fine the drawing is, Alyosha, my pigeon-widgeon, such tiny figures, but each standing separate. This one's called Twelve Holidays,' with the Feodorovsky Virgin in the middle—such a dear kind lady! And this one—'Weep not,oh mother, beside my grave....'"

Sometimes it seemed to me that she played with the icons as seriously and credulously as my cowed cousin Katerina played with her dolls.

Often she saw devils, both' singly and in droves.

"One night in Lent I was walking past the Rudolfs' house— everything bright with moonlight—and suddenly I saw something dark straddling the roof near the chimney. Big and shaggy it was, with its horns bent down into the chimney, a-sniffing and a-snorting, lashing its tail over the roof and shuffling its big feet. I made the sign of the cross and said, 'Christ shall rise again to the mortification of His enemies!' Straightaway he gave a little squeak and slid down into the yard—mortified he was! Likely the Rudolfs were cooking something to break their fast and he sniffed it gloating. . . ."

I laughed at the thought of the devil somersaulting down into the yard, and she laughed with me.

"Don't they like mischief though, just like little children! One night, getting on to midnight, I was doing the wash in the bath-house. All of a sudden the door of the stove swung open and out they came—little ones, and littler ones—red ones, green ones, black ones—like roaches. I rushed to the door, but they wouldn't let me reach it. There I was, locked up with those devils, millions of them, filling the whole bath-house—under my feet, up my legs, pinching, biting, stinging 'til I couldn't so much as make the sign of the cross to shoo them away. Soft and warm and furry they were, like little kittens, always up on their hind legs, a-turning and a-tumbling, baring their little mice teeth, flashing their little green eyes, tossing their heads with the little knobs where the horns were coming through, twisting their little pigs' tails. . . . Lordy, what a time I had! Lost my senses, I did, and when I came to, the candle was most burnt up, the wash water all cold, and the wash scattered all over the floor. 'Phooh!' thinks I, 'the plague on you, devils that you be!' "

I closed my eyes and could see the door of the grey stone stove open, letting out a stream of tumbling imps who crowded the bath-house, blowing at the candle and sticking out their vixenish pink tongues. This too was amusing, but terrifying as well. My grandmother shook her head and was silent for a minute, until again she was seized by a flare of imagination:

"And I've seen folks with the curse on them, too; that was also during the night, in the winter, with a blizzard raging. I was crossing the Dukov gully, where remember I told you Yakov and Mikhailo wanted to drown your father through a hole in the ice of the pond. That's where I was going; I had just come down the path to the bottom of the gully when all of a sudden such a whistling, such a screeching I heard! I looked up, and there's a troika of black horses galloping down on me with the coachman, a round little devil in a pointed red cap, standing up on the seat with his arms stretched out, driving them with chains instead of reins. And when the horses couldn't get through the gully they made straight for the pond in a cloud of snow. And those in the sleigh were also devils, whistling and shouting and waving their caps. Seven troikas went flying past me like fire-wagons, and the horses of all of them black as sable, and the people in all of them accursed of their fathers and mothers! Such people are good sport for the devil. The devils seek them out, riding them and driving them through the night for their merrymaking. Reckon it was a devil's wedding I saw that night. . . ."

Grandmother spoke with such simplicity and conviction that it was impossible not to believe her.

But best of all were the verses she recited about how the Holy Virgin walked the thorny path through this world, exhorting the "Robber-Princess" Yengalycheva not to rob and flail Russians; verses about Alexei, the man of God, and about Ivan-the-Warrior; tales about Vasilisa-the-Wise, about Pope-the-Goat and the godly Godson; fearful legends about Marfa-the-Possadnitsa, about Baba Usta, the Robber Chief, about Maria, the Egyptian sinner, and about the grief of the Robber's Mother. Her stock of tales, legends, and verses was inexhaustible.

She was not afraid of people, including my grandfather, or devils, or any other dark power, but she was deathly afraid of roaches, and sensed their presence even at a great distance. Sometimes she would wake me up in the middle of the night, whispering:

"Alyosha darling, there's a roach crawling. Kill it, for the love of Christ!"

Only half awake, I would light the candle and crawl about on my hands and knees in search of the enemy; but my efforts were not always successful.

"There isn't any," I would say, but she would gasp from where she lay motionless, her head covered by the quilt.

"Oh, yes there is! Keep hunting, I beg you! It's there, I know it is!"

And she was always right. Usually I would find the roach somewhere far away from the bed.

"Have you killed it? Ah, praise the Lord! And thank you, my love," she would say, throwing the quilt off her head with a happy smile.

But if I failed to find it, she would be unable to sleep, and I would feel her body trembling at the slightest rustle in the silence of the night and hear her whispering with bated breath:

"There it is at the door... now it's under the trunk "

"Why are you so afraid of roaches?"

"What are they good for anyway?" she would answer sensibly enough. "Only go crawling about, crawling about, the black devils! God gave the least of His creatures some purpose in life—the thousand-legger shows there's dampness in the house; the bedbug shows the walls are dirty; if you catch a louse on you, it means you'll be sick—that's all clear enough! But as for them—who can tell what they're for; what right have they to be alive?"

Once when she was on her knees carrying on an animated conversation with God, grandfather flung open the door and cried hoarsely:

"Well, mother, a visitation from the Lord, all right! The workshop's on fire!"

"What!" cried my grandmother, struggling to her feet. Both of them rushed noisily into the darkness of the large parlour.

"Yevgenia, take down the icons! Natalya, dress the children!" ordered my grandmother in a firm, loud voice.

"Ah-h-h!" wailed my grandfather.

I ran into the kitchen; the window over-looking the yard was bright as gold, while golden patches slithered and slid over the floor; my Uncle Yakov pulled his boots on his bare feet and then jumped about on the spot as though they burned his soles, crying:

"Aha! It's Mikhail set us on fire; set us on fire and ran away!"

"S-s-s, you cur!" said my grandmother, giving him such a push through the door that he nearly fell.

Through the frost on the windowpane I could see the burning roof of the workshop and the flames whirling through the open door. Red blossoms of fire bloomed smokeless in the quiet night; only high up in the air did a smoke cloud hover, without blotting out the silver trail of the Milky Way. The snow glowed red with the flames and the walls of the outhouses swayed and trembled as though straining toward the corner of the yard where the fire was burning merrily, lighting up the broad cracks in the workshop and thrusting its bright twisted tongues through them. Red and gold ribbons of flame quickly slid over the dry boards of the roof where the slender clay chimney thrust up noticeably, pouring a thin stream of smoke into the air. A soft crackling and silken rustling beat at the windowpane; the fire grew, and its splendour transformed the workshop into beauty like that of the iconostasis in the church, luring the watcher with irresistible power.

I threw a heavy sheepskin over my head, pulled on somebody's boots, and staggered into the entranceway, then out onto the porch, where I stood stunned—blinded by the brilliance of the fire; deafened by its roar and the shouts of my grandfather, my uncle, and Grigori; frightened by the behaviour of my grandmother. She threw an empty sack over her head, wrapped herself in a horse blanket, and ran into the blazing workshop, shouting:

"The sulphuric acid, you fools! The sulphuric acid'll blow up!"

"Stop her, Grigori!" wailed my grandfather. "Oh, she's done for!"

But grandmother was back already, all smoking and shaking her head, bending under the weight of a demijohn of sulphuric acid.

"Lead out the horse, father!" she cried hoarsely, between coughs. "Pull this thing off me—can't you see I'm a-fire?"

Grigori took the smouldering horse blanket off her shoulders, then grabbed up a spade and bent double to smash the huge hunks of snow at the door of the workshop. My uncle kept jumping about him with an axe in his hands, my grandfather followed at the heels of my grandmother, throwing snow at her. She buried the demijohn in a snowdrift and ran to open the gates of the yard.

"Save the granary, neighbours!" she cried, bowing to the people who came running up. "It'll spread to the granary and the hayloft—all our buildings will burn to the ground, and yours will be next. Chop off the roof and throw the hay into the garden! Grigori, throw the snow up high—what good's it on the ground? Be done with your running, Yakov, give the people spades and axes! Good people, work together, and God will be our help!"

She was as fascinating as the fire. Lighted by the flames which seemed to strike out at her, she darted like a black shadow about the yard, being everywhere at once, noticing everything and giving everybody orders.

Sharap ran into the yard and reared up on his hind legs, throwing my grandfather off his feet; the horse's rolling eyes flashed red in the fire light; he snorted and balked, and was so unmanageable that grandfather let go the reins and jumped aside.

"Hold him, mother!" he cried.

She threw herself under the very feet of the rearing horse and stood motionless with outstretched arms. The horse neighed plaintively and settled down, casting furtive glances at the fire.

"Don't be afraid," said grandmother in a deep voice as she patted the animal's neck and took the reins in her hands. "Would I leave you at such a fearful moment? You silly little mouse!"

The little mouse, three times her size, followed meekly to the gate, neighing as it looked into her flushed face.

Nanny Yevgenia led out the children, all bundled up and mumbling into their wrappings.

"Vasili Vasilyevich, I can't find Alexei!" she cried.

"Get along, get along," answered grandfather, while I hid under the porch steps so that Yevgenia would not lead me away too.

The roof of the workshop caved in, leaving a pattern of smoking, glowing rafters against the sky; from inside the structure came explosions of red, green and blue flames which licked out into the yard, reaching toward the crowd of people who were trying to extinguish this enormous bonfire by throwing snow at it. The vats boiled furiously, giving off thick clouds of smoke and steam which filled the yard with strange odours and brought tears to the eyes; I climbed out from under the steps and landed at my grandmother's feet.

"Get away!" she cried. "You'll get crushed! Get away!"

Into the yard dashed a horseman in a plumed metal helmet. His sorrel steed was foaming at the mouth and he lifted his whip as he shouted threateningly:

"Make way!"

Little bells jingled merrily and everything was gay and festive. My grandmother pushed me up on the porch.

"Didn't you hear me? Get away from here, I tell you!"

It was impossible not to obey her at this moment. I went into the kitchen and again took my stand at the window, but the dark crowd of people cut off my view of the fire. The only thing I could see was the flash of metal helmets among the dark winter hats and caps.

The fire was quickly extinguished by beating it down and pouring water on it. The policemen drove away the people, and at last my grandmother came into the kitchen.

"Who's here? You? Not asleep? Afraid? Don't be afraid. It's all over now."

She sat down next to me and began rocking back and forth without a word. It was pleasant to regain the quiet night and the darkness, but at the same time I regretted the loss of the fire.

My grandfather appeared in the doorway.

"Mother?"

"Ah?"

"Get burned?"

"Nothing much."

He scratched a sulphur match, and the blue flame illuminated his chipmunk face, black with soot. He lighted the candle on the table and sank down heavily next to my grandmother.

"You might have a wash," she said. She was also covered with soot and smelled of smoke.

"Sometimes the Lord shows you His mercy," sighed my grandfather. "Sends you a flash of reason."

He patted her on the shoulder and added with a grin:

"Just for brief minutes, for little spells, but still He sends it."

Grandmother also laughed and was about to say something, but grandfather frowned.

"Have to get rid of that Grigori. It's all his carelessness. That muzhik's done for, outlived his time. Yakov's sitting out there on the porch crying, the fool. You'd better go out to him . . ."

She got up and went out, holding up one hand and blowing on the fingers.

"See it all, from the very beginning?" asked my grandfather without looking at me. "What did you think of that grandmother of yours, eh? And don't forget she's an old woman. . . . Beaten and broken. . . . There's something for you! As for the rest of them—phooh!"

He bent down and said nothing for some time. Then he got up and broke off the burnt end of the candle wick as he asked:

"Were you afraid?"

"No."

"That's right. Nothing to be afraid of."

He took off his shirt with an irritated movement and went to the washstand in the corner.

"Stupid to have a fire!" he said in a loud voice, stamping his foot. "Anyone who has a fire should be thrashed out in the public square as a fool or a thief! That's what they ought to do with such people and then there wouldn't be any more fires! . . . Get back to bed! What you sitting here for?"

I went out, but there was no more sleeping for me that night; I had just crawled back into bed when I was galvanized into life by an inhuman wail. Once more I ran into the kitchen; I found my grandfather standing in the middle of the room, shirtless, holding a candle in his hand; the candle trembled; he kept shifting his feet but did not budge from the spot.

"Mother, Yakov, what's that?" he gasped.

I jumped up on the stove and crouched back in the corner. Once more everything became topsy-turvy inside the house, like during the fire. The wails beat in rhythmic waves against the walls and ceiling, ever louder and more insistent. My grandfather and uncle began running about like madmen; my grandmother shouted them out of the kitchen. Grigori made a great noise with

the logs he was stuffing into the stove. He filled some boilers
with water and walked about nodding his head like an Astrakhan
camel.

"First get the fire going!" commanded my grandmother.

Grigori climbed up on the stove for some kindling, touched
my foot, and shouted in fright:

"Who's there? Phooh, what a scare you gave me! You're
always where you don't belong!"

"What's happening?"

"Your Aunt Natalya's giving birth," he answered calmly,
jumping down off the stove.

I remembered that my mother had not wailed like that when
she had given birth.

When Grigori had put the boilers on the stove, he climbed
up beside me and took a clay pipe out of his pocket.

"Started smoking to cure my eyes," he said, showing me the
pipe. "Your grandmother says to take snuff, but I figure it's better
to smoke."

He sat with his feet swinging over the edge of the stove,
staring at the meagre light of the candle; his ear and cheek were
smudged with soot, his shirt was torn, so that I got a glimpse of
his ribs sticking out like hoops. One glass of his dark spectacles
was cracked and a large piece had fallen out, giving a glimpse of
a moist red eye that looked like a sore.

He stuffed his pipe with leaf tobacco and sat listening to the
moans of the woman, muttering to himself as though he were drunk:

"Seems your grandmother got some burns after all. How's
she going to do the delivering? Hear how your aunt's going on?
They forgot all about her; she started her moaning soon's the fire
broke out—out of fright.... Just look how hard it is to bring a
living creature into the world, and still nobody holds a woman of
any account. But a woman should be respected—a mother, that
is—and don't you ever forget it!"

I dozed off, but was awakened by a slamming of doors, the
drunken cries of Uncle Mikhail, and a general rumpus. I heard
strange words being said:

"Time for the Gates of Heaven to swing wide...."

"Give her some lamp oil with rum and soot in it: half a glass of oil, half a glass of rum and a tablespoon of soot. . . ."

"Let me have a look at her," Uncle Mikhailo kept asking.

He was sitting on the floor spitting between his widespread legs and striking the floor with his hands. The heat became unbearable on top of the stove, so I climbed down. But when I came up to my uncle he grabbed me by the leg and yanked it so that I fell, striking my head on the floor.

"Fool!" I cried.

He jumped to his feet, snatched me up and swung me into the air with a roar.

"I'll smash you against the stove!"

When I came to I was lying on my grandfather's knees in the parlour. He was sitting in the icon corner, rocking me back and forth, his eyes fastened on the ceiling as he muttered:

"And there'll be no forgiving us, any of us. . . ."

The icon lamp burned brightly above his head and a candle was lighted on the table in the centre of the room, while a hazy winter morning glanced through the window.

"What hurts?" asked my grandfather, bending over me.

Everything hurt. My head was damp, my body like lead, but I did not wish to talk about it—everything about me was so strange: unfamiliar people were occupying most of the chairs in the room—a priest in a purple robe, a grey-haired old man in glasses and a military uniform, and many others; they were all sitting motionless, like wooden figures, frozen in expectation as they listened to a splashing of water somewhere close at hand. Uncle Yakov was standing erect in the doorway with his hands behind his back.

"Here, take him to bed, Yakov," said my grandfather.

My uncle beckoned to me and we went on tiptoe to my grandmother's room. When I had crawled up on the bed he whispered:

"Your Aunt Natalya has died. . . ."

This did not surprise me—for some time she had not been seen around the house—had not entered the kitchen or come to the table for her meals.

"Where's grandmother?"

"In there," he answered with a wave of his hand. He went out as he had come in—tiptoeing in his bare feet.

I lay in bed glancing anxiously about me. Blind, hoary faces were glued to the window-pane; my grandmother's dress was hanging in the corner over the trunk—I knew this, but now it seemed to me that the dress was some living creature lurking there in the shadows. I hid my head in the pillow, keeping one eye on the door; I wanted to jump up and run away; it was hot in the room, and the house was filled with a stifling odour reminding me of how Tsiganok had died and the blood had flowed over the kitchen floor. My head, or perhaps my heart, seemed to swell up; everything I had witnessed in that house dragged through me like a sledge along a wintry road, pressing me down, blotting me out. ...

Slowly the door of the room was opened and my grandmother edged through. Pushing the door closed with her shoulder, she remained leaning against it her arms outstretched toward the blue flame of the icon lamp.

"My poor hands . . . how they hurt. . ." she whispered in a plaintive, childlike voice.

V

The division of property was made that spring; Yakov remained in town and Mikhail went across the river. My grandfather bought himself a fine new house on Polevaya Street, with a saloon on the first floor, a cosy little room in the attic, and a garden overlooking a ravine bristling with bare willow shoots.

"Plenty of whips!" said my grandfather with a merry wink at me as we walked together down soft, thawing paths on an inspection of the garden. "Soon I'll begin teaching you your letters, and then the whips'll come in handy."

The whole house was crowded with tenants; my grandfather left only one large room on the upper floor for himself and the reception of guests, while my grandmother and I had our quarters in the attic. The window of this room gave onto the street, and by leaning out I could watch the drunkards come out of the saloon in the evening and on holidays. They would go stumbling down the street, roaring and falling in the gutter. Sometimes they would be thrown out of the saloon like sacks of flour, but they always crawled back to the door, which would slam with a jarring of glass and a shriek of the rusty pulley. Then a fight would begin. It was amusing to watch all this from up above. Every morning my grandfather went to his sons' workshops to help them get started, returning in the evening, tired and depressed and irritable.

My grandmother sewed and got the meals and dug in the garden, bustling about all day long like a huge top driven by invisible springs. She would take her snuff, sneeze appetizingly, and observe as she wiped her perspiring face:

"Praised be the saints and the angels to the end of time! At last we've come to a quiet life, Alyosha, my pigeon-widgeon! Everything's so nice for us now, thanks to the Holy Virgin."

But I did not find our life very quiet. From morning to night the tenants kept running about the yard and through the house; neighbours kept popping in, always hurrying somewhere, always being late for something, always getting ready for something.

"Akulina Ivanovna!" they would call to my grandmother.

And Akulina Ivanovna would smile upon all of them in her friendly way and listen attentively to all of them as she pushed the snuff up her nose with her thumb and wiped it neatly with a large red-checked handkerchief.

"To get rid of the lice?" she would say. "To get rid of the lice you must wash often at the bath-house, my dear, and best to take a steaming with oil of peppermint. But if the lice be under the skin, then take a tablespoon of goose fat—the very purest—a teaspoon of bichloride of mercury, and three drops of mercury; mix it all together seven times with a china pestle and then rub it on. Never to use a bone or a wooden spoon, else the mercury will spoil; and never to touch it with copper or silver—that's very harmful."

Sometimes, after careful consideration, she would say:

"You'd best go to Asaf-the-Recluse at the abbey, my good woman. Your question be too much for me to answer."

She served as a midwife, as arbiter in family quarrels, treated sick children, recited "The Virgin's Dream" so that the women could learn it "for good luck," and gave advice in household matters:

"The cucumbers themselves know when it's time to be pickled; soon as they stop smelling of earth and the like, that's when to begin salting them down. To set good kvass, its temper must be stirred: being's kvass can't abide anything sweet, throw in a few raisins, or some sugar—a teaspoonful to a pail-full. There's different tastes in *varenets,* * there's the Danube way to make, it, and the Shpanish, and then there's the Caucasian. . . ."

All day I trotted at her heels, in the yard or the garden, or at the neighbours', where she would sit for hours drinking tea and recounting tales; it was as if I had grown to be part of her, and during that period of my life I can remember nothing but that kind, indefatigable old woman.

Sometimes my mother would put in her appearance for brief stretches. She was still proud and stern and looked upon everything with eyes as cold and grey as winter sunlight. She

---

* Varenets—baked milk curds.—Trans.

never stayed long, and went away without leaving any remembrance of herself.

One day I said to my grandmother:

"Are you a witch?"

"There now, whatever made you think of such a thing!" she laughed. But presently she became very serious and added, "Who am I to be a witch? Witchcraft takes lots of learning, and here am I without even knowing my letters! Look what a learned man your grandfather is, but the Blessed Virgin didn't see fit to make me wise."

Then she confided another bit of her life to me:

"I too grew up an orphan. My mother was without husband, and a cripple in the bargain. Frighted she was by the lord who owned her when still a maid. So she threw herself out the window at night, hurting her side and her shoulder so that her arm withered after that, her right one, the main one, and she an expert lacemaker. After that the nobleman had no use for her and let go—to make her way as best she could—but how could she make her way with only one arm? So a beggar she became. But at that time the people of Balakhna were richer and better—such brave carpenters they were, and lacemakers, each one better than the other! So we used to go a-begging, my mother and me, through the town in autumn and winter; but when the Archangel Gabriel raised his sword and drove off the frost, and the spring came over the earth, then off we'd go, far as feet would carry, to Murom we went, to Yurievets, and up along the Volga and the quiet Oka. How nice it is to walk the earth in spring and summer—with the ground so soft and the grass like velvet! And there in the fields the Virgin has sprinkled flowers for your joy, and there lie the great spaces for your heart's delight! And then my mother would half close her blue eyes and her song would go winging away to the heaven—a soft voice she had, and a sweet one—and everything around would get quiet and breathless with listening. How good it was to go a-begging then! But when my tenth year came my mother was ashamed to take me with her begging; a disgrace it was, so she settled down in Balakhna; there she'd go alone from door to door, and on Sundays on the porch of the church, while I sat home learning to make lace. I couldn't learn fast enough, so anxious was I to help my poor mother; and when the pattern wouldn't turn out, there I'd sit with the tears rolling down my cheeks. In a bit over two years, mind, I learned the lacemaking, and my fame spread throughout the town. Whenever some special work was wanted, they'd come to us—'Well, Akulya, start your bobbin working!' Didn't that make me happy though! To be sure it wasn't me to take the credit, but my mother for teaching me. If she couldn't work herself with her one hand, she knew how to teach, and a good teacher is worth ten workers. I was so proud! 'You can stop your begging now, mother,' says I. 'I can feed you now with the work of my hands.' But 'Hush, you,' says my mother. 'Don't you know it's a dowry you must lay by for yourself with that money?' Soon after that your grandfather put in his appearance—a very noticeable young man: only twenty-two and overseer of the *burlaks* already. So his mother looked me over. She saw how poor I was—the daughter of a beggarwoman, which made it sure I would make a dutiful wife. Hm-m . . . And she herself a bun-seller, and an evil-spirited woman ... but why speak ill of the dead? The Lord sees all that without our help; the Lord sees it, the devil needs it. . . ."

She laughed her hearty laugh; her nose quivered comically and her eyes caressed me with musing tenderness, conveying much more than words.

I remember one quiet evening when my grandmother and I were having tea in my grandfather's room; he himself was not well, and sat on the bed without any shirt on, his shoulders covered by a long towel with which he frequently wiped the perspiration off his brow. His breathing was hoarse and rapid, his green eyes were filmy, his face red and puffy. His sharp little ears were particularly red, and when he reached out for a glass of tea his hand shook pitifully. He was very meek and not at all like himself.

"Why don't you give me any sugar?" he complained to my grandmother in the tone of a spoiled child.

"Because honey's better for you," she answered gently but firmly.

He swallowed down the hot tea with much grunting and blubbering.

"Watch out I don't die," he said.

"That's it. If I should die now it would be like I never lived at all—all for nothing."

"Lie down and stop talking."

For a minute he lay quiet with his eyes closed, smacking his blue lips. Suddenly he jumped up as though someone had pinched him.

"Have to marry off Yakov and Mikhail soon as possible. Maybe wives and some more children will tame them down, eh?"

He began naming over the eligible young women in the town while my grandmother sat drinking glass after glass without making any comment. My grandfather had forbidden me to go out because of some misdemeanour, so I sat at the window watching the fading sunset and its bright reflection in the windows of the houses.

Down in the garden flocks of beetles were buzzing about the birches. A cooper was hammering away in the next yard, while not far away I could hear the wheel of a scissors-grinder. From the ravine beyond the garden came the shouts of children playing among the thick bushes. I had a desperate longing to be out there with them, and my heart was heavy with the sadness of twilight.

Suddenly my grandfather took out a brand new book, slapped it against his palm, and called to me in a cheerful voice:

"Hey, you young whippersnapper, you cabbage ears, you, come on over here! Sit down, Tatar face! See that sign? That's 'a' for apple, Say it—'a' for apple. 'B' for butter. 'C' for cellar. What's this?"

" 'B' for butter."

"Right. And this?"

" 'C for cellar."

"Wrong! 'A' for apple. Look close: 'd' for dinner, 'e' for ever, T for father—what's this?"

" 'E' for ever."

"Right. And this?"

" 'D' for dinner."

"Fine. And this?"

" 'A' for apple."

My grandmother interrupted.

"Be better for you to lie quiet, father."

"Silence! This is just what I need to keep my mind off my worries. Go on, Alexei!"

He threw his hot, moist arm about my neck and pointed to the letters, while with the other hand he held the book under my very nose. He effused a smell of vinegar, sweat, and baked onion which nearly suffocated me. He became strangely excited and shouted into my ears:

" 'K' for kitchen, 'l' for lady!"

The words were familiar, but the Slavonic letters in no way resembled them. The "l" looked more like a worm than a lady; the "f" looked like humpbacked Grigori rather than father; the bulging "b" reminded me of my grandmother and me together, while there was something about all the letters that resembled my grandfather. He kept drilling me on the alphabet, taking the letters in order and out of order; he infected me with his excitement, so that I too broke into a sweat and began to shout at the top of my voice. This struck him funny and his laugh brought on a fit of coughing.

"Just look how he's took to it, mother," he gasped, clutching his breast and the book. "Phooh, you Astrakhan plague, you! What you hollering about?"

"It's you that's hollering. . . ."

It delighted me to watch him and my grandmother, who sat with her elbows on the table, her fists at her cheeks, laughing quietly as she watched us.

"Enough of shouting your heads off!" she said.

My grandfather turned to me in friendly explanation:

"I'm shouting because I'm sick, but what you shouting for?"

Then he shook his perspiring head and said to my grandmother:

"The late Natalya was wrong when she claimed he had a bad memory. He's got a memory like a horse! Go on, snubnose!"

At last he jokingly pushed me off the bed.

"That's enough. Hang on to the book. Tomorrow you'll tell me the whole alphabet without a mistake, and for that I'll give you five kopeks."

When I reached for the book, he drew me toward him and said sadly:

"What did your mother have to go and abandon you for, sonny?"

"Now, father, no sense in talking like that," put in my grandmother.

"Wouldn't talk like that if the hurt of it didn't make me. . . . Ah, what a girl to go wrong!"

He pushed me away with a brusque movement.

"Go on out and play! But not in the street—only in the yard or the garden, hear!"

The garden was just the place I had been longing to be: I knew that as soon as I put in my appearance up on the embankment, the boys down in the ravine would start throwing stones at me, and I wanted nothing more than to pay them back in kind.

"There's the pug!" they cried on catching sight of me. "Here goes!" And they hurriedly collected ammunition.

I had no idea what a "pug" was, so the name carried no insult; but it was a joy to find myself pitted against so many and to see how a well-aimed stone would put the enemy to flight or make them hide in the bushes. Such fights held no malice and left no feeling of injury.

I learned my letters quickly, and perhaps it was this that made my grandfather pay more attention to me and stop whipping me so often, though in my opinion I deserved more lickings than ever before. As I became older and bolder, I began to violate my grandfather's rules and orders, but he only scolded, or shook his fist at me.

It seemed to me that he had often beaten me without cause, and one day I told him so.

He gave me a light tap under the chin and blinked into my eyes.

"Wha-a-at?" he drawled, adding with a chuckle:

"You little heretic, you! Who are you to decide how many lickings you deserve? I'm the only one can know that! Scat!"

But he caught me by the shoulder as I turned and once more looked me in the eye.

"You being sly, or just a simpleton?"

"I don't know."

"Don't know, don't you? Well, then I'll tell you: you be sly— that's better than to be a simpleton. A calf's a simpleton, understand? Now go on out and play."

Soon I was reading the Psalter letter by letter. Usually we studied after tea in the evening, and each time I had to read an entire psalm.

" 'B' for butter, 'l' for lady, 'e' for ever, 's' for sugar, 's' for sugar—bless; 'e' for ever, 'd' for dinner—ed: blessed. Blessed is he. . ." I spelled, running my index finger along the line. The boredom of it gave rise to all kinds of questions.

"Who is blessed? Uncle Yakov?"

"I'll give you a whack over the head and then you'll know who is blessed!" answered my grandfather with an angry snort. But I sensed that his anger was not genuine; it was only assumed by force of habit, and for decency's sake.

And I was not mistaken; a minute later my grandfather grumbled, without a thought for me:

"Hm-m, when it comes to singing and playing, he's a regular King David, but when it comes to working, he's no better than an Absalom. A songster, a trickster, a jester—phooh! 'Dancing merry o'er green!' Well, and how far does that dancing get you? Not very far!"

I stopped reading to listen to him, glancing up into his frowning, worried face; his narrowed eyes were gazing off into the distance, and they were filled with a warm sadness thawing his usual severity. His golden eyebrows quivered and his stained fingernails glistened as he tapped nervously on the table.

"Grandfather!"

"Eh?"

"Tell me a story."

"You go on with your reading, lazybones," he grumbled, rubbing his eyes as though he had just waked up. "You'd rather hear all kinds of fairy tales than the Psalter."

I suspected that he too would rather hear fairy tales than the Psalter, though he knew the latter almost by heart, having taken a vow to read part of it out loud every evening before going to bed, chanting like the deacon chanted the breviary in church.

But I pressed him for the, story, and finally the old man gave in.

"Oh, all right. You'll be having the Psalter with you all your life, but soon I'll be going to meet my Maker at the judgment seat."

Leaning against the needle-point of the old armchair, he threw back his head, fixed his eyes on the ceiling, and lost himself in recollections of old times. Once a robber band had come to Balakhna to loot the shop of the merchant Zayev. My grandfather's father had run to the belfry to give the alarm, but the robbers overtook him, slashed him with their swords, and threw his remains down from the belfry.

"I was only a little chap at that time; I didn't see what happened and I don't remember it; I only remember from the time the French came, in 1812—when I was just twelve. They drove about thirty prisoners into Balakhna at that time—all of them little and skinny, dressed in whatever they could lay hands on—worse than beggars—shivering in their skins, some of them with their arms and legs froze, so they couldn't even stand up. The muzhiks wanted to kill them off, but the convoy wouldn't let them. Then the troops from the garrison came and drove the muzhiks to their huts. After that they got used to each other; the Frenchmen turned out to be a shrewd, nimble lot, and jolly in the bargain, singing their songs whenever the mood struck them. The quality used to drive down from Nizhni in troikas to have a look at them. Some of those who came would curse the French and shake their fists at them, even strike them; others would talk kind to them in their own tongue and give them money and old clothes to cheer them up. I remember one old man—a gentleman he was—who covered his face with his hands and started crying:

'Just see what that fiend Napoleon has done to the French!' he says. Think of that—a Russian, and a gentleman at that, with such a kind heart—taking pity on foreigners that way. . . ."

For a moment he was silent, closing his eyes and stroking down his hair. Then he continued cautiously, rummaging through his memories of the past:

"Winter, with a blizzard raging and the cold pressing down hard on the huts, and the Frenchmen running to our window and calling to my mother—she used to make buns to peddle—they'd knock at the window, jumping about and shouting for buns. My mother wouldn't let them into the hut; she'd hand them their buns through the window. They'd grab them, all hot and steaming, right from the oven, and stick them inside their shirts, tight against their frozen bodies, right to their hearts; how they ever stood it! Lots of them died of the cold—people from a warm country, not used to such frosts. Two of them lived in our bathhouse, down in the garden—an officer and his adjutant named Miron; the officer was tall and thin, nothing but skin and bones, and he went around in a woman's cloak that came to his knees. He was a gentle soul, but a regular drunkard. My mother brewed beer on the sly and sold it; he'd buy himself beer and drink himself drunk and start singing his songs. He learned to babble a bit in our tongue. 'Your land's not white,' he would say. 'It's black and harsh.' He spoke very broken, but you could understand what he meant, and it's the truth—nothing gentle about our northern parts. If you go down the Volga the land gets warmer and softer, and down past the Caspian seems there's no snow at all. You can be sure of this, seeing's how you'll not find anything about snow or about winter in the Gospels, or the Acts, or the Psalter, and it was down in that country Christ lived. . . . Soon's we finish the Psalter, you and me'll start reading the Gospels."

Again he became silent and seemed to doze off; when his mind was fixed on something, he would stare out the window with his eyes narrowed, his whole figure little and sharp.

"Go on," I urged quietly.

"Ah well!" he said with a start. "What was it I was talking about? The French? Well, they're also humans, no worse than us sinners. They'd go shouting after my mother, 'Madame, madame!' which means 'my dame' in their tongue, but that there 'dame' would go toting home a sack of flour weighing no less than five poods if an ounce. Strong as an ox she was; it meant nothing for her to go flinging me around by the hair right up until I was twenty years old. And I was no weakling myself at that time. That adjutant Miron was a great lover of horses: he'd go from yard to yard making signs, asking to be allowed to groom the horses. At first people were scared—an enemy—might ruin the horses. But after a while the muzhiks used to ask him themselves: 'Hi there, Miron!' and he'd laugh and duck his head like a bull and come running. His hair was red as a carrot, and he had a big nose and thick lips. He was a fine groom and knew how to cure the horses of various ailments; later he became a groom in Nizhni, but he went off his head and the firemen beat him to death. As for the officer, he sort of went into a decline when spring came, and on the day of Saint Nicholas he died quiet like: sat dreaming at the window of the bath-house and passed away, just sitting there with his head out the window. I felt sorry for him; even shed a few tears; a gentle soul he was; used to take me by the ears and whisper something soft in his own tongue. I couldn't understand his words, but they sounded nice. Not too much human kindness in. this world. Once he started teaching me how to talk his language, but my mother forbid it. She even took me to the priest and he ordered me a beating and put in a complaint about the officer. People were strict in those days, brother! You don't have to suffer what we did— others have suffered it for you, and don't you ever forget it! Take me, for example—what I've suffered!"

It grew dark. My grandfather strangely expanded in the dark and his eyes shone like those of a cat. He recounted his story quietly, cautiously, musingly, but when he spoke of himself he became animated and boastful. I did not like to hear him speak of himself and I did not like his constant admonitions:

"Remember that!" "Don't you forget it!"

There were many things he told me which I would have been glad to have forgotten, but they stuck in my mind like painful splinters, even without his admonitions. He never told me fairy tales—only accounts of true happenings. I had observed that questions annoyed him, and so I made a point of putting them:

"Who's better—Russians or Frenchmen?"

"Who can tell? I never saw Frenchmen in their own country," he answered with irritation, adding:

"Even a rat's all right in its own hole."

"Are Russians all right?"

"Some are, some aren't. They were better when they were serfs—like wrought iron. Now the chain's off their feet, but they've nothing to eat. To be sure the gentlefolk are a hardhearted lot, but they've got more sense than the muzhik. Can't say that about all of them, but once a gentleman's good, he's very good. Some are the veriest fools—like sacks—hold whatever you stuff them with. Too many empty shells among us—at first glance looks like a human being, but on looking a little closer you see the worms have eaten out all the kernel—nothing left but a shell. What we need is some learning; need to sharpen our wits, but there's nothing to sharpen them on. . . ."

"Are Russians strong?"

"Some are, but it's not strength that counts, it's skill; the strongest man is weaker than a horse."

"Why did the French fight us?"

"Well, now—wars—they're the business of the tsar. It's not for simple folk like us to understand why."

But I shall never forget my grandfather's answer when I asked him who Bonaparte was:

"He was a brave fellow who wanted to conquer the whole earth, so's everybody could live equal—no lords and officials, but just like that—all the same. The names would stay different, but the rights equal for everybody. And the same faith for everybody. No sense in that, of course; it's only crabs are all alike. Take fish, now—even they're all different: the salmon's no friend of the catfish, and the sturgeon's not making up to the herring. We've had our own Bonapartes—Stepan Razin, for example, and Yemelyan Pugachov—but I'll tell you about them another time...."

Sometimes he would stare at me wide-eyed for a long time, as though he had never seen me before, and this was very unpleasant.

But he never spoke to me about my father or mother.

Sometimes grandmother would enter during these conversations. She would quietly take a seat in the corner and say nothing until suddenly she would ask a question in her caressing voice:

"Remember, father, how fine it was that time you and me made a pilgrimage to Murom to pray to the Virgin? What year was that?"

"Don't remember exactly, but it was before the cholera— the year they combed the forest for the Olonchans."

"That's right. I remember how scared we were of them. . . ."

"Hm-m."

I asked who the Olonchans were and why they hid in the forest. My grandfather answered reluctantly:

"The Olonchans were simply muzhiks— serfs who ran away from work at the factories."

"How did they catch them?"

"How do you suppose? Like when the boys play—some of them run, others catch them. Once they're caught, they get licked with whips and thongs; used to get their nostrils slit too, and brands put on their foreheads to show they were punished."

"What for?"

"Who knows? That's a dark business, and it's hard to say who was at fault, the ones who did the running or the ones who did the catching."

"Remember, father," put in my grandmother once more, "how it was after the great fire?"

"Which great fire?" asked my grandfather with a stern insistence on accuracy.

Lost in their reminiscences, they became oblivious of my presence. Their voices went on quietly, and with such measured rhythm that at times it seemed they were singing a song, a gruesome song about fires and illnesses and the thrashings dealt to human beings, about accidental deaths and clever swindles, about religious fanatics and irascible gentlemen from the upper classes.

"How much we've seen! How much we've lived through!" muttered my grandfather.

"And has it been a bad life?" asked my grandmother. "Just think what a fine spring it was when Varvara was born!"

"That was in '48, the year of the march on Hungary; day after we had Varvara baptized they drove off her godfather Tikhon. . . ."

"And he never came back," sighed my grandmother.

"Never came back. From that day on God's mercy slipped past us like water over a raft. Ah, Varvara. ..."

"Enough, father. ..."

"Why enough?" he answered angrily. "Turned out bad, our children, however you look at them. Our strength all poured away into nothing. You and me thought we were putting things by in a sound basket, but the Lord saw fit to slip a sieve into our hands. . . ."

He cried out as if he had been branded, running about the room, moaning, denouncing his children, shaking his bony little fist at my grandmother.

"And it's all your spoiling that sent them to the dogs, you softy! You witch, you!"

The extremity of his bitterness drove him into the icon corner, where he beat himself on his thin, sounding breast and wailed tearfully:

"Why, oh Lord? Am I so much worse than anybody else?"

His wet eyes glistened with pain and indignation, and his whole body trembled.

My grandmother remained sitting in the darkness, silently crossing herself. Finally she went over to him.

"Why torture yourself like this?" she said persuasively. "The Lord knows what He's about. There be not many children better than ours. It's the same everywhere, father—quarrels and fighting and fussing. All mothers and fathers wash away their sins with their own tears. You're not the only one. . . ."

Sometimes her words would calm him, and he would wearily slip into bed, while my grandmother and I would steal away to our attic.

But once when she went over to him with her gentle words, he whirled around and struck her a sounding blow in the face with his fist. My grandmother swayed and pressed her hand to her lips. When she had sufficiently recovered, she said in a calm, quiet voice: "You fool . . ." and spat the blood at his feet. He raised his arms over his head and shrieked twice:

"Get out before I kill you!"

"Fool!" repeated my grandmother, going toward the door. He threw himself after her, but she unhurriedly stepped over the sill and slammed the door in his face.

"The old hussy," hissed my grandfather, red as a glowing coal, as he clutched the jamb, scratching at it with his nails.

I sat on the bunk built against the stove more dead than alive, scarcely believing my own eyes. This was the first time he had ever struck my grandmother in my presence, and I was crushed by the repulsiveness of it. His act revealed a new quality in him, something which nothing could justify and which bore down on me with an awful weight. He kept standing there, hanging on to the doorjamb, shrinking and going grey, as though dusted with ashes. Suddenly he went to the centre of the room, fell on his knees and slumped forward, supporting himself on his arm. Then he straightened up, beat himself on the breast with both hands, and cried. . . .

"Oh God, oh God . . ."

I slid off the warm tiles of the bunk as though they were ice and ran out. Upstairs my grandmother was walking up and down, rinsing her mouth.

"Does it hurt?"

She went over to the corner and spit the water into the waste bucket.

"It's all right," she answered calmly. "My teeth are whole— just a cut on the lip."

"Why did he do it?"

"Lost his temper," she answered, glancing out the window. "It's hard for him, old man that he is, so much misfortune.... You go to bed and forget about it. ..."

I asked her about something else, but with unwonted sharpness she replied:

"Didn't you hear me? Go to bed! Such a disobedient lad...."

She sat down by the window and sucked at her lip, frequently spitting into her handkerchief. I kept looking at her as I undressed: a sprinkling of stars could be seen in the square of night sky above her head. Everything was quiet outside, everything dark inside.

When I was in bed she came over to me and quietly stroked my forehead.

"Sleep in peace," she said. "I'm going down to him. . . . Don't you feel too sorry for me, pigeon-widgeon, a lot of it's my own fault. ... Go to sleep!"

She kissed me and went out, leaving me with a choking sadness. I jumped out of the soft, hot bed and went to the window, where I stood glancing down into the empty street, numbed by unbearable pain.

VI

Once more life became a nightmare. One evening after tea, when my grandfather and I were reading the Psalter and my grandmother was washing up the dishes, my Uncle Yakov rushed into the room. He was as dishevelled as ever, looking like a worn-out broom. He threw his cap into the corner and without a word of greeting began to speak with wild gestures:

"Mikhail's on a rampage, pa! He had dinner at our place, drank himself drunk and went raging mad: broke the dishes, tore up a woollen dress belonging to a customer, broke the window, and cursed me and Grigori. He's coming here and swore he'd get you: Til pull all the hairs out of pa's beard!' he yelled. Til kill him!' he cried. You better watch out. . . ."

Grandfather leaned on the table and slowly pulled himself to his feet, his face all drawn toward his nose, making it look for all the world like a hatchet.

"Hear that, mother?" he squeaked. "What d'ye think of that, eh? Coming to kill his own father! There's a son for you! Well, the time's come! The time's come, fellows . . . "

He squared his shoulders and began pacing the floor. Then he went to the door and fastened it with a heavy hook.

"The both of you are still after that dowry of Varvara's, I know," he said, turning to Yakov. "Well, here's how you'll get it!" and he snapped his fingers under my uncle's nose.

"Why jump on me, pa?" said the latter, springing back and speaking in an offended tone.

"You? I know you too!"

Grandmother said nothing as she hurriedly put the cups in the cupboard.

"I came to protect you!"

"Ha!" laughed my grandfather scornfully. "That's a good one! Thanks, son! Here, mother, give this foxey something to work with—a poker or a flatiron! And you, Yakov Vasilyevich,

soon as your brother breaks the door open you'll give it to him—on my head!"

My uncle thrust his hands in his pockets and slunk off to one side.

"Well, if you don't want to believe me. . . ."

"Believe *you*?" shouted my grandfather with a stamp of his foot. "I'd believe a cat, or a rat, or a kangaroo—but not you! It's you that gave him the liquor and egged him on—I know! Well, now beat him up! Take your choice—him or me!"

Grandmother turned to me and whispered:

"Run upstairs and watch for Uncle Mikhail through the window. Soon's you see him, come tell us! Be off, hurry!"

So up I went and planted myself at the window, a bit intimidated by the thought of what my raging uncle would do when he got here, but swelling with pride at the responsible task entrusted to me. The street was wide, and covered with a thick layer of dust, through which the curves of the cobbles protruded. It extended far to the left, crossing a ravine and coming out on Ostrozhnaya Square, where the grey building of the old jail with its four towers stood firmly implanted in the clay soil. There was a certain melancholy beauty and impressiveness about this building. To the right, three houses from ours, the street ran into Sennaya Square, bounded on the opposite side by yellow barracks for prisoners and the ogling fire tower, at the top of which the watchman walked round and round like a dog on a chain. The square was cut up by gullies and ditches, the bottom of one of which was filled with green slime, while to the right lay Dukov Pond. It was there, according to my grandmother, my uncles had once thrown my father through a hole in the ice. Almost opposite my window was a bystreet lined with little, motley houses; it ended in the church of the Three Saints, a thick structure crouching against the earth. On looking straight out of the window, the roofs seemed to be boats upturned on the green waves of the orchards.

The dusty houses of our street, faded by the winds of long winters, washed by endless autumn rains, stood huddled together like beggars on a church porch, glancing about furtively with their bulging windows as though, like me, they were waiting for something. The few people in sight walked as unhurriedly as meditative roaches climbing the stove. A stifling heat rose to my window, bringing with it the detested odour of *pirog* stuffed with spring onions and carrots.

To the present day I find this odour intolerable. The scene was oppressive—oppressive in a peculiar way which was almost unbearable. My breast became filled with liquid lead, which pressed against my ribs and chest until it seemed that I was being blown up like a bubble which could not be contained in this tiny room with its coffin-like ceiling.

Suddenly I caught sight of Uncle Mikhail glancing out from behind the grey house on the corner of the by-street. He had pulled his cap down so that it made his ears stick out. He was wearing a short brown coat and knee boots all covered with dust; one hand was in the pocket of his checked pants, the other holding on to his beard. I could not see his face, but he was standing as though he meant to leap across the street and dig his black, hairy claws into grandfather's house. I should have run downstairs and told them that he had come, but I could not tear myself away from the window. I saw him steal cautiously across the street, as though he were afraid to dirty his grey boots, and heard the jarring of glass and the squeaking of hinges as he opened the door of the saloon.

I ran downstairs and knocked at the door of my grandfather's room.

"Who's there?" he cried gruffly, without opening. "You? Well? Went into the saloon, you say? All right, go back where you came from!"

"I'm afraid...."

"Can't be helped!"

I went. It was getting dark; the dust of the street became thicker and darker; oily yellow lights appeared in the windows; from the house across the street came the sound of string music playing something fine and mournful. Someone was singing in the saloon; whenever the door was opened I could hear a tired, broken voice which I knew to belong to the one-eyed beggar Nikitushka, a bearded old man whose left eye was tight shut and whose right one resembled a red-hot coal. The slamming of the door would chop off his song like the blow of an axe.

My grandmother envied the beggar; whenever she heard him sing she would sigh and say:

"How lucky he is to know so many wonderful songs!"

Sometimes she would call him into our yard. He would sit on the porch leaning on his cane, singing and reciting verses, while my grandmother would sit next to him, interrupting him with an occasional question.

"You mean to say the Holy Virgin has been in Ryazan?"

"She's been everywhere—in all the gubernias. . ." he would answer convincingly.

A sleepy exhaustion crept imperceptibly along the street, pressing down on my heart and closing my eyes. If only my grandmother would come! Or even my grandfather! What sort of person must my father have been, that my uncles and grandfather should have disliked him so, while my grandmother and Grigori and nanny Yevgenia should speak so well of him? And where was my mother?

Of late I kept thinking more and more often of my mother, envisioning her as the heroine of all my grandmother's tales and legends. The fact that my mother did not want to live with her family only raised her in my estimation. I imagined that she was living with a band of highwaymen at an inn, and that they robbed the rich and divided the spoil among the poor. Or perhaps she was living in a cave in the forest, again with a band of kind-hearted robbers for whom she cooked and guarded stolen gold. Or still another version was that she was wandering over the earth counting its treasures like the "Robber-Princess" Yengalycheva, accompanied by the Holy Virgin, who kept saying to her as she said to the "Robber-Princess":

It is not for thee, thou greedy one,
To strip the earth of its silver and gold;
It is not for thee, thou grasping one,
To hide thy shame neath the treasures of earth!

And my mother answered her in the words of the "Robber-Princess":

Forgive me, O Virgin Immaculate,
And pity my soul for its sinful ness,
Not for myself do I plunder so,
For the sake of my son, my beloved one....

Then the Holy Virgin, who was as kind hearted as my grandmother, forgave her, and said:

Ah, thou vixen, thou Varyushka,
Ah, thou Tatar incorrigible!
Go, if thou must, thy chosen path:
Choose the way; rue the day.
But touch not the folk of this Russian land,
On a forest trail a Mordovian flail,
Or a Kalmyk slay on the steppelands grey....

I lost myself in recollections of these legends as in a dream, from which I was roughly awakened by a bustling and shuffling and roaring coming from the hair and the yard down below. Leaning out of the window I saw my grandfather and Uncle Yakov and the funny saloonkeeper Melyan pushing my Uncle Mikhail through the gate out into the street; he fought his way back, but they kicked him and beat him on the arms, the back, the shoulders, and at last he went flying into the dust of the street. The gate was slammed, locked and bolted, his battered cap tossed over the fence, and everything became quiet.

After lying still for a while, my rumpled, tattered uncle sat up, picked up a cobblestone, and hurled it at the gate, producing a dull thud like a blow on the bottom of a barrel. Dark-faced people came crawling out of the saloon and started bellowing and waving their arms; heads appeared in the windows of the houses; the street became lively with yells and laughter. This too was like a fairy tale—fascinating, but unpleasant and even frightening.

Suddenly everything was over, everyone had gone, all was quiet.

On the trunk by the door sat my grandmother, all hunched over, motionless, scarcely breathing; I was standing in front of her stroking her soft, warm, wet cheeks, but apparently she was unaware of it, and only sat there muttering miserably:

"Dear Lord, wasn't there enough good sense to go around when it came to me and my children? God help us. . . ."

It seems to me that my grandfather lived not more than a year in this house on Pole-Vaya Street—from spring to spring. But in so short a time the house managed to become notorious; almost every Sunday the urchins would come running to our gates, joyfully announcing to the entire block:

"Another fight at the Kashirins'!"

Usually Uncle Mikhail would come in the evening and remain the whole night, keeping the house in a state of siege, its inhabitants in a state of alarm. Sometimes he would bring two or three assistants along—desperate young bucks from the Kunavino workshop. They would climb up the ravine into the garden and there give full rein to the dictates of their drunken imagination. They pulled up all the raspberry and currant bushes, and one night they ruined the bath-house, breaking everything in it that was breakable—the shelves, the benches, the boilers. They took the stove apart, pulled up some of the floor boards, ripped off the door and the jamb.

My grandfather stood at the window silent and lowering, listening to them destroy his property; my grandmother ran out into the yard, where she became lost in the darkness. But her voice came back pleadingly:

"Mikhail! Think what you're doing, Mikhail!"

In reply came a string of foul and idiotic Russian oaths, the meaning of which must have been beyond the comprehension and feeling of the beasts vomiting them forth.

There could be no thought of following grandmother at such a moment, but it was frightening without her. I went down into grandfather's room.

"Out of here, anathema!" he shouted at me hoarsely.

I ran back to the attic and stared out into the darkness of the garden, trying not to lose sight of my grandmother, crying and calling to her, afraid that they would kill her. She did not come, but on hearing my voice, my drunken uncle addressed some filthy oaths to my mother.

On one such evening my grandfather was ill. He lay in bed and kept crying plaintively as he rolled his head back and forth over the pillow:

"Is this all I lived for, sinned for, hoarded for? If it wasn't so shameful, I'd call the, police and haul them up before the governor. . . . What a disgrace! Who ever heard of parents sicking the police on their own children? So there's nothing you can do but keep lying here, old man!"

Suddenly he threw his legs over the edge of the bed and went staggering to the window.

"Here, where you going?" cried my grandmother, catching him by the arm.

"Give me a light!" he ordered, his breath coming in great gasps.

When my grandmother had lighted the candle, he held it in front of him like a gun and shouted mockingly through the window:

"Phooh, Mishka, thief in the night, mad as a dog with the scurvy!"

Immediately the upper pane of the window was shattered and half a brick fell on the table next to my grandmother.

"Missed!" yelled my grandfather, and began either to laugh or to cry.

My grandmother picked him up in her arms as though he were me and laid him on the bed, muttering in a frightened voice:

"What are you doing, for the love of Christ! If anything should happen, it'd be Siberia for him; do you think he realizes it means Siberia when he's in such a state?"

My grandfather lay with his legs jerking as he sobbed hoarsely: "Let him kill me...."

A roaring and stamping came from outside. I took the brick off the table and ran to the window, but my grandmother managed to snatch me up and thrust me in the corner, hissing:

"You crazy little brat!"

Another time my uncle mounted the back porch and began swinging a huge club at the entrance door. My grandfather stood in the hall waiting for him, supported by two lodgers with clubs in their hands and the large wife of the saloonkeeper wielding a rolling pin. Behind them pressed my grandmother.

"Let me reach him," she pleaded. "Let me have a word with him."

My grandfather held his club upraised and stood with one foot forward like the muzhik with the spear in the painting "The Bear Hunt." When my grandmother rushed over to him, he silently pushed her away with his foot and his elbow. All four of them stood in menacing poses of expectation; a lamp hanging on the wall above them lighted their faces with its fitful flame. I stood watching from the attic stairs, anxious to take my grandmother away.

My uncle kept furiously beating the door. The lower hinge was already broken, and scraped unpleasantly, leaving the door hanging by only the upper hinge, which also threatened to give way. Grandfather spoke to his supporters in the same sort of scraping voice:

"Beat him over the hands and the legs, but not on the head, mind."

Next to the door was a little window, just large enough to stick a head through; my uncle had already broken the glass of this window, leaving it to gape darkly, fringed with splintered glass, like an empty eye socket.

My grandmother ran to the window, thrust her arm through, and waved to Mikhail as she cried:

"Misha, for Christ's sake, go away! They'll cripple you for life! Go away!"

He struck her over the arm with his club; I could see something heavy flash across the window and fall on her arm, after which my grandmother sank to the floor, just managing to cry once more, "Run, Misha . . ." before she became limp and silent.

"Ah, mother!" wailed my grandfather in a dreadful voice.

The door opened, my uncle jumped through the black opening, but was immediately thrown out onto the porch like a spadeful of dirt.

The wife of the saloonkeeper took my grandmother to grandfather's room; he soon followed.

"Is the bone broken?" he asked unhappily, going over to her.

"Looks like it's broken," she replied without opening her eyes. "But what have you done to him—to him!"

"Come to your senses, woman!" cried my grandfather angrily. "What do you think I am, a beast? We tied him up and he's lying out in the shed. I poured a bucket of water over him. There's a fiend for you! Where does he get it from?"

My grandmother groaned.

"I've sent for the bonesetter already; try to bear it a while," said my grandfather, sitting down next to her on the bed. "They'll be the death of us yet, mother; bring us to our graves before our time."

"Give them everything."

"And what about Varvara?"

They spoke for a long time, grandmother in a quiet, plaintive voice, my grandfather noisily and angrily.

Then a little, hunchbacked old woman put in her appearance. She had a mouth stretching from ear to ear; her lower jaw trembled, her mouth hung open like a fish's, and her upper lip was bisected by a sharp nose. Her eyes could not be seen, she could scarcely move her legs and kept shuffling across the floor with her crutch, jingling the little bundle she carried.

This, I thought, was Death come to my grandmother. I ran over to the old woman and shouted at the top of my lungs:

"Get out of here!"

My grandfather grabbed me up and hauled me unceremoniously to the attic.

VII

At a very early date I realized that my grandfather had one God, my grandmother another.

On waking in the morning, grandmother would usually sit for a long time on the bed combing her amazing hair, jerking her head, clenching her teeth as she pulled out whole locks of the long black silk, and cursing under her breath so as not to wake me up:

"A pox on you, a plague on you, damn you!"

When she had managed to untangle it more or less, she would braid it and wash herself hurriedly, with angry spluttering. Without having washed the irritation from her large face, all wrinkled with sleep, she would kneel in front of the icons. Then would begin her true morning ablutions which left her completely refreshed.

Straightening her spine and throwing back her head, she would glance affectionately into the round face of the Virgin of Kazan and cross herself fervently as she whispered:

"Blessed Virgin, pour thy blessings on the coming day. . . ."

Then she would bow to the very floor, raise herself slowly, and again whisper with growing fervour:

"Fount of all joy, beauty inexpressible, like an apple tree in full bloom   "

Almost every morning she found new words of praise and adoration, and this made me listen to each of her prayers with strained attention.

"Dear heart, so pure, so divine! Light of my soul, guardian of my hearth, sun of heaven, so bright, so golden, precious mother of God, save us from the onrushings of evil, save us all from needless abuse, and me from being offended without cause. . . ."

A smile hovered in the depths of her dark eyes, and she seemed to have become younger as she again crossed herself with a slow movement of her heavy hand.

"Dear Jesus, son of God, be merciful to me, a sinner, for thine own mother's sake. . . ."

Her prayers were always a laudatory offering, a pean of praise coming from a simple and sincere heart.

In the morning is he did not linger long over her prayers: it was necessary to put up the samovar, since my grandfather no longer kept a servant, and if she made him wait for his morning tea, she was rewarded by violent and endless reproaches.

Sometimes, if he had awakened earlier than my grandmother, he would climb up to the attic and find her at her prayers. He would stand listening silently, with a contemptuous smile at the corners of his thin, dark lips, remarking later at the breakfast table:

"How many times have I taught you how to pray, you thickhead, but on you go, in your stubborn way, muttering along like a heretic! How God ever puts up with it is more than lean understand!"

"He understands," answered my grandmother confidently. "No matter what you say to Him, He's sure to understand."

"Crazy as a Chuvash, that's what you are! Phooh!"

Her God was with her all day long. She even told the animals about Him. I could see that it was easy for all creatures—people, dogs, birds, bees, and even growing things—to submit to that God. He was equally kind and equally dear to everything on earth.

One day the mischievous tomcat belonging to the saloonkeeper's wife—a lovely, grey, golden-headed beast which was a favourite in the yard in spite of the fact that it was a toady and a sly glutton—caught a starling. My grandmother took the tortured bird away from the cat and said angrily:

"No fear of God in your heart, that's what's the trouble with you, you horrid beasty!"

The janitor and the saloonkeeper's wife laughed at my grandmother for these words, but she shouted at them angrily:

"You think the animals have no knowledge of God? The least of them knows Him as well as you, you hardhearted creatures!"

While harnessing the fat, listless Sharap, she would murmur:

"Why so unhappy, servant of God? Getting old I guess. . . ."
The horse would sigh and shake its head.

Yet she did not utter the name of God as often as did my
grandfather. I could understand my grandmother's God and was
not afraid of Him, yet I dared not lie in His presence. That would
have been shameful. Because of this shame, I never lied to my
grandmother. It was quite impossible to hide anything from so
kind a God, and so far as I can remember, I never had any
inclination to do so.

One day the saloonkeeper's wife had a quarrel with my
grandfather, and included my innocent grandmother in her
vituperations, even throwing a carrot at her.

"And it's a fool you are, my fine lady!" retorted grandmother
calmly. But I was deeply offended for grandmother's sake and
decided to take revenge.

For some time I considered what would be the best way to
injure this fat, redheaded woman with the double chin and no
eyes to speak of.

In the internecine wars waged by our neighbours, I had
observed that vengeance was wreaked by chopping off the tails
of cats, poisoning dogs, killing chickens, or by stealing into the
enemy's cellar at night and pouring kerosene into barrels of
sauerkraut or pickles, or pulling the stoppers out of kegs of kvass.
But none of these means satisfied me. It was necessary to think
up something more bold and terrible.

And so I decided on the following measure: when the
saloonkeeper's wife climbed down into the cellar, I closed the
hatch after her, locked it, did a dance of vengeance on top, and
threw the key up on the roof. Then I rushed into the kitchen where
my grandmother was cooking. At first she could not understand
my ecstasy, but when she discovered its cause, she slapped me
on the parts provided for that purpose, dragged me out into the
yard, and sent me up on the roof for the key. Crushed by her
reaction, I silently procured the key and then ran into a corner of
the yard, from where I watched my grandmother free the prisoner
and then come walking toward me in the company of the hated
one, both of them laughing amiably.

"I'll give it to you yet!" threatened the saloonkeeper's wife, shaking her fat fist at me, but her eyeless face was smiling good-naturedly. My grandmother took me by the scruff of the neck and led me into the kitchen.

"What did you do that for?" she asked.

"Didn't she throw a carrot at you?"

"Aha! So it was on my account you did it, eh? I'll show you, you little whippersnapper! I'll shove you under the stove with the mice, and then you'll get some sense in you! A fine champion you make! Come, everybody, and take a look at this little bubble before it bursts! If I tell your grandfather, won't he take the skin off your behind for you though! Get up into the attic now and have a look at those books of yours!"

She did not speak to me for the rest of the day, but in the evening before saying her prayers, she sat down on the side of my bed and said these unforgettable words:

"Listen, pigeon-widgeon, just remember this: never butt into the affairs of grownups. Grownups are a spoiled lot—tried by toils and temptations. But you're not—not yet. So you just go on living according to your child lights, until the Lord sees fit to touch your heart and show you your task, leading you out onto the path you must trod. Is that clear? As for who's to blame for what—that's none of your business. God will judge and punish. That's for Him, not for us."

She was silent for a minute, during which she took some snuff, and then she narrowed her right eye and added:

"Sometimes the Lord Hisself is hard put to tell who's to blame."

"Why, doesn't He know everything?" I asked in surprise.

"If He did," she replied sadly, "there's lots of things people wouldn't be a-doing. He sits up there in heaven, watching us sinners down below, and sometimes he breaks into such tears, such sobbing! 'Ah, my people, my people, my own dear people!' he weeps. 'How my heart bleeds for you!' '

She herself was weeping, and without bothering to dry her tears, she went to the icon corner to pray.

From that time on her God became even dearer and more comprehensible to me.

At his lessons my grandfather also taught me that God was all-knowing, all-seeing, and ever present, a help to man in all his trouble. But grandfather did not pray like grandmother.

Before going to the icon corner in the morning, he would carefully wash and dress and comb his red hair and beard; only after adjusting his blouse in the mirror and tying the black cravat he wore inside his vest would he creep stealthily toward the icons. He would always come to a halt at one and the same knot in the floor board which resembled the eye of a horse, his arms stiff at his sides like a soldier's. After a moment's silence, during which he stood with bowed head, thin and straight, he would say impressively:

"In the name of the Father and of the Son and of the Holy Ghost!"

It always seemed to me that the room became particularly quiet after these words—even the flies seemed to buzz with a certain veneration.

Now his head was thrown back, his eyebrows bristling, his golden beard horizontal with the floor. He said his prayers in a firm voice, as though reciting a lesson, pronouncing the words emphatically and demandingly:

"Cometh the Judgment Day when no man knoweth, to expose the deeds of men. . . ."

Beating himself lightly on the chest, he would press his request:

"Against Thee, Thee only, have I sinned. . . . Hide Thy face from my sins. .. ."

Every word was stressed as he recited the "Creed," and he beat time by jerking his right leg. He stood there neat and clean and commanding, drawing his whole body toward the icons, seeming to grow taller and thinner and harder.

"Thou, who hast borne the Great Healer, cleanse my heart of all evil; hark to the groaning of my soul and have mercy, O Mother of God!"

Then he would wail thinly, the tears gleaming, drawing his whole body toward the icons:

"Let my faith be accounted for works, O my God, and lay not a burden beyond my strength to bear. . . ."

He crossed himself again 'and again, quickly and convulsively, nodding his head like a butting goat and speaking in a wheezing, whimpering voice. When in later life I had occasion to visit a synagogue, I realized that my grandfather prayed like a Jew.

The samovar had long since been steaming on the table, the room was filled with the scent of hot rye cakes stuffed with cottage cheese, and my stomach was roaring with hunger. My grandmother stood leaning against the doorjamb, sighing and frowning, with her eyes fastened on the floor; the sun glanced merrily through the window, the dew shone like pearls on the trees, the morning air bore the fresh scent of dill, currants, and ripening apples, but my grandfather still continued to rock and wail at his prayers:

"Quench the fire of my passion, for I be base and accursed!"

I knew all his matins and all his vespers by heart, and would follow him with intense concentration to see whether he made a mistake or left out anything.

Such occasions were rare, but they always roused in me a malicious sense of triumph.

When my grandfather had finished his prayers, he turned to me and my grandmother and said:

"Good morning."

We bowed, and at long last took our places at the table.

"You left out 'sufficient,' " I said, turning to my grandfather.

"Sure you're not lying?" he asked sceptically.

"No. You should have said, 'And may my faith be sufficient into my need,' but you left out 'sufficient.' '

"Humph!" he exclaimed, blinking guiltily.

Some day he would repay me with interest for that remark, but for the present I took my fill of pleasure in his embarrassment.

One day my grandmother said jokingly:

"Must be boring for God to listen to your prayers, father—always saying one and the same thing."

"Wha-a-t?" he drawled menacingly. "What's that you're gibbering?"

"It's never a word from your own soul you offer your Maker, that's what I'm saying."

Trembling and flushing, he jumped up on a chair and threw a saucer at my grandmother.

"Get out of here, you old witch!" he screeched like a saw on glass.

Whenever he spoke about the strong arm of God, he emphasized its ruthlessness: once, for example, when people sinned they were drowned in a flood; another time their cities were burned and destroyed; people were punished by famine and plague. For him, God was a raised sword, a lash held over the heads of the wicked.

"Any as violates the laws of God are sure to come to some bad end!" he warned me, tapping the table with his bony fingers.

It was difficult for me to believe in the cruelness of God. I was suspicious that grandfather had invented this in order to make me afraid of himself, rather than of God.

"Is it to make me obey you that you tell me this?" I asked candidly.

"Of course," he replied with equal candour, "A fine thing it would be if you didn't obey!"

"What about grandmother?"

"Don't you listen to that old fool," he said sternly. "She's been that way all her life—crazy and unlearned. I'll let her know she's not to talk to you about such important things. Now answer me this: how many ranks are there among the angels?"

I answered and then asked:

"What does it mean, 'A person of high rank'?"

"Have to know everything, don't you?" he snorted, dropping his eyes and chewing his lips. On second thought he explained reluctantly:

"That's got nothing to do with God, that's human business—people of high rank—government officials and the like. An official is one as lives off the law—chews it up and swallows it down."

"What's the law?"

"The law? That's, so to speak, what people take on as their habit," answered the old man, his sharp, clever eyes twinkling with relish. "People live together and come to an agreement among themselves: that, for example, is the best way to do something or other, so they take it on as a habit, make it a rule, or a law, as they call it. Like when the boys get together to play a game and decide among themselves how they'll play. What they decide on is the law."

"And the officials?"

"They're like the bad boys who come and break the law."

"Why?"

"That's not a thing for you to understand," he said with a frown. "The Lord stands over all the affairs of men. They want one thing; He wants another. Nothing sure about human affairs. Just one little breath from the Lord, and everything gets scattered to the wind lake so much dust."

There were many reasons why I was interested in officials, so I kept pressing my point:

"There's that song Uncle Yakov sings:

"The holy angels—servants of God,
"The state officials—slaves of Satan!"

My grandfather closed his eyes, lifted his beard on his palm and stuck it into his mouth. From the trembling of his cheeks, I could tell he was laughing inside.

"Have to put you and Yakov in a sack and throw you in the river," he said. "He has no business singing such songs and you have no business listening to them. That's a song made up by dissenters and heretics—a bad sort of joke." He looked past me in a moment's meditation, then added with a sigh, "Phooh! What people!"

While in his conception God stood high and menacing above the affairs of men, he, like my grandmother, considered that the Lord had a hand in all his business—He and an endless number of saints. The only saints my grandmother seemed to recognize were Nicholas, Yuri, Frol and Lavr, who were kind and good, spending their time wandering from village to village, from town to town, helping people and sharing all their human qualities. Almost all of my grandfather's saints, on the other hand, were martyrs who had torn down idols and pitted themselves against the Caesars, as a result of which they had been tortured, burned at the stake and skinned alive.

Sometimes my grandfather would say wistfully:

"If only the Lord would help me sell this house for a profit of even five hundred rubles, I'd hold a service for Nicholas-the-Martyr!"

My grandmother would laugh and say to me:

"The old fool! Like as if Nicholas had nothing better to do than sell houses for him!"

For many years I kept my grandfather's church calendar with various remarks written in his hand. Opposite the days of Iochim and Anna he had Inscribed in red ink:

"Saved by their mercy from great misfortune."

I remember what that misfortune was. In his efforts to help his worthless sons he had secretly begun to lend money, taking various articles of value as security. Someone reported this, and one night the police came to search our house. There was great excitement, but everything ended happily. My grandfather prayed until sunrise, and in the morning he wrote those words on the calendar in my presence.

Before supper he had me read the Psalter, the prayer book, or the heavy volume of Yefrem Sirin. After supper he once more began to pray, and in the evening silence his monotonous words of repentance went on and on:

"It is Thine to give, and Thine to take away, most merciful immortal King   Lead us not into temptation. . . . Protect us from the wicked. . . . Let my tears absolve me of sin. . . ."

Often my grandmother would say:

"Oh, how tired I am! Looks like I'll be going to bed without saying my prayers to-night!"

My grandfather took me to church: on Saturdays to vespers, on Sundays to late mass. Even at church I could tell which God people prayed to: the priest and the deacon prayed to grandfather's God, but the choir always sang to grandmother's.

To be sure, I have given a crude picture of the childish distinction I drew between the two Gods, a distinction which I remember having caused me much spiritual conflict. I feared and disliked grandfather's God, who loved no one and kept a stern eye on everyone. He was primarily interested in unearthing something wicked and vicious in man. It was clear that he did not trust people, was ever waiting for them to repent, and took pleasure in meting out punishment.

During those days my mind dwelled primarily on God, the only beauty I found in life. All other impressions repulsed and saddened me with their filth and cruelty. God—my grandmother's God, friend to all living things—was the brightest and best of all that surrounded me. And naturally I could not understand why grandfather was blind to God's goodness.

I was not allowed to play out in the street because this excited me too much. I became almost drunk from the impressions gained from playing there and was often the instigator of some fight or disorder. I made no friends; the neighbours' children were hostile toward me. I hated to be called a Kashirin, and knowing this, they insisted on shouting the name to each other:

"Here comes the grandson of Kashirin, the miser! Take a look!"

"Knock him down!"

And the fight would begin.

I was exceptionally strong for my age and a good fighter. Even my enemies admitted this and never attacked me single-handed. So I always took a good beating at their hands, and returned home with a bloody nose, cut lips, and torn clothes.

Grandmother would meet me with fright and commiseration.

"What! Been fighting again, you little brat? I'll show you all right! Where'll I begin?"

She would wash my face and put a coin, or some herbs, or a lotion on my injuries, saying the while:

"What in the world makes you fight like this? Such a quiet lad at home, but a very demon once you get out in the street! For shame! I'll tell your grandfather not to let you out!"

Grandfather always noticed the bumps and bruises, but he never got really angry about them, simply muttering:

"Got on your medals again! Such a brave warrior! But don't let me catch you out in the street again, hear?"

I had no desire to go out in the street when everything was quiet there, but when I heard the merry voices of the children I would forget my grandfather's warning and run out of the yard. I did not mind the bumps and bruises, but I could never get used to the brutality of the boys' fun, a brutality with which I had become only too familiar and which nearly drove me mad. I could not bear to see them set cocks and dogs fighting each other, torture cats, chase the goats belonging to Jews, tease drunken beggars and the pious "Igosha, Death-in-the-Pocket."

The latter was a tall, lean, grimy person with a bristling beard on his bony face. His stooped figure in a long sheepskin coat swayed strangely as he moved down the street, his eyes fixed on the ground. His dark face with its sad little eyes inspired me with awe and respect. It seemed to me that this person must be engaged in some very solemn task which was not to be interrupted.

But the boys ran after him and threw stones at his hunched back. For some time he would pay no attention to them, as if he did not feel the blows, but all of a sudden he would stop, throw back his head and look around, adjusting his shaggy cap with a convulsive movement as if just aroused from sleep.

"Igosha, Death-in-the-Pocket! Igosha, where you bound? Just look in your pocket—see that death there?" cried the boys.

Grabbing hold of his pocket, he would bend over, pick up a stone or a lump of earth and wave his long arm clumsily, cursing under his breath. He always used the same three swear words— the boys' vocabulary was incomparably richer. Sometimes he would run limping after them; his long coat would get in his way and he would fall on his knees, supporting himself with grimy arms that looked like two dry sticks. Then the boys would pelt him with stones, while the bolder ones would run up to him, throw a handful of dust on his head and dodge away.

Perhaps the most painful sight the street had to offer was that of our former master-workman Grigori Ivanovich. He had gone completely blind and spent his days wandering through the city begging. Tall and silent and comely, he was led by a grey little old woman who would stop at every window and say in a squeaky little voice:

"Help a blind beggar, for the love of Christ. . . ."

Grigori Ivanovich would say nothing. His black glasses looked straight into the wall of the house or the window or the face of anyone he met; his dye-saturated hand would quietly stroke his broad beard, but his lips were always tightly closed. I often saw him, but never did I hear a sound from those tight lips, and this silence oppressed me more than anything else. I never went up to him—I could not make myself do this—but whenever I saw him I would run home and say to my grandmother:

"Grigori is coming!"

"Ah!" she would exclaim with pained agitation. "Here, run and give him this!"

I rudely refused. Then she herself would go out the gate and stand talking to him for a long time. He would laugh and shake his beard, but say scarcely a word.

Sometimes grandmother would bring him into the kitchen and feed him. Once he asked where I was. Grandmother called me, but I ran away and hid in the wood pile. I could not meet him. I felt horribly ashamed in his presence, and I knew that my grandmother felt the same. Only once did she and I speak about Grigori. When she had seen him out the gate, she came walking slowly back through the yard weeping, her head bent down. I went over to her and took her hand.

"Why do you always run away from him?" she asked quietly. "So fond he is of you, and a good man...."

"Why doesn't grandfather feed him?" I asked.

"Grandfather?"

She stopped and drew me to her and whispered almost prophetically:

"Remember my words: the Lord will send us a bitter punishment for this! A bitter punishment!"

She was not mistaken. Some ten years later, when my grandmother had already gone to her rest, my crazed grandfather himself walked the streets of the city begging miserably at the windows for something to eat.

"Good folks, give me a piece of *pirog*—just a little piece. . . Phooh, such people!"

That bitter, heart-rending "Phooh, such people!" was the only thing left of his former self.

In addition to Igosha and Grigori Ivanovich, there was the profligate old woman Voronikha, the very sight of whom was enough to drive me off the street. She put in her appearance every Sunday—huge, dishevelled, drunken. She had a peculiar walk, as though she did not move her feet or touch the ground, but sailed like a storm cloud, shrilling her lewd songs. The people on the street fled before her, hiding in stores, around corners, behind fences. She swept the street clean. Her face was blue and bloated like a balloon; her bulging grey eyes rolled frighteningly. Sometimes she would wail:

"Where are my children, my children?"

I asked my grandmother what that meant.

"It's not for you to know," she said at first, but then she explained in a few words: it seems the woman's husband had once been an official named Voronov. In order to be promoted to higher rank, he had sold his wife to his chief, who took her away for two years. When she returned, her children—a boy and a girl—were dead, her husband had gambled away public funds and was in jail. In her grief she began to drink and lead a profligate life. Now the police took her off the streets every Sunday.

There was no doubt about it—home was better than on the streets. It was particularly pleasant during the hours after dinner when grandfather went to visit Uncle Yakov and grandmother would sit at the window telling me stories and reminiscences of my father.

She had clipped the broken wing of the starling rescued from the cat and cleverly attached a little stick to the stump of the bird's leg. Now that it was well, my grandmother tried to teach it to talk. For a whole hour she would stand before the cage on the

window sill—and keep repeating the words she wanted to teach
the bird.

"Come now, say: birdy wants some porridge!"

The bird would cock its round eye at her like the proverbial
humourist, knock its wooden leg against the floor of the cage,
stretch its neck and whistle like an oriole, imitate a jay and a
cuckoo, attempt to meou like a cat, or bark like a dog, but it had
a hard time reproducing human sounds.

"Enough of your nonsense!" my grandmother would say very
seriously. "Try it now: birdy wants some porridge!"

If the feathered monkey would screech something faintly
resembling my grandmother's words, she would laugh with joy
and feed it a bit of oat porridge from her finger.

"Oh, I know you all right, you trickster!" she would tease.
"You can say anything if you want to!"

And she actually taught it to speak: after some time it asked
for porridge quite clearly, and on seeing my grandmother would
cry something which sounded extremely like "Hello!"

At first the bird hung in my grandfather's room, but soon he
outlawed it to our attic, because it began to imitate him; my
grandfather enunciated his prayers very distinctly, and the starling
would poke its yellow beak through the bars of the cage and say:

"True, true, oo, oo, tru-u-ue, oh, too true!"

This offended my grandfather. One day he interrupted his
prayers, stamped his foot and cried angrily:

"Take that devil out of here before I kill it!"

There was much that was interesting and much that was
amusing in our house, but sometimes I was overwhelmed by a
vast longing. It was as though a great burden were weighing me
down, and I went on living at the bottom of an inky pit, bereft of
sight and hearing and feeling—blind and only half alive.

VIII

Quite unexpectedly my grandfather sold our house to the saloonkeeper and bought another one, on Kanatnaya Street. This street was clean and quiet, unpaved and overgrown with grass. It led directly out into the fields and was lined with little, brightly painted houses.

The new house was more pleasant and cheerful than the old one. The facade was painted a dark, warm red, against the background of which the blue shutters of the three downstairs windows and the lattice-work shutter of the attic window stood out vividly. The left side of the roof was fretted by the branches of elms and limes. There were many enticing corners in the yard and garden, which seemed to have been especially designed for playing hide-and-seek. The garden was delightful— not very large, but charmingly overgrown with shrubbery. In one corner stood the bath-house, small and neat as a toy. In another corner was a wide, shallow pit overgrown with weeds, from which protruded the charred remains of a former bathhouse. On the left the garden was bounded by stables belonging to Colonel Ovsyannikov; on the right by outhouses belonging to the Betlengs. The extreme end joined the property of the dairy-woman Petrovna, a fat, red-faced, noisy creature who resembled a large bell. Her little house, dark and rickety, had settled comfortably into the earth and become overgrown with moss. Its two windows glanced out over fields, cut up by deep gullies and banked by the blue haze of the distant forest. All day long soldiers drilled on these fields, their bayonets flashing like white lightning in the autumn sun.

Our house was filled with people I had never seen before: the front apartment was occupied by a military man, a Tatar by birth, and his round little wife who laughed and shouted and played a gaily decorated guitar from morning to night. The song she sang most often in her high, ringing voice, was the following:

To love when you despise?
Oh no! If you are wise,

You 'll seek another girl.
I hope you get your prize,
And that she 77 be a pearl!
A ve-e-e-ery w-o-o-n-drous pearl!

Her husband, who was as round as a ball, would sit at the
window with his blue cheeks blown up as he puffed on his pipe,
rolling his merry little brown eyes and coughing with a strange
bark:

"Ar-r-uff! Ar-r-ruff-uff-uff!"

Two draymen and a tall, glum Tatar orderly named Valei
lived in the warm quarters built over the storehouse and stable.
One of the draymen was a little, grey man whom they called
Uncle Pyotr; the other was his deaf and dumb nephew Styopa.
Styopa was sleek and smooth, with a face like a brass tray. All
these people were new to me and presented rich possibilities.

But the person I found most interesting was our boarder,
"That's Fine," who occupied a room next to the kitchen in the
back of the house. It was a long room with two windows in it,
one looking out onto the garden, the other onto the yard.

The boarder was tall and bent, with a black, parted beard
accentuating the pallor of his face. He had kind eyes and wore
glasses. In general he was quiet and unobtrusive, and when he
was told that tea or dinner was ready, he would always answer:

"That's fine!"

My grandmother began to call him "That's Fine" behind his
back, and even to his face.

"Go tell That's Fine' to come have tea, Alexei," she would
say, or: "Have some more, That's Fine,' you're not eating very
much."

His room was piled high with wooden boxes and secular
books, a kind I had never seen before. Everywhere stood bottles
filled with different coloured fluids, bits of copper and iron and
lumps of lead. He was always dressed in a brown leather jacket
and grey-checked pants, all spotted with paint and smelling
unpleasantly. From morning to night he would stand there
smelting lead, soldering copper, weighing something on his tiny

scales, grunting, burning his lingers, blowing on them, stumbling over to diagrams hanging on the wall, wiping his glasses and examining the diagrams so closely that he almost touched them with his chalklike nose. Sometimes he would stand stockstill in the centre of the room or beside the window and remain thus for a long time with his eyes closed, his head lifted, silent and motionless.

I climbed up onto the roof of the shed across the yard and observed him through the open window. I could see the blue flame of the alcohol lamp burning on the table and his dark figure bending over it; I could see him write something in a worn notebook, his glasses shining coldly, like bits of blue ice. The necromancy of this man kept me up on the roof for hours, possessed by a torturing curiosity.

Sometimes he would stand framed in the window, his hands behind his back, staring directly at the roof; but he never seemed to see me, and this offended me. Suddenly he would jump back to his table and bend double as he rummaged nervously through papers and objects there.

I might have been afraid of him had he been rich and well dressed. But he was poor: the dirty, wrinkled collar of his shirt stuck out of his leather jacket, his pants were patched and stained, the shoes he wore on his bare feet were much the worse for wear. There was nothing dangerous or frightening about poor people— this I had learned from the pity my grandmother showed them and the contempt in which my grandfather held them.

Nobody in our house liked "That's Fine." Everyone spoke of him with ridicule—the jolly wife of the military man called him "Chalk Nose," Uncle Pyotr called him a chemist and wizard, while my grandfather called him a "pharmacer," a dealer in black magic.

"What does he do?" I asked my grandmother, but she answered abruptly:

"None of your business. Know when to keep your mouth shut."

One day I gathered all my courage and went to his window.

"What are you doing?" I asked, scarce able to hide my excitement.

He started and gave me a long look over his glasses. Then he held out his burned and scarred hand and said:

"Here, climb in."

The fact that he invited me to enter through the window rather than through the door raised him considerably in my estimation. He sat down on one of the boxes, placed me in front of him, moved me first to one side, then to another, and finally asked:

"Where did you come from?"

The question was strange enough, inasmuch as I sat beside him at the kitchen labile four times every day.

"I'm the grandson here," I answered.

"Ah, yes," he said, and relapsed into silence as he studied one of his fingers.

I decided it was necessary to make things more clear.

"But I'm not a Kashirin—I'm a Peshkov."

"Peshkov?" he repeated with the wrong stress. "That's fine."

He pushed me aside, got up and went back to the table.

"Well, sit down and don't make any noise."

I sat there for a long time observing how he made filings from a piece of copper which he held in pincers. When he had enough, he gathered the golden dust into a little heap which he placed in a thick mug; then he took some powder as white as salt out of a can, added it to the filings, and poured some dark liquid over it. The mixture in the mug began to hiss and smoke and give off an acrid odour that made me cough violently.

"Smell bad?" asked the wizard boastfully.

"Yes!"

"Aha! That's good, brother, that's very good!"

I failed to see any cause for boasting.

"If it's bad, it can't be good!" I said severely.

"You don't say," he cried, blinking his eyes. "Well, now, that's not always true, brother! Do you like to play knucklebones?"

"Dibs?"

"That's right, dibs."

"Sure I do."

"How'd you like me to smelt a filler for you? Make a good beater."

"I'd like it."

"Let's have the knucklebone then."

Again he came over to me, holding the smoking mug in his hand.

"If I fill it up for you, promise you won't come back any more?" he said, glancing at me out of one eye.

This injured me deeply.

"I'll never come back as it is!" I retorted and went into the garden.

There I found grandfather placing manure about the roots of the apple trees; it was autumn, and the leaves had long since begun to fall.

"Here, clip the raspberry bushes," said my grandfather, handing me the shears.

"What is That's Fine' making?" I asked.

"Just a mess," he answered angrily. "Spoiling the room: he's burned the floor already and stained the wallpaper, even tore a piece off. Have to give him notice."

"That's right," I assented as I tackled the raspberry bushes.

But I was in too much of a hurry.

On rainy evenings, if my grandfather was out, my grandmother would hold parties in the kitchen. She would invite all the lodgers, including the draymen, the adjutant, and even a gay young woman lodger; often the lively Petrovna would come, and always "That's Fine" would be found in the corner by the stove, where he would sit silent and motionless. The deaf-mute Styopa would play cards with the Tatar Valei, who would cuff him on his broad nose and say:

"You old devil, you!"

Uncle Pyotr would bring a huge loaf of white bread and a jar of raspberry jam, slice the bread, spread it thickly with jam, and hold the pieces on his outstretched palms as he offered them to the guests.

"Be so kind as to help yourselves," he would say with a low bow. Whenever anyone took a piece, 'he would examine his dusky palm and lick off any drops of jam which might be there.

Petrovna brought cherry wine and the gay young lodger donated nuts and candy. A feast would begin which was my grandmother's favourite form of entertainment.

My grandmother held such a party shortly after "That's Fine" had offered me a bribe to stay away from his room. A dreary autumn rain was failing, the wind was blowing, the trees sighing and scratching at the walls of the house. It was warm and cosy in the kitchen; the people drew close together and were somehow particularly quiet and well-disposed. My grandmother was more lavish with her tales than usual.

She sat on the edge of the stove bunk with her feet resting on the step, and leaned down toward the people, her face illuminated by a little tin lamp. She always chose a seat up on the stove when she was inspired.

"I have to talk down from up above; it's easier somehow when you talk down," she explained.

I sat at her feet on a lower step, just above the head of "That's Fine." Grandmother told the charming story of Ivan-the-Warrior and Miron-the-Hermit; rhythmically flowed the rich, measured language:

> Once on a time lived the evil Gordion,
> Black was his soul, stony his heart.
> Hating of truth, stinting of ruth,
> Living a mole in an evil hole.
> Of all whom he hated, this Gordion,
> Miron-the-Hermit he most abhorred,
> Miron, who peace and love adored,
> Of blessed truth a champion.
> Now summoned this Gordion, Captain-of-War,
> His warrior bold dubbed Ivánushka.
> Get thee hence to old Miron,
> Slaughter the ancient, the haughty one,
> Strike off his head, be not afeared,
> Lift it aloft by its hoary beard,
> And bring it me, a feast for my hounds.

Forth went Ivan, obedient
Forth to the task, bitterly ruing:
Not of mine own, of another's will
Do I this deed, decreed of God.

Under the floor he hid his sword,
Came to the hermit, courteous bowing.
Greetings, O ancient, how forest thou?
Many the blessings shed by the Lord?

  Smiled the knowing one, Miron the ancient,

Spake in his wisdom to Ivan-the-Bold:
Why thou deceives! I know not, in sooth,
For Jesus our Saviour is wise to all things,
Goodness and evil both dwell in His hand,
And surely He knoweth thine evil intent.

  Shame filled the heart of Ivdnushka:

Feared he the vengeance of Gordion.
Snatched he his sword from its leathern sheath,
Boldly he burnished the baneful blade.
Fain would I spare thee the sight of this,
Keep thee in blissful unknowingness,
But now thou hast seen—on thy knees, old man!
Pray the last time to the Fountain Head,
Pray for all men, and for me and thyself.
Then shall I sever thy hoary head!
  Down on his knees sank the ancient one,
  There on his knees 'neath a sapling oak.
  Over him benddd the branches green,
  Soft spake the ancient, smiling the while:
  Consider, Ivan: long shall thou wait me,
Endless the prayer for the souls of all men,
Better have done with my life undelaying,
Make thou an ending and hasten away.
  Here Ivan frowned at him wrathfully,

Here he did answer him boastfully:
Nay! As decreed, thus shall it be!
Pray while I wait for you, even an age!
Prayed then the hermit till coming of nightfall,
Prayed he from nightfall 'til breaking of dawn,
Prayed from the summer straight through to the spring.
Year followed year, and still the good hermit
Kneeled 'neath the oak, now grown to the sky,
'Round him a forest up-sprang from the acorns,
Still his petition ascended on high.
Thus to this day, there in the forest,
Pleadeth untiring the hermit Miron,
Asking God's help for all of the people,
Beseeching the Virgin to smile upon men.
Near him reclineth Ivan-the-Warrior,
Sword and its sheathing rotted to dust,
Chain mail and armour eaten by rust,
All of his garments gone to decay.
Consumed by the heat—yet unconsumed;
Devoured by pests—yet undevoured.
Shunned by the wolves, shunned by the bears,
Spared by blizzards, spared by the frost,
Powerless he to move from that place,
To lift a hand, or even to stand.
And this, I wist, be a punishment,
That he hearkened so to such evilness,
That he bent his will to another's will.
Still the prayers of the ancient one
Flow up to God for us sinning ones,
Flow like a stream to the ocean-sea.

At the very beginning of the tale I noticed that for some reason "That's Fine" was greatly agitated: he kept making strange convulsive movements with his hands, taking off and putting on his glasses, waving them in rhythm to the verse, nodding his head, pressing his fingers against his eyes, and wiping the sweat pouring

off his forehead and cheeks. If anyone moved or coughed or
scraped his feet across the floor, he would whisper impatiently:
"Sh!"

When grandmother had finished, he jumped up noisily with
a waving of his arms, and began to walk about in circles,
muttering:

"That's a wonderful thing! It must be written down by all
means! How very true it is. . . ."

Now I could plainly see that he was crying: his eyes were
filled with tears that flowed over and streamed down his cheeks.
This was strange and very touching. He ran about the kitchen in
funny little hops, trying to put on his glasses, but unable to hook
them behind his ears. Uncle Pyotr let out a laugh, but everyone
else was silent with embarrassment.

"Well, go ahead and write it down," said grandmother
hurriedly. "No sin in that. I know lots of others like it."

"Oh, no! Just this one. It is so very—Russian," cried the
boarder excitedly. Suddenly he came to a halt in the middle of
the kitchen and began to speak in a loud voice, waving his right
hand and holding his glasses in his trembling left one. He spoke
heatedly and at length, emphasizing his words by raising his voice
and stamping his foot.

"It's wrong to let someone else act as your conscience!" he
repeated over and over again.

All of a sudden his voice broke off, and with a glance at the
faces around him he stole away, quietly and guiltily, with hanging
head. People sniggered and glanced at each other uneasily. My
grandmother retired into the shadows of the bunk and gave a
deep sigh.

"What's wrong with him? Mad about something?" asked
Petrovna, passing her hand over her thick red lips.

"No," replied Uncle Pyotr. "That's just his way."

Grandmother climbed down off the stove and began to put
up the samovar.

"The gentles are all like that—capricious!" added Uncle
Pyotr calmly.

"That's what comes of being a bachelor," put in Valei.

Everyone laughed, and Uncle Pyotr said:

"See him cry? Hard to come down to herring when you're used to sturgeon!"

It became dull in the kitchen; a sad dreariness pricked at my heart. "That's Fine" had greatly surprised me, and I pitied him. I could not get the memory of his brimming eyes out of my mind.

He spent the night away from home, returning after dinner the next day. He seemed chastened and embarrassed and was badly rumpled.

"I made a scene yesterday," he said to my grandmother with the guilty manner of a little boy. "Are you angry?"

"Why should I be?"

"For having my say like that."

"You didn't hurt anybody."

I felt that grandmother was afraid of him. She did not look at him and spoke too softly to be natural.

He went over to her and said with utter simplicity:

"You see I am terribly alone. I have no one in the world. And when a person's forever silent like that, there comes a moment when all that's going on in his soul has to break loose. Then he's ready to speak to even the rocks and the trees.

"Why don't you get married?" asked grandmother, moving away from him.

"Ah!" he cried, with a wave of his hand, and went out frowning.

My grandmother watched him leave, then took a pinch of snuff and turned to me.

"Don't you go hanging around him," she said sullenly. "No telling what he's like."

But again I was drawn to him.

I had noticed the change which came over his face as he said, "I am terribly alone." There was something comprehensible to me in those words which touched my heart, and I went to seek him.

I glanced through the window of his room—it was empty, and cluttered with stange and useless things—as strange and useless as their owner. I went into the garden and found him in the pit, sitting all hunched over on a charred beam, his elbows on his knees and his hands locked behind his neck. The beam was covered with dirt and one end of it stuck up in the air above the nettles and wormwood and burdock. It was obviously uncomfortable for him to sit there, and this fact made me feel all the more drawn to him.

For some time he sat staring past me with the unseeing eyes of an owl, but suddenly he asked with a touch of annoyance:

"Come for me?"

"No."

"Then what?"

"Nothing special."

He took off his glasses and wiped them with a handkerchief stained black and red.

"Well, climb down."

When I had taken my place next to him, he gave me a tight hug.

"Sit here. We'll just sit and say nothing, all right? Like this . . . . You a stubborn fellow?"

"Yes."

"That's fine."

We sat there without speaking for a long time. It was a shy, quiet evening, one of those melancholy evenings of Indian summer when the flowering fades and withers before your very eyes; when the earth has exhausted the lush smells of summer and exudes only the chill odour of dampness; when the air is strangely transparent, and the daws plunge in the rosy sky, giving rise to oppressive thoughts. Everything was hushed and mute, so that the slightest sound—the rustle of a bird's wing, the falling of a leaf—was so resounding as to cause one to start up and glance about, only to relapse once more into the engulfing silence.

Such moments give rise to thoughts which are particularly pure, but fragile and transparent as a spider's web, defying capture in words. They flash and fade like falling stars, searing the soul with sadness, or fondling it, disturbing it, causing it to seethe and crystallize into permanent contours. At such moments character is moulded.

Snuggling against the warm body of my companion, I glanced with him through the black filigree of apple boughs and saw the linnets planning in the flushed sky, saw the goldfinches pecking at the dry turnip tops in search of spicy seeds, saw the ragged grey clouds with lurid borders strain across the fields, while beneath them the crows headed for their nests in the churchyard. All of it was good, and comprehensible to an unwonted degree.

Sometimes my companion would utter a deep sigh and remark:

"Fine, isn't it, brother? Humph! But isn't it damp? Aren't you cold?"

When the sky had darkened and everything merged in nightfall, he said:

"Well, guess that's enough. Come on. . . ."

He stopped when we reached the garden gate.

"That grandmother of yours is a wonderful woman," he said. "Ah, what a world!"

Then he closed his eyes and smiled, and repeated very softly and distinctly:

> *And this, I wist, be a punishment,*
> *That he hearkened to such evilness,*
> *That he bent his will to another's will. . . .*

"Remember that, brother!" he admonished, pushing me ahead. "Can you write?"

"No."

"Learn. And once you learn, put down what your grandmother recites—that's very important."

We became friends after that. From that day on I used to visit "That's Fine" whenever I wished. I would sit on a box filled with rags and watch him unmolested while he smelted lead or heated copper; when it was molten, he would forge plates on a little anvil with a fancy handle, and work on them with a rasp, sandpaper, and various files, one of which was as fine as a hair. He would weigh everything on a delicate copper scale. He would mix various liquids in thick white porcelain vessels, filling the

room with acrid smoke. He would frown as he looked into a
thick book, muttering and biting his red lips, or sighing gently:

Ah, rose of Sharon. . . .

"What are you making?"

"A certain thing, brother."

"What thing?"

"Now you see, I wouldn't know how to explain so that you
would understand. . . ."

"Grandfather says you're probably making counterfeit
money."

"Grandfather? Hm. That's all nonsense. Money, brother, is
not worth bothering about."

"Now, can you buy bread without it?"

"That's right, can't buy bread without it."

"See? Or meat.. .."

"Or meat either."

He laughed in a quiet way I found delightful, and rubbed me
behind the ear as if I were a kitten.

"Can't get the better of you, brother," he said. "You push me
into a corner every time. So let's not talk any more."

Sometimes he would stop working and come sit down beside
me at the window, where we would watch the apple trees shedding
their leaves or the rain on the roof and in the yard, all overgrown
with weeds. "That's Fine" was sparing of words, but what he
said always seemed to be to the point. Most often he would draw
my attention to something he wanted me to notice by nudging
me and indicating the object with a wink and a glance.

I could see nothing remarkable about our yard, but from
those nudges and his occasional words everything I saw assumed
particular significance and became engraved on my memory. A
cat went running across the yard and stopped to watch its
reflection in a puddle, raising its paw as though to strike the image.

"Cats are proud and sceptical," said "That's Fine" softly.

The red-gold rooster Mamai flew up on the fence, fluttered
its wings, nearly lost its balance, became annoyed, and began to
cluck angrily as it stretched its neck.

"He's important, is the General, but he hasn't got much sense."

The clumsy Valei picked his way through the mud like an old horse, raising his broad, puffy face to squint at the sky; a ray of pale autumn sun struck him on the chest and set the brass buttons of his jacket aflame. The Tatar stopped and touched them with his crooked fingers.

"As if he'd just had a medal pinned on his chest."

Soon I found that my attachment to "That's Fine" had grown very deep. He became essential to me in all my joys and sorrows. Though he himself was silent by nature, he never stopped me from saying anything that was on my mind. My grandfather, on the contrary, was always interrupting me:

"Stop your chatter, you windbag!"

My grandmother was so full of her own thoughts that she could not absorb other people's.

But "That's Fine" always listened to me attentively, and often he would say with a smile:

"But that's not true, brother. You just made that up!"

His brief remarks were always apt and timely. It was as though he could see what was going on in my heart and mind, could see what was false and superfluous before the words passed my lips, and seeing it, slew it with three sharp words, fondly spoken:

"You're lying, brother."

Sometimes I would intentionally test his magic powers by making up stories and relating them as fact. But after listening a minute he would inevitably shake his head and say:

"You're lying, brother."

"How do you know?"

"Oh, I know all right!"

Often grandmother would take me with her when she went to fetch water from the pump on Sennaya Square. One day we saw five townsmen beating a muzhik. They had him down on the ground and were going at him like a pack of dogs. My grandmother took the pails off her yoke, flourished it like a club, and rushed at the townsmen, shouting to me:

"Get away!"

But I was afraid and ran after her. I began to throw stones at the enemy, while she bravely poked them with her yoke, and thumped them on head and shoulders. Other people joined in the fray, and the townsfolk were driven off. Grandmother began to wash the muzhik whose face was badly battered. To this day I shudder at the recollection of how he pressed his dirty fingers to a torn nostril, coughing and howling while the blood spurted from between his fingers into my grandmother's face and on her breast. She also howled and trembled from head to foot.

When I got home I ran to the boarder and began to tell him all about it. He stopped working and stood in front of me holding a long file upraised like a sword. He looked at me sternly and steadily from under his glasses, then suddenly interrupted, saying with unusual emphasis:

"Splendid! That's exactly how it was! Very good!"

I was so taken up by what I had seen that I went on talking without realizing what he had said, but he put his arm around me and began pacing the floor.

"That's enough, that's enough," he admonished. "You've said all that you had to say, understand? Enough!"

I stopped talking. At first I was hurt, but on considering the matter I realized to my amazement that he had stopped me just in time, that I had, in fact, told everything.

"Don't let your mind brood over such things," he said. "Try to forget them."

Sometimes he would quite unexpectedly say things that I have remembered all my life. Once I told him about my enemy Klushnikov, one of the warriors from Novaya Street. He was a fat, large-headed boy who could no more get the better of me than I could of him. "That's Fine" listened to my trouble, and then said:

"Nonsense! Strength like that is no strength at all! Real strength lies in quickness of movement; the quicker you are, the stronger—understand?"

On the following Sunday I tried using my fists quicker, and had an easy time licking Klushnikov. That made me prize the boarder's words even more.

"You have to know how to take hold of things, understand? And that's very difficult—to know how to take hold of things."

I did not understand the meaning of what he said, but I remembered these and similar words. I remembered them because there was something irritatingly mysterious in their simplicity: What could be difficult about taking hold of a stone, or a piece of bread, a cup, or a hammer?

The people in our house came to dislike "That's Fine" more and more. Even the friendly cat belonging to the gay young lady lodger would not climb up onto his knee as it would onto the knees of other people, nor would it answer his gentle call. I beat it for this and shook it by the ears, almost weeping as I tried to convince the cat not to be afraid of this man.

"My clothes smell of acid, and that's why it won't come to me," he explained. But I knew that everybody else, including my grandmother, had a different explanation. They were hostile to him, and I found this wrong and painful.

"Why are you forever hanging around him?" asked my grandmother angrily. "Watch out, or he'll go teaching you tricks!"

My grandfather, the mean redhead, whipped me cruelly every time he heard that I had visited the boarder. Naturally I did not tell "That's Fine" that I had been forbidden to visit him, but I frankly told him what people thought of him.

"Grandmother's afraid of you; she says you go in for black magic, and grandfather too. He says you're against God and it's dangerous for people to have anything to do with you."

He jerked his head as though chasing a fly; his pallid face flushed with a smile that made my heart contract and my head reel.

"I can see all that, brother," he said quietly. "Too bad, isn't it, eh?"

"Yes."

"Too bad, brother."

Finally they drove him away.

One morning after breakfast I found him sitting on the floor packing his things in a box and humming: "Ah, rose of Sharon."

"Well, good-bye, brother. I'm leaving."

"Why?"

He studied me intently for a moment before answering.

"Didn't you know? This room is needed for your mother."

"Who said so?"

"Your grandfather."

"He's lying."

"That's Fine" drew me toward him, and when I was sitting on the floor beside him, he said quietly:

"Don't be angry! I thought you knew and just didn't say anything, brother, and I didn't like it."

For some reason I was hurt and annoyed.

"Listen," he said with a smile and almost in a whisper. "Remember my telling you not to visit me?"

I nodded.

"Hurt your feelings then, didn't I?"

"Yes."

"I didn't mean to, but I knew they would scold you if you started making friends with me."

He spoke as though he were my own age, and his words made me very happy. It seemed to me I had long since known what he just told me.

"I knew that long ago," I said.

"Good. Well now, so that's how it is, brother. Hm."

My heart ached unbearably.

"Why doesn't anybody like you?"

He hugged me tightly and blinked hard as he replied:

"Because I'm not like them, understand? That's the whole thing. I'm not like them!"

I plucked at his sleeve, not knowing what to say.

"Don't be angry," he said, and then whispered in my ear, "and don't cry either."

But the tears were stealing down his own cheeks from under his filmy glasses.

We sat there for a long time in silence, as was our wont, occasionally exchanging brief words.

That evening, after taking a fond farewell of everyone and **embracing me warmly**, he went away. I slipped through the gate and saw him jouncing on top of the cart as the wheels struck the frozen ruts in the road. As soon as he had left, my grandmother set to work cleaning the dirty room while I made a point of getting in her way by running from corner to corner.

"Get out!" she cried on stumbling over me.

"Why did you put him out?"

"That's none of your business!"

"You're all fools, the whole bunch of you!" I said.

She began slapping me with a wet rag and crying:

"Have you gone plumb crazy, or what?"

"They're all crazy but you," I corrected, but this did not appease her.

"Well, thank God he's gone!" said grandfather at the supper table. "Every time I saw him it was like a knife in my heart. Had to get rid of him."

In my rage I broke a spoon, for which I was duly chastised.

Thus ended my friendship with the first of that innumerable company of people—strangers in their native land—who represent its finest sons.

IX

I might liken myself as a child to a beehive to which various common, ordinary people brought the honey of their knowledge and views on life, each of them making a rich contribution to the development of my character. Often the honey was dirty and bitter, but being knowledge, it was honey nonetheless.

After the departure of "That's Fine," I became friendly with Uncle Pyotr. He resembled my grandfather in that he was thin and neat and clean, but he was smaller in stature and in every other way. He reminded me of a young boy dressed up like an old man just for the fun of it. His face was a basketwork of fine leather thongs, forming a cage from behind which his merry eyes twinkled like two little birds. His grey hair was curly, and his beard lay in ringlets; he smoked a pipe whose smoke was the colour of his hair and curled about him as did his quaint speech. He spoke in a buzzing voice that seemed to be kind and gentle, but I always had the impression that he was ridiculing people.

"At the beginning of things, the countess who owned me— Tatyan by name, Alexeyevna by patronymic—says, 'It's a smith you'll be,' but no sooner had I taken to smithing than she says, 'Be the gardener's assistant.' I had no objections, but as the saying goes, 'If you don't belong, everything's wrong.' When that didn't work out, she says, 'Try your hand at fishing, Petrushka!' Again it's all right by me; I takes up with the fish, but just I get a hankering for them, when it's good-bye fish and I'm sent to town to serve as drayman. So it's drayman I'll be and anything else you like, but before she gets a chance to like anything else along comes 'mancipation and there I be, left with the horse on my hands, and to this very day I follow the horse instead of the countess."

The horse was old and white and looked as if a drunken painter had slung a mottled brush at it. It was a crazy quilt with bandy legs. Its bony head set with filmy eyes hung sorrowfully from a neck scarce connecting it to the body by stretched sinews and flaccid hide. Uncle Pyotr was most respectful to his horse; he called it "Tanya" and never beat it.

"Why should you give your beast a Christian name?" my grandfather once asked him.

"But it's not, Vasili Vasilyevich—not at all," he replied. "Tanya's no Christian name—the Christian name's Tatyana."

Uncle Pyotr was also literate and had a thorough knowledge of the Scriptures. He and my grandfather were always arguing as to which of the saints was the most saintly. They were relentless in passing judgment on sinners mentioned in the Bible, condemning Absalom above all others. Sometimes their arguments assumed a purely grammatical aspect: my grandfather said "wickedism," "lawless-ism," "idolitism," white Uncle Pyotr claimed they should be pronounced "wickedry," "lawlessry," "idolitry."

"Your way's one thing—mine's another!" bellowed my grandfather all red in the face. "A fig for your '-ry's'!"

But Uncle Pyotr sat unperturbed, with the smoke curling about his head.

"And what's better about your '-isms'?" he drawled spitefully. "Not a bit better in the sight of God. Maybe when the Lord listens to them prayers of yours He thinks to Hisself, 'The prayer is big, but not worth a fig!' '

"Get away from here, Alexei!" my grandfather shouted at me, his green eyes flashing.

Pyotr was very fond of order and cleanliness. Whenever he walked through the yard, he would kick away sticks and bones and chips, muttering reprovingly:

"No good for anything but just to get in the way."

He was very loquacious and gave the impression of being kind and merry. But at times his eyes would become filmy and staring like those of a corpse. And frequently he would be found sitting off somewhere in a dark corner as sullen and silent as his nephew.

"What's the matter, Uncle Pyotr?"

"Go away," he would answer with dull severity.

Into one of the houses on our street moved a gentleman with a lump on his forehead and a very strange habit: on Sundays he would sit at the window and fire his shotgun at dogs, cats, chickens and crows, and even at passersby if they did not

strike his fancy. One day he poured grapeshot into "That's Fine." It did not penetrate his leather jacket, but some of the shot landed in his pocket. I remember watching the boarder examine the pieces he held in his hand. My grandfather urged him to put in a complaint, but he tossed the shot into a corner of the kitchen and said:

"Not worth the trouble."

Another time the sniper put some shot into my grandfather's leg; my grandfather was enraged, reported the offence and began mobilizing witnesses. But all of a sudden the gentleman disappeared.

Every time his shots were heard out on the street, Uncle Pyotr would hastily pull on the faded, large-visored cap he wore on Sundays and rush through the gate. Once out on the sidewalk, he would put his hands under his coattails to make them stick up like a rooster's tail, poke out his belly, and stride importantly past the sniper's window. If the first stroll remained uneventful, he would repeat it a second and a third time. All the people from our house would crowd at the gate to watch, with the military man and his blond wife peering at the window. People also came out in the yard of the Betlengs' house. Only the grey house belonging to the Ovsyannikovs remained lifeless.

Sometimes Uncle Pyotr's efforts were futile—the hunter refused to consider such game worthy of his attention. But sometimes the double-barrelled gun went off.

"Bang-bang!"

Without quickening his steps, Uncle Pyotr would come over to us and report with the greatest satisfaction:

"Got me in the coattails."

One day the shot landed in his neck and shoulder.

"Why should you egg on such a wild creature!" asked grandmother as she removed the lead with a needle. "He'll shoot your eyes out yet!"

"Oh no, Akulina Ivanovna!" replied Pyotr contemptuously. "He's no shot at all!"

"Why give him the satisfaction?"

"Satisfaction? I just do it to tease the gentleman!"

As he examined the wounds in his hand, he added, "No shot at all. The countess, now, Tatyan Alexeyevna, once had temporary marriage ties—she changed her husbands like her footmen— once had these ties, I'm saying, with an army man named Mamont

Ilyich. Well, *he* was a shot all right! What he could do with a gun, grandmother! He'd place the feeble-minded Ignashka way off-some forty steps or so—and tie a bottle to his belt so's to hang down between his legs, and Ignashka would plant his feet wide apart and laugh like the idiot he was. Then Mamont Ilyich would take aim and—bang! right into the bottle. Only once a horsefly must've bit Ignashka or something—the boy goes and jerks and gets the bullet in his knee—right in the cap. They call the doctor and quick as a wink he has the leg off—just like that! They buried it . . ."

"And Ignashka?"

"Oh, he was all right. An idiot has no use for arms and legs— lives by his idiocy. Everybody's ready to help an idiot— they're a harmless lot like the saying goes, 'No sense—no offence.' "

This story did not impress my grandmother—she knew dozens like it. But it gave me the creeps.

"Could one of the gentlefolk kill a person to death?"

"Why not? He could, all right. Sometimes the gentlefolk even kill each other. Once a lancer came to visit Tatyan Alexeyevna and got into a fight with Mamont. They both grabbed their pistols, went to the park and there on the path by the lake the lancer gave it to Mamont—bang!—right in the liver. Well, Mamont went to glory, the lancer to the Caucasus, and that was the end of that! There, you see? Killing their own selves. As for the muzhiks and their kind—phooh! Many as you like! Especially nowadays, when they don't own them no more. Used to be more careful—after all, the muzhik was their property!"

"Didn't care much then either," put in my grandmother.

"True enough," agreed Uncle Pyotr. "Property, all right, but cheap property."

He was always gentle with me and spoke more kindly to me than to the grownups, without dropping his eyes. But there was something about him I did not like. When he treated us to his favourite jam, he would spread my bread thicker than that of the others. He would bring me ginger cookies and poppy seeds when he went to town, and he always spoke with me quietly and seriously.

"Well, what we going to be when we grow up, my man? A soldier, or a clerk?"

"A soldier."

"Good for you. Not hard to be a soldier these days. The priests have it easy too—just go around shouting, 'Praised be the Lord,' and there's an end to it. Even easier to be a priest than a soldier. But the easiest of all is to be a fisherman. He don't need to know anything at all—just get the habit, that's all."

He gave an amusing imitation of how the fish circle around the bait and how a bass, a bream, and a mackerel struggle when they are hooked.

"You get mad, now, when your grandfather gives you a beating, don't you, though?" he said consolingly. "But there's no reason at all to get mad in a case like that, my man. They're all for your own good, those beatings, and they're just childish beatings. But take my Tatyan Alexeyevna, for instance. There was a person for you when it came to beatings! She kept a special man for such business—Christopher was his name—such an expert he was that the owners of neighbouring estates used to send to the countess: be so good, Tatyan Alexeyevna, as to lend us your Christopher for a beating or two. So she'd send him over."

He gave an unimpassioned and detailed account of how the countess would sit in a red armchair on the columned porch of her estate, resplendent in a sheer white dress with a blue scarf about her shoulders, supervising the lashings Christopher administered to her serfs of both sexes.

"That Christopher person came from Ryazan—something like a gypsy or a *Khokhol** he was, with moustaches from ear to

* KhoKhol: Russian nickname for Ukrainians.— Trans.

ear, but his face all bluelike, from shaving his chin. And there was no telling whether he was really half-witted or just made believe to be so's to make life easy for hisself. He'd go into the kitchen and fill a basin with water, catch a fly, or a roach, or some kind of a beetle, and I was well acquainted with stories like this, having heard many of them from my grandfather and grandmother. But with all their variations, they were the same in that they told of human torture and humiliation. I was sick of such stories.

"Tell me about something else," I said.

The drayman gathered all his wrinkles about his mouth, then shifted them to his eyes as he gave his consent drown it by pushing it down with the end of a stick—keep drowning it for a long time. Or sometimes catch the vermin under his own collar and drown it. .

"All right, greedy. Here's something else. Once we had a cook. . . ."

"Who had?"

"Countess Tatyan Alexeyevna."

"Why do you call her Tatyan, like a man, instead of Tatyana? She wasn't a man, was she?"

"Of course not—she was a lady, but still she had a moustache. A little black one. She was a black German by birth—a tribe something like the Negroes. Well, then this cook of ours— this is going to be a funny story, my man. . . ."

The funny story was an account of how the cook had spoiled a pie and was punished by being made to eat the whole thing at one sitting, as a result of which he became sick.

"That's not funny," I said with annoyance.

"So what's funny? Come on, let's hear."

"I don't know."

"Then keep your mouth shut."

Once more he started spinning his dull tales.

Sometimes my cousins would come for a visit on Sundays— Uncle Mikhail's sad and lazy Sasha, Uncle Yakov's neat and knowing Sasha. One day, when the three of us were exploring the roofs of the outhouses, we saw a gentleman sitting on a woodpile in the Betlengs' yard, playing with some puppies. He was wearing a green long coat lined with fur, but his little yellow bald head was uncovered. One of my cousins suggested that we steal one of the puppies, and we immediately thought up a plan: my cousins were to go out in the street and wait at the Betleng gate while I was to frighten the man. When he ran away, my cousins would dash into the yard and grab a puppy.

"How shall I frighten him?"

"Spit on his bald head," suggested one of my cousins.

I found nothing particularly wicked about spitting on a bald head—I had seen and heard about greater crimes being committed, so I did not hesitate to fulfill the task entrusted to me.

But the act created a tremendous fuss. A whole army of men and women from the Betlengs' house invaded our yard, led by a handsome young officer. And since my cousins were innocently playing out in the street at the moment when the crime was perpetrated, I was the only one to receive the beating which my grandfather performed with great gusto in order to propitiate the insult offered the house of Betleng.

While I lay bruised and aching on the bunk in the kitchen, Uncle Pyotr came to see me, all dressed up and in a cheerful mood.

"That was a clever thing to think up, young man," he whispered. "Serves him right, the old goat. Spit on the bunch of them! Better to have thrown a brick at his rotten head!"

I remembered the round, hairless, childlike face of the gentleman in the green coat, and how he had squealed softly and plaintively as a puppy as he wiped his yellow pate with his little hands. This had made me hate my cousins and feel frightfully ashamed of myself at the time, but now I forgot it as I looked into the basketwork face of the drayman, which was trembling in the same frightening and repulsive way my grandfather's had when he gave me the beating.

"Get out!" I cried, pushing Pyotr away with my hands and feet.

He chuckled and winked and got up off the bunk.

From that time on I never had any desire to talk with him. I began to avoid him, and at the same time to keep a suspicious eye on him, as though I were vaguely expecting something.

This incident was shortly followed by another. For some time I had nurtured a secret interest in the quiet house belonging to the Ovsyannikovs. It seemed to me that a mysterious fairy tale existence went on in that grey house.

The Betleng house was always noisy and cheerful. A number of attractive young girls lived there courted by students and officers who were always talking, laughing, singing and playing. The house itself had a gay look, with its flashing windows through which the green of the plants shone with particular vividness. My grandfather did not like this house.

"Infidels! Heretics!" he called the occupants in general, while he applied a particularly filthy word to the women—a word which Uncle Pyotr once explained to me in a gloating, filthy manner.

But grandfather was impressed by the stern and silent house of the Ovsyannikovs.

It was high and one-storied and ran far back into a clean, open yard carpeted with grass. In the centre of the yard stood a well, covered by a roof supported by two columns. The house stood back from the street, as though hiding from it. Three narrow arched windows whose panes were turned to rainbow hues by the sun, decorated the facade. A barn to the right of the entrance gate also had three windows matching those of the house, but they were imitation windows, formed by moulding tacked to the wall, with frames and sashes painted in white. There was something unpleasant about these blind windows, and the barn seemed to emphasize the fact that the house wanted to hide away and live its life unobserved. The entire property, including the empty stables and empty barns with their huge gates, breathed a sense of quiet injury, or silent pride.

Sometimes a tall, beardless old man with white moustaches bristling like needles could be seen limping about the yard. Occasionally another old man with side whiskers and a crooked nose led a grey horse out of the stable. Once out in the yard, the narrow-chested, thin-ankled horse would nod to everything about it like a modest nun. The lame old man would slap it noisily, whistle and sigh deeply, then send the horse back into the dark stable. It seemed to me that the old man wanted to escape from the house, but was held there by some evil spell.

Almost every day from noon to evening, three little boys played in the yard. They were all dressed alike in grey pants and blouses and similar hats, and they themselves were so much alike, with their round faces and grey eyes, that I could distinguish them only by their size.

I watched them through a chink in the fence, but to my disappointment they did not notice me. It was pleasant to see in what a happy, friendly manner they played games that were unfamiliar to me. I liked the way they were dressed and the way they took care of each other, especially the older ones in relation to the youngest—a sturdy, amusing little fellow. If he fell down, they laughed as people always laugh at anyone who falls down, but there was nothing mean about their laughter; they would immediately help him get up and brush off his hands and knees with burdock leaves or their handkerchiefs.

"You clumthy thing!" the middle one would say.

They never fought or played tricks on each other, and all three of them were strong and agile and full of energy.

One day I climbed a tree and whistled to them. They stopped at the sound of the whistle, then drew together with their eyes on me and held a consultation. I expected them to start throwing stones, so I descended, filled my shirt and pockets with missiles, and once more climbed the tree. But they were already playing again in a far corner of the yard and apparently had forgotten all about me. That was regrettable, but I did not want to be the first to declare war. Presently, someone called from the window:

"Home, children—quick!"

They turned obediently but unhurriedly, and marched off like geese.

Many times I sat on the tree above the fence, hoping they would invite me to play with them, but they never did. In my imagination I often joined them in their games, even calling out and laughing aloud in my enthusiasm. At such times all three of them would look at me and quietly pass remarks to each other, while I would slip embarrassedly down the tree.

One day they began to play hide-and-seek. The middle brother was "it," and he stood at one corner of the barn with his hands over his eyes, without peeking, while his two brothers hid. The oldest boy quickly climbed into a sledge sheltered by the overhanging roof of the barn, but the little fellow ran round and round the well, not knowing where to hide.

"One!" cried the boy who was "it." "Two. . . ."

The little one climbed up on the edge of the well, grabbed hold of the rope, and jumped into the empty bucket, which immediately disappeared, knocking dully against the sides of the well.

I was frozen with horror as I saw the rope quickly and noiselessly unwinding. But I immediately realized what might be the result and jumped down into the yard, shouting:

"He fell in the well!"

The middle brother reached the well at the same time I did, and grabbed the rope, which lifted him off his feet and burned his hands, but I took hold, and by that time the eldest boy came running and helped me haul up the bucket.

"Not so fast, please," he said.

We rescued the little one, who was badly frightened. Blood was flowing from the fingers of his right hand, one of his cheeks was also badly scratched, he was soaked to the waist and deathly pale, but he smiled and said with a shudder:

"How I fel-l-l!"

"You craythy thing!" lisped the middle brother, hugging him and wiping the blood from his face, while the eldest frowned and remarked:

"Come on, we can't hide it anyhow, so we may as well go now."

"Will you get a licking?" I asked.

He nodded and held out his hand.

"You ran mighty fast," he said.

I was so overwhelmed by his praise that before I could take his hand he was saying to the middle brother:

"Come on, or he'll catch cold. We'll say he simply fell down. No sense telling about the well."

"Yes," agreed the little one. "We'll just say I fell in a puddle." And they went away.

Everything had happened so fast that when I glanced up at the branch on which I had been sitting it was still shaking, scattering its yellow leaves.

For about a week after that the brothers did not appear in the yard, and when they did, they were noisier than ever. As soon as the eldest boy saw me, he cried in a friendly tone:

"Come play with us!"

We climbed into the sledge and sat there or a long time getting acquainted.

"Did they beat you?" I asked.

"We got it, all right," answered the eldest.

It was hard to believe that these boys also took beatings like mine, and I thought it unfair.

"Why do you catch birds?" asked the little one.

"Because they sing nice."

"Don't catch them any more. Let them stay free to go where they want."

"All right, I won't any more,"

"Only first catch one and give it to me."

"What kind?"

"A cheerful kind—to put in a cage."

"That'll be a chaffinch."

"The cat'll kill it," said the middle brother. "And father won't let uth keep it."

"That's right," agreed the eldest.

"Haven't you got a mother?"

"No," answered the eldest, but the middle brother corrected him:

"We have, only another one—not ourth—ourth died."

"That kind's called a stepmother," I said, and the eldest nodded.

"That's right."

All three of them fell into a brooding silence.

I had learned what a stepmother was from grandmother's tales, and so I could understand their silence. They sat there huddled together, as like as three peas. I recalled the story of the witch stepmother who resorted to foul means to take the place of the real mother, and I tried to console the boys by saying:

"Don't worry, your real mother will come back yet."

"How can she, once she's dead? That never happens," said the eldest with a shrug of his shoulders.

Never happens? Heavens, how many times a sprinkling of living water had brought back to life not only those who were merely dead, but even those who had been chopped into a hundred pieces! And how many times death turned out to be not a real death, sent by God, but the work of witches and wizards!

I began an enthusiastic recounting of grandmother's stories, but the eldest laughed contemptuously and said:

"We've heard those—they're just fairy tales!"

His brothers listened in Silence, the little one with a frown on his face and his lips compressed, the middle brother with one elbow on his knee, the other arm crooked about the little one's neck, drawing him toward me.

It was already well on toward evening; rosy clouds had settled low over the roofs, when the old man with white whiskers appeared among us. He was wearing a long brown coat like a priest and had a shaggy fur cap on his head.

"Who's that?" he asked, pointing his finger at me.

The eldest boy rose and nodded toward my grandfather's house.

"He's from over there," he said.

"Who asked him to come?"

All three of the boys immediately climbed silently out of the sledge and went home, once more reminding me of obedient geese.

The old man took me firmly by the shoulder and led me through the yard to the gate. I was on the verge of tears from fright, but he strode ahead so quickly that I found myself out in the street before I had time to cry. He stood at the gate shaking his finger at me and saying:

"Don't dare come see me again!"

"I never came to see you, you old devil!" I retorted angrily.

His long arm reached out for me once more, and he led me down the sidewalk, reiterating the same question, like hammer blows over my head:

"Is your grandfather at home?"

Unfortunately for me, he was. He stood before the menacing old man, his head thrown back, his beard sticking out, looking up into eyes as round and dull as kopek pieces.

"His mother's away, I'm busy, nobody to look after him begging your pardon, Colonel!" he said hastily.

The Colonel gave a roar that could be heard all over the house, swung around on his heel and marched away. Some time later I was thrown out into Uncle Pyotr's cart.

"Got it again, my man?" asked the drayman as he unharnessed the horse. "What was the beating for this time?"

When I had told him the story, he flared up and hissed through his teeth:

"What do you want to make friends with the likes of them for? They're gentlefolk's spawn; see what you took on their account? Hereafter you give it to them!"

He kept on muttering to himself, and at first, rankled by my injuries, I sympathized with what he said. But his basketwork face trembled so disgustingly that I was reminded of the fact that those boys would also be flogged, and that they had in no way offended me.

"No reason why I should give it to them," I said, "and what you're telling is just a pack of lies."

He glanced at me sharply, then suddenly shouted:

"Get out of my cart!"

"Fool!" I cried, jumping down.

"A fool, am I? A liar, am I? I'll show you . . ." and he began chasing me around the yard, but was unable to catch me.

My grandmother appeared on the kitchen porch. I ran to her, and he began to complain about me:

"I get no peace with that brat around! Don't spare his words—calls me all sorts of filthy names, and me five times his senior . . ."

When people lied in my very face, I was stunned out of mind. Now I stood there at an utter loss for words, but my grandmother said firmly:

"Now, there, Pyotr, aren't you taking a little too much rope? You can't tell me as he called you filthy names."

My grandfather would have believed the drayman.

From that day on the relationship between me and the drayman was one of silent, vicious war. He would try to find opportunities for poking me or striking me with the reins as if by chance; he set my birds free and one day he sicked the cat on them. He was always complaining to my grandfather about me, invariably exaggerating the cause. I found it impossible to look upon him as anything but a boy like myself dressed up like an old man. In my turn I would unravel his bast sandals and untwist the cording, so that it would break when he was lacing them. One day I sprinkled pepper in his cap, and he went about sneezing for a whole hour. In general, I did everything in my power to give him measure for measure. On Sundays he would spend the entire day spying on me, and more than once he caught me in illegal communication with the spawn of the gentlefolk, on which occasions he straightway reported the fact to my grandfather.

I had continued my acquaintanceship with the boys, and derived more and more pleasure from it. Between the wall of my grandfather's house and the Ovsyannikovs' fence there was a little corner shaded by an elm and a lime and overgrown with elderberry bushes. Behind these bushes I had cut a little opening in the fence, to which the brothers would come in turns or pairs, to talk quietly with me. One of them always watched to see that the Colonel did not catch us.

They told me about the dull life they lived, and this made me very sad. We talked about my birds, and about many childish interests, but so far as I can remember they never mentioned their father or their stepmother. Most often they simply asked me to tell them stories, and I conscientiously related all the tales I had heard from my grandmother. If I forgot anything, I would ask them to wait while I ran to her to be prompted. She was only too glad to do this.

I often told them about my grandmother. One day the eldest boy gave a deep sigh and said:

"All grandmothers must be nice. We used to have a nice grandmother too. ..."

He so often and so sadly repeated the expressions: "used to be," "used to have," "once upon a time," that it seemed he had lived a hundred years, instead of only eleven. I remember that he had slender hands with long thin fingers. He himself was slender and fragile with eyes as shy and clear as the icon lamps in church. I was fond of his brothers as well. They won my sympathy and inspired me with the desire to do something nice for them. But I was most fond of the eldest.

So absorbed would I become in our conversation that I often failed to notice the approach of Uncle Pyotr, who would startle us with his long-drawn-out:

"What-a-t! At it again?"

I could see that he was becoming more and more subject to fits of sullenness. I even learned how to determine the mood in which he returned from work: ordinarily he opened the gates unhurriedly, so that the hinges gave a prolonged creak. But if the drayman was in a bad mood, the hinges would let out a sharp, sudden shriek, like a cry of pain.

His mute nephew left for the country to get married. Pyotr went on living alone in a low-ceilinged room over the stable containing one tiny window and smelling of tar, old leather, tobacco and sweat. I could never visit him because of this odour. These days he slept without extinguishing his lamp, a thing which displeased my grandfather very much.

"Watch out or you'll be burning the place down, Pyotr."

"No danger of that. I always stand the lamp in a basin of water at night," he answered, glancing off to one side.

He was always glancing about shiftily nowadays, and he no longer attended grandmother's parties or treated us to jam. His face had become dried up, the wrinkles had grown deeper, and he swayed like a sick man when he walked.

One morning when my grandfather and I were shovelling the snow which had fallen abundantly during the night, the latch on the gate clicked with particular importance, a policeman entered the yard, closed the gate, stood with his back to it, and beckoned to my grandfather with a fat grey finger. When my grandfather went over to him, he stuck his big nose into his face and said something to which my grandfather hastily replied:

"Here? When? If only I can remember. . . ."

Suddenly he started comically and cried:

"Merciful God! Not really?"

"Sh!" warned the policeman.

Grandfather glanced about and caught sight of me:

"Take the shovels and go home!"

I hid around the corner of the house and watched them enter the drayman's quarters in the stable. The policeman took the glove off his right hand and began slapping his left with it.

"He understands all right; abandoned his horse and went into hiding."

I ran into the kitchen to tell my grandmother all I had seen and heard. She nodded her flour-dusted head as she kneaded the dough.

"Must've stole something or other," she said calmly when I had finished. "Go out and play. What's it to you?"

When I ran out into the yard again, grandfather was standing at the gate with his hat off and his eyes raised to heaven, crossing himself. His face was angry and bristling and one of his legs was jerking.

"Didn't I tell you to get in the house?" he cried, stamping his foot.

He followed me into the kitchen.

"Come here, mother!" he said.

They went into the next room and whispered together for some time. One look at grandmother's face when she returned told me that something dreadful had happened.

"What are you scared of?" I asked.

"You just keep your mouth shut," she replied softly.

A strained and awed atmosphere hung over the house the rest of the day; my grandmother and grandfather kept exchanging furtive glances and short, incomprehensible words which heightened the feeling of alarm.

"Light all the icon lamps, mother," ordered my grandfather, clearing his throat.

They ate dinner hurriedly, but without appetite, as if expecting someone. Grandfather wearily blew out his cheeks, cleared his throat, and murmured:

"Satan's too strong for a man to pit hisself against. Take him, for instance—a godly, pious man to all appearances, but look what he's done!"

Grandmother sighed.

The silvery winter day dragged on interminably, while the atmosphere at home became more uneasy and oppressive with every hour.

Towards evening another policeman came. He was fat and redheaded and sat drowsing on a bench in the kitchen, nodding and snuffling.

"How did they find out?" my grandmother asked.

After a short pause he replied gruffly:

"Don't worry, they find out everything."

I remember sitting at the window heating an old coin in my mouth in order to make an impression of St. George the Victorious on the frosted windowpane.

Suddenly there was a great bustling in the entranceway and the door burst open. Petrovna stood on the threshold and shouted:

"Go have a look at what's out on your property!"

On catching sight of the policeman she rushed back into the entranceway, but he caught her by the skirt and also shouted in fright:

"Wait a minute! Who are you? What's out there?"

She fell on her knees and began to cry, swallowing down her words and her tears:

"I went out to milk the cow, and all of a sudden I sees something like a pair of boots in the Kashirins' yard."

"That's a lie, you hussy!" shouted my grandfather in a rage. "You couldn't see anything in our yard—the fence is too high and there's no holes in it! You're lying! There's nothing out there!"

"Ah me!" wailed Petrovna, stretching out one hand to him and holding her head with the other. "It's the truth when he says

I'm lying. I was walking along and all of a sudden I sees tracks leading up to your fence and the snow all trampled down in one place, so I climbs up and looks over the fence, and there he is lying there...."

"Who-o-o?"

The cry came frightful and long-drawn and meaningless. Then all of a sudden, as though they had lost their senses, everyone went running and shoving out of the kitchen into the yard. There in the snow-filled pit lay Uncle Pyotr, his back against a charred beam, his head drooping on his breast. Just below his right ear was a great gash resembling a red mouth with bluish fringes sticking up like teeth. I closed my eyes in horror, and through my lashes I saw Uncle Pyotr's saddle knife lying on his knee with the twisted darkened fingers of his right hand alongside, while his left hand was buried in snow. The snow had melted under his slight figure, which lay deep in the white fluff, looking more childlike than ever. On his right the snow was stained with a strange red design that looked like a bird, while on his left it remained unspotted, and lay smooth and glistening. His head, so meekly bowed, rested on his chest, pushing up his curly beard, beneath which hung a large brass cross framed by rivulets of dried blood. My head swam from the confusion of voices; Petrovna shouted without interruption; the policeman shouted to Valei to go somewhere; my grandfather shouted:

"Don't spoil the tracks!"

Suddenly he frowned and dropped his eyes.

"No sense in yelling like that, officer," he said in a loud, authoritative voice. "This is the hand of God, the judgment of God, and you with your silly business—fie on you!"

All the people became silent, sighing and crossing themselves and staring at the dead man.

Others climbed over the fence from Petrovna's side and came running across the yard, falling and muttering, but making little noise, until my grandfather glanced around and cried in despair:

"You're breaking all the raspberry bushes, neighbours! Aren't you ashamed of yourselves?"

My grandmother took me by the hand and led me into the house.

"What did he do?" I asked.

"Didn't you see?" she answered, whimpering.

All that evening and until late in the night strange people moved about the kitchen and the room adjoining it. The police gave orders, and a man who looked like a deacon made notes in a book and kept quacking like a duck:

"What's that? What's that?"

Grandmother served tea to everybody. At the kitchen table sat a round, bewhiskered, pock-marked man who said in a squeaky voice:

"Nobody knows his real name. The only thing they know is that he comes from Elatma. But that there deaf mute is no more deaf than you nor me, and he come out with the whole story. And the third chap squealed too —seems there was a third one. They been robbing churches ever so long—that was their main specialty...."

"My God!" exclaimed Petrovna, all moist and red.

I lay up on the bunk looking down on them, and they all appeared short and fat and ugly. . . .

X

Very early one Saturday morning I went into Petrovna's garden
to catch bullfinches. Some time passed, but the proud, red-
breasted creatures would not enter my snare. Vaunting their
beauty, they would step importantly over the silver snow crust,
or fly into the bushes, where they would sway on the hoarcovered
branches like bright flowers among blue sparkles of snow dust.
All this was too lovely to allow of my feeling disappointment in
the hunt. In general I was not a very impassioned hunter; I always
took greater pleasure in the process than in the result. I was most
interested in observing and meditating on the lives of the birds.

What could be more pleasant than to sit alone at the edge of
a snowy field and listen to the chirping of the birds in the crystal
silence of a winter's day, while somewhere far away in the distance
sounded the bells of a passing troika—that melancholy lark of
the Russian winter.

When I was chilled to the bone and felt that my ears were
freezing, I gathered up my snares and cages, climbed the fence
into grandfather's garden, and went toward the house. The gates
were open, and a huge muzhik was leading three horses hitched
to a large, closed sleigh out into the street. Clouds of steam rose
from the horses, the muzhik Whistled gaily, and my heart stood
still.

"Who did you bring?" I asked.

He turned, glanced at me from under his hand, jumped up
into his seat, and said:

"The priest!"

That did not concern me—if the priest had come, he was
probably visiting one of the tenants.

"Get going, my chickens!" cried the muzhik as he touched
the horses with the whip, causing them to spring ahead and set
the air ringing with bells. I watched them go, then closed the
gates and went into the house. When I entered the kitchen I heard
my mother's deep voice coming from the adjoining room:

"Well, what now? Off with my head—is that it?"

I threw down my cages and rushed out into the entranceway without taking off my coat, but my grandfather caught me. He looked at me with wild eyes, swallowed painfully, and gasped:

"Your mother's come—go in to her! Wait!"

He shook me so that I could scarcely retain my footing, then pushed me toward the door.

"Go on, go on," he said.

I fumbled at the door, scarcely able to lift the latch with my frozen, trembling fingers; when at last I opened it, I stood speechless on the threshold.

"Ah, so here he is!" said my mother. "Heavens, how big you've grown! Don't you recognize me? The way you dress him! And look, his ears are frozen! Give me some goose grease—hurry, mother!"

She stood bending over me in the middle of the room, taking off my clothes and turning me around like a ball. Her large body was clothed in a soft, warm red dress as wide as a man's cloak, with large black buttons descending diagonally from the shoulder to the waist, and then down to the very hem. I had never seen such a dress before.

Her face seemed to have grown smaller and paler, her eyes larger and deeper, and her hair more golden. She threw aside the clothes she took off me, drawing down the corners of her red lips disdainfully and saying in an imperious tone:

"Well, why don't you say something? Aren't you glad? Phooh, what a dirty shirt!"

Then she rubbed goose grease on my ears. It hurt, but the pain was compensated by the refreshing, delightful scent which emanated from her. I pressed up close and looked deep into her eyes, unable to utter a word in my agitation. As a background to what she was saying, I heard my grandmother softly complaining:

"He's gotten clean out of hand, don't even fear his grandfather any more. Ah, Varya, Varya. . . ."

"Stop whining, mother! Everything will be all right!"

In contrast to my mother, all the surroundings seemed little and old and drab. I myself felt as old as my grandfather.

She held me tightly between her knees as she stroked my head with a warm, heavy hand.

"Need a haircut," she said. "And time for you to be going to school. Do you want to study?"

"I've already studied."

"There's more to be learned. But what a sturdy little fellow you are!" And she laughed a rich, warm laugh as she fondled me.

My grandfather came in, grey and bristling, with bloodshot eyes. She pushed me away with a single gesture and asked in a loud voice:

"Well, what am I to do, father? Leave?"

He stood at the window scratching the ice with his nail and saying nothing. The atmosphere was so strained that I could feel my eyes and ears expanding until they seemed to comprise my whole being, while my breast was nigh to bursting with the impulse to scream.

"Get out of here, Alexei," said my grandfather dully.

"Why?" asked my mother, once more drawing me to her.

"You'll not leave! I forbid it!"

My mother got up and soared about the room like a lurid sunset cloud.

"Listen, father" she said, halting behind his back.

"Silence!" he shrieked.

"I won't allow you to shout at me!" said my mother quietly.

"Varvara!" cried my grandmother, rising from the couch and shaking a warning finger, while my grandfather sank weakly onto a chair, muttering to himself:

"What's this? What's this, eh? Who am I? What do you call this?"

Suddenly he let out a roar like a wounded beast:

"You've disgraced me, that's what you've done, Varka!"

"Go away," said my grandmother to me. Deeply unhappy, I went into the kitchen and climbed up onto the stove, from where I could hear the sounds coming from the other room—now everyone talking excitedly, now everyone silent, as though suddenly fallen asleep. They were talking about a baby my mother had given birth to and left with someone. But it was impossible to tell whether my grandfather was angry because my mother had given birth without his consent, or because she had not brought him the baby.

Finally he came into the kitchen, red and dishevelled and exhausted, followed by my grandmother, who was wiping the tears from her cheeks with a corner of her blouse. He slumped down on a bench, leaning on his hands, biting the grey lips of his twitching face. My grandmother fell on her knees before him.

"Forgive her, father, for the love of Christ, forgive her! Even better sleighs have broken down. Don't such things happen among the gentlefolk too, and among the merchants? Just see what a woman she is! Forgive her, father—none of us are perfect. . . ."

Grandfather leaned back against the wall and looked her in the eye as he whimpered:

"Oh yes, of course! Why not? You'd forgive anybody. You'd forgive anything. Phooh! Fie on you!"

Then he leaned toward her, grabbed her by the shoulder and shook her.

"But what about the Lord?" he said in a rapid whisper. "He doesn't forgive anything, eh? Here we are at the brink of the grave, and the punishments we get—our last days, and no peace, no joy, and none to hope for. Beggars we'll die—mark my words— beggars!"

My grandmother took his hands in hers, sat down beside him, and laughed softly.

"What of it? Why you so scared to be a beggar? So we'll be beggars. You can sit home and I'll go out with the cup. Nobody'll refuse me—we'll not go hungry! Stop worrying yourself with all this business!"

Suddenly he snorted, turned his head like a goat, grabbed my grandmother about the neck and hugged her up tight, little and crumpled and blubbering:

"You fool! You blessed little fool! The only person left to me! You'd be willing to lose everything, simpleton that you are! Just remember how we worked for our children, how I sinned for them! And now at the end, not to have anything, not even a little bit. . . ."

At this point I could stand it no longer; I jumped off the stove with the tears streaming down my face and ran to their side, sobbing with joy that my mother had come, that they should be speaking together with such unprecedented tenderness, and that they allowed me to share their grief with them, both of them embracing me, fondling me, bathing me in their tears.

"So you're here too, you little scoundrel," whispered my grandfather into my ear. "Now your mother's come you won't be needing me, your grandfather, the old devil,. eh? Nor your grandmother, the old harpy that only knows how to spoil you. Phooh, fie on vou!"

He waved us off with his hands and stood up.

"Everybody leaves us—everybody tries to get away—each for himself. . . . Well, call her in," he said angrily. "Hurry up!"

Grandmother left the kitchen and grandfather went over to the icon corner.

"Merciful God—just see—to think of it!" he muttered with bowed head, striking himself vauntingly on the chest. I did not like this, and in general I did not approve of the way in which he spoke to God, always so boastful. My mother entered, filling the room with the cheer of her red dress. She sat on the bench at the table with grandmother and grandfather on either side of her, the full sleeves of her dress draped over their shoulders. She spoke to them softly and seriously, and they listened without a word. Both of them looked so small beside her that it seemed she was the mother and they the children.

Worn out with emotion, I fell fast asleep on the bunk.

That evening both the old people dressed up in their best clothes and went to vesper service. Grandmother merrily winked at my grandfather, who was resplendent in the suit of a master-workman and a racoon coat.

"Just see what a neat little goat your father is," she said, nudging my mother.

Mother laughed gaily.

When she and I were alone in her room, she sat on the couch with one leg drawn up under her and called me over, patting the couch next to her.

"Here, come sit down. Well, how are things? Not very good?"

How were they? I didn't know.

"Does your grandfather beat you?"

"Not so much any more."

"Really? Well, tell me anything you like."

I had no desire to talk about my grandfather, so I began to tell her that a very nice man had lived in the room we were in, but nobody had liked him and grandfather had finally put him out. Apparently this story did not interest my mother, and she said:

"Tell me something else."

I told her about the three little boys and how the Colonel had chased me out of his yard.

"What a nasty man," she said with a hug.

Then she became quiet, studying the floor through narrowed eyes and shaking her head.

"Why is grandfather so angry with you?" I asked.

"I am to blame."

"You should have brought him the baby. . . ."

She started up, frowned, and bit her lip, then burst out laughing and hugged me again.

"You little silly! But don't say a word about that again, hear? Not a word—and don't even think about it!"

For some time she spoke words that were quiet and stern and unintelligible. Then she got up and began to pace the floor, tapping her chin with her fingers and moving her heavy brows.

A wax candle burned and melted on the table and was reflected in a mirror. Dirty shadows crept across the floor, an icon lamp glowed in the corner, and the frost-covered window was silver with moonlight. Mother glanced about as though searching for something on the empty walls and ceiling.

"When do you go to bed?"

"A little later."

"That's right, you had a nap this afternoon," she remembered with a sigh.

"Do you want to go away?" I asked.

"Where to?" she replied with some surprise, then she lifted my head and gazed for so long into my eyes that I could not hold back the tears.

"Why are you crying?"

"My neck hurts."

But my heart hurt more. I realized that she could not live in that house, that she would surely go away. . . .

"You will look like your father some day," she said, tossing the carpet aside with her foot. "Has grandmother told you about him?"

"Yes."

"She was very fond of Maxim—very. And he was fond of her. . . . "

"I know."

Mother looked at the candle, frowned, and put it out.

"That's better," she said.

It seemed fresher and cleaner in the room without the candle. The dirty shadows on the floor were replaced by patches of blue moonlight, while golden reflections glittered on the windowpane.

"Where did you live before you came here?"

She mentioned the names of several towns as though remembering something long forgotten, all the while circling about the room like a hawk.

"Where did you get such a dress?"

"I made it myself. I do everything for myself."

It was pleasant to find her so different from everybody else, but I regretted that she spoke so little. If I did not ask her questions, she said nothing.

Once more she sat down next to me on the couch, and we remained there without speaking, holding tight to each other, until the old folks returned smelling of wax and incense, gravely quiet and gentle.

Supper was a solemn and elevated affair. We spoke little and cautiously, as though afraid of awakening someone from a light sleep.

Soon mother energetically undertook my "secular" education: she bought me a few books, one of which was called "A Russian Primer." From this book I learned the secular alphabet in a few days. But mother immediately had me learn poetry by heart, and this was the beginning of mutual torture.

Here is the first verse I had to learn:

A winding road, an endless road,
A road past fields and man's abode,
No pick or spade the path has laid,
But countless hoofs the bed have made.

When I recited it I always said "binding" instead of
"winding," "blade" instead of "spade" and "by" instead of "but."

"But just think," protested my mother, "how could a road be
'binding,' silly? 'Winding'—that's what you must say.'

I understood, and yet I kept saying "binding," to my own
consternation.

Mother became angry and insisted that I was stubborn and
stupid. That was a very bitter accusation to hear, and I strained
every effort to remember the accursed lines. Mentally I recited
them without a mistake, but when I said them out loud I invariably
mixed up the words. I came to hate these illusive lines, and began
to distort them for spite, thinking up a whole series of words in
alliteration, which gave me the greater pleasure the less sense
they made.

But this amusement cost me dear: one day at the end of a
successful lesson, mother asked me to recite the poem, and in
spite of myself I began to mutter:

A road was sowed and blowed with toad,
No pixies, twixies, fixed the rixies. . . .

I realized what was happening only too late: my mother rose
with her hands on the table and asked, enunciating each word
separately:

"Where did you get that?"

"I don't know," I answered, thoroughly shocked.

"Oh yes you do! Tell me!"

"Just like that."

"Just like what?"

"For fun."

"Get into the corner."

"What for?"

"Into the corner!" she repeated threateningly.

"Which corner?"

Without answering, she gave me such a look that I completely lost all sense of what I was doing or what she wanted me to do. In the icon corner stood a round table containing a vase filled with sweet-scented dried flowers and grasses. In another corner stood a trunk covered with a rug. A bed occupied the third corner while the fourth was taken up by the door.

"I don't know what you want me to do," I said, with a desperate effort to understand.

She sank into a chair, silently rubbing her brow and cheek.

"Hasn't grandfather ever stood you in the corner?"

"When?"

"At any time," she cried impatiently, striking the table twice.

"No, not that I remember."

"Don't you know that it is a punishment—to be stood in the corner?"

"No. Why is it a punishment?"

"Dear me!" she said with a sigh. "Come here."

"Why are you shouting at me?" I asked, coming over.

"Why do you make a point of mixing up the poem?"

I explained to the best of my ability that when I shut my eyes I remembered the poem as it was written, but when I said it out loud, other words came out.

"Aren't you just making that up?"

I swore I was not, but immediately I began to wonder whether I was or not. Suddenly, taking my time, I recited the poem without a mistake. That amazed and overwhelmed me.

I felt my face flushing, my ears burning. I stood there in front of my mother consumed with shame, and through my tears I could see her face darken with disappointment, her lips tighten, her brows lower.

"What does that mean?" she asked in a strange voice. "So it seems you actually did make it up!"

"I don't know. I had no intention to. . . ."

"You're a hard person to deal with," she said, lowering her head. "Go away."

She began to give me more and more poems to learn, but my mind refused to absorb them. The desire to distort these rhythmic lines and to fit different words into them grew more viciously intense. I had no trouble in doing this—the unwelcome words came to my mind in droves, quickly substituting themselves for the required ones. Often whole lines refused to be captured by my visual memory however much I tried. One plaintive verse—by Prince Vyazemsky, it seems—caused me particular trouble.

> 'Til late at night from early morn,
> Old folks and orphans and widows
> Beg for a crust 'neath the windows.

I always left out the third line:
Stretch out their hands and in voices forlorn.

In exasperation my mother told my grandfather about my freaks of memory.

"Spoiled, that's what he is!" he said angrily. "There's nothing wrong with his memory; knows all the prayers better than me. His memory's like stone—once a thing's cut into it, it's there for good. Try giving him a licking!"

My grandmother confirmed his opinion:

"He remembers fairy tales and songs, and songs be the same as poetry."

All this was true, and I felt that I was to blame, but as soon as I undertook the learning of a poem, other words would come crawling out like a flock of roaches and line themselves up:

> Night and morning, to our gate,
> Cripples, orphans come and wait,
> Wait and whine and beg for bread,
> Take it to Petrovna's shed,
> Sell it for her cows, and then,
> Wallow drunken in the glen.

At night as I lay alongside of my grandmother, I would tell her all I remembered from the books and all that I myself made up. Sometimes she would laugh, but mostly she reproved me:

"Just see what you can do if you want! But you hadn't ought to make fun of beggars. Christ was a beggar, and so were all the saints."

I replied by muttering:

> *Beggars I hate,*
> *And grandfather too,*
> *So help me God.*
> *What can I do*
> *To escape my fate*
> *And grandfather's rod?*

"May your tongue wither at the roots, you wicked boy!" exclaimed grandmother. "What; if your grandfather hears it?"

"Let him!"

"Why ever should you be a-worrying of your poor mother? Hard enough it is for her without you making it worse," coaxed grandmother gently.

"Why is it hard for her?"

"Hold your tongue! It's not for you to understand such things!"

"I know it's grandfather that. . . ."

"Hold your tongue I tell you!"

I was unhappy almost to the point of despair, but for some reason I wanted to hide the fact. And so I became bold and unruly. My mother's lessons increased and became more difficult. I had no trouble with arithmetic, but I could not bear to write and understood nothing about grammar. The thing which oppressed me above everything else was the knowledge that my mother was so miserable living in my grandfather's house. She became more gloomy with every day, looking upon everyone with alien eyes and sitting for hours at the window gazing into the garden, seeming to wither away. The first few days after her arrival she was quick and full of life, but now there were dark circles under her eyes and she neglected her appearance, going-about the whole day long in a wrinkled, unbuttoned blouse without combing her hair. It hurt me to see her so unattractive—she always should have been neat and clean and beautiful, the most beautiful person in the world.

During our lessons she stared past me at the wall or through the window, asking her questions in a tired voice and forgetting to listen to the answers. She had become very irritable and often shouted at me. This also hurt my feelings: a mother should be more just than other people, like the mothers in fairy tales.

One day I said to her:

"Are you unhappy with us?"

"Get on with your work," she replied sharply.

I also observed that my grandfather was preparing to do something which frightened my grandmother and my mother. Often he would lock himself up with my mother in her room and screech like shepherd Nikanor's horrible wooden whistle. On one such occasion my mother shouted so loud as to be heard throughout the house:

"That will never be, never!"

She slammed the door and my grandfather howled.

That was in the evening. My grandmother was sitting in the kitchen making grandfather a shirt and muttering under her breath as she sewed. When the door slammed she listened, and then said:

"Oh Lord, she's gone to the tenants!"

Suddenly my grandfather rushed into the kitchen, struck my grandmother over the head, and hissed as he nursed his stinging hand:

"When you going to learn to hold your tongue, you old witch?"

"It's a fool you be," answered my grandmother calmly, adjusting her hair. "Think you're going to get me to hold my tongue? You can be sure I'll always be telling her anything I find out about your scheming. . . ."

He threw himself at her and began to pummel her head. Grandmother made no resistance, but kept saying:

"Go ahead and beat me, you fool! Harder, harder!"

From the bunk where I was sitting I began throwing pillows and blankets and boots at him, but in his rage my grandfather did not notice it. Grandmother fell on the floor, and there he kicked her head until he himself stumbled and fell, overturning a pail of water.

He jumped up, spitting and sputtering. With a wild glance around, he ran out of the kitchen and up to his room in the attic. Grandmother got up with a groan, sat down on the bench, and began straightening out her tangled hair. I jumped down off the bunk on the stove.

"Gather up these pillows and things and put them back on the stove," she said angrily. "A fine thing to go throwing the pillows about! Learn to be minding your own business! And that old devil going off his head like that too!"

Suddenly she let out a little cry, frowned, and called me over.

"Look here," she said, lowering her head. "What is it hurts so here?"

I lifted her heavy hair and discovered that a hairpin had been driven into her scalp. I pulled it out and found another. I went weak all over.

"I better call mother," I said. "I'm afraid."

"What you saying—Til call mother!'" she cried with a wave of her hand. "Thank the Lord she didn't see or hear it, and you'll be calling her! Get out of here!"

With the deft fingers of a lacemaker, she herself began feeling through her heavy black mane for the imbedded hairpins. Gathering all my courage, I helped her pull out two more.

"Does it hurt?"

"Not specially. Tomorrow I'll heat up the bath-house and wash all the hurt away. But don't you go telling your mother he beat me, pigeon-widgeon," she coaxed tenderly. "They're angry enough with each other as it is. You won't, now, will you?"

"No."

"Don't forget! Now let's straighten up here. Can you see anything on my face? No? That's good. So everything's neat as daisies."

She began to wipe up the floor, and I said from the bottom of my heart:

"You're like one of the saints—they beat you and torture you, and you don't pay any attention to it."

"What nonsense is that! A saint! A fine place to go looking for a saint!"

She kept on muttering as she crawled about on all fours, while I sat on the doorstep figuring out how I could pay back my grandfather for what he had done.

This was the first time he had shown such violence to grandmother in my presence. There in the twilight I seemed to see his red face with the red hair waving about it. My heart was burning with indignation, and I suffered from the inability to think up a fitting revenge.

Two days later, on entering his room in the attic, I found him sitting on the floor in front of an open chest going through some papers. On a chair beside him lay his favourite calendar of saints—twelve sheets of heavy grey paper divided into squares for the days of the month, with figures of the saints in the squares. My grandfather prized this calendar highly, allowing me to look at it only on those rare occasions when he was particularly pleased with me. And I always contemplated those attractive little grey figures with a peculiar emotion. I knew the lives of some of them: Kirik and Ulita, Varvara-the-Martyr, Pante-leimon, and many others. I was especially moved by the sad life of Alexei, Man-of-God, and the splendid verses about him which my grandmother often recited to me with deep feeling. When you looked at these hundreds of saints, it brought the quiet consolation that there had always been martyrs.

But now I decided to cut up this calendar, and when grandfather went over to the window to read a blue paper embossed with eagles, I grabbed up several sheets, quickly ran downstairs, took the scissors from grandmother's table, climbed up on the stove and began cutting off the heads of the saints. When I had decapitated one row, my heart was touched with pity for them, so I began to merely cut along the lines dividing the sheet into squares. Before I had cut up the following line my grandfather appeared on the doorstep.

"Who gave you permission to take the calendar?" he asked.

Suddenly he caught sight of the little squares scattered over the bunk. He grabbed them up, peered at them, discarded them for others, and when he realized what was happening, his jaw clamped, his beard began to quiver, and he breathed so hard that, the papers went flying.

"What have you done!" he shouted at last, yanking me off the stove by the leg. I somersaulted into the air, but my grandmother caught me.

"I'll kill you!" shrieked my grandfather, pummeling both me and my grandmother.

Suddenly my mother appeared and I found myself in the corner with her in front of me.

"Stop this nonsense!" she cried as she warded off grandfather's blows. "Come to your senses!"

"I'm done for," wailed my grandfather, sinking down on the bench by the window. "You're all against me—all of you!"

"You should be ashamed of yourself for putting on such a show!" came my mother's low voice.

Grandfather shouted and kicked the bench, his eyes tight closed and his beard pointing ridiculously toward the ceiling. It seemed to me that he really was ashamed of the show he was putting on in the presence of my mother, and that was why he closed his eyes.

"I'll paste these pieces together on some calico and the calendar will be better than ever—stronger," said mother as she straightened out the sheets of paper. "See, they're all wrinkled and worn and falling to pieces."

She spoke to him in the same tone she used during our lessons when I did not understand. Suddenly grandfather got up, straightened his shirt and his vest with great importance, cleared his throat, and said:

"See that you paste them together today. I shall bring you the other sheets."

He went to the door, but turned at the threshold.

"He deserves a licking!" he said, shaking a crooked finger at me.

"Yes, he does" agreed my mother. "Why did you ever do such a thing?" she asked, bending over me.

"I did it on purpose. If he ever beats grandmother again, I'll cut his beard off!"

Grandmother, who was in the act of taking off her torn blouse, shook her head.

"It's holding your tongue you should be, like you promised!" she said, spitting in disgust. "May it swell up so's it can't go wagging any more!"

Mother glanced at her, then turned to me.

"When did he beat her?" she asked.

"Have some shame on you, Varvara, asking him about such things! It's none of your business!"

"Ah, mother, you blessed creature" cried my own mother, embracing her warmly.

"Hm, a fine sort of a mother for you! Here, let me go. . . ."

They looked at each other in silence for a minute, then moved apart. My grandfather could be heard moving about in the entrance-way.

From the very first day of her arrival, my mother was friendly with the gay wife of the army man, and went to visit her almost every evening. There she met people from the Betlengs' house—pretty young girls and brave officers. My grandfather did not like this, and often as he sat over his supper in the kitchen he would shake his spoon in their direction and grumble:

"Another party on, curse them! There'll be no sleeping the night through!"

Soon he asked the tenants to move, and when they had gone he brought two loads of odd furniture from somewhere, placed it in the empty apartment, and locked the door.

"Don't need those tenants any more—going to be entertaining guests myself from now on."

And on Sunday the guests began to arrive. Among them were grandmother's sister, Matryona Ivanovna, a noisy, large-nosed laundress wearing a striped silk dress and a golden scarf on her head. With her came her two sons, Vasili, a draughtsman, long-haired and dressed in grey—a jolly, good-natured fellow; and

Victor, who had a horsy head and a narrow face sprinkled with freckles. While he was taking off his rubbers out in the entrance-way I heard him piping like a clown:

"Andrei-papa, Andrei-papa. . . ."

This surprised and frightened me.

Uncle Yakov came with his guitar. He also brought along a quiet, bald-headed, one-eyed watchmaker, dressed in a long black coat that made him look like a monk. He always sat smiling in the corner with his head tipped to one side, and one finger supporting his cloven, clean-shaven chin. He was dark, and his one eye gazed at everyone with particular intensity. He spoke little and constantly repeated the same phrase:

"Please not to trouble yourself—it's all the same...."

When I first saw him I suddenly remembered the time, long ago (we were still living on Novaya Street), when I had heard the drums beating ominously out in the road and seen a high black cart surrounded by soldiers and people move from the jail to the public square. On a bench in the cart sat a man with a round cap on his head and chains on his hands that jingled with the swaying of his body. A black sign hung about his neck with something written on it in large white letters. The man's head hung down as though he were reading it. . . .

"This is my son," said my mother, introducing me to the watchmaker, but I edged away in fright, holding my hands behind my back.

"Please not to trouble yourself," he said, stretching his mouth to his right ear in a frightful way. Catching me by the belt, he yanked me toward him and whirled me about with a quick, deft movement.

"He's all right, a sturdy chap," he said in approbation as he let me go.

I took up my position in a leather armchair large enough to sleep in. Grandfather always boasted that this chair had belonged to Prince Gruzinsky. From the corner I observed with what an effort the grownups tried to be jolly and how strangely and suspiciously the watchmaker changed his facial expressions. His face was thin and greasy, all melted and running. When he smiled, his thick lips shifted to the right and his little nose moved like a dumpling in a stew. His large, protruding ears also moved, now rising along with the brow above his one eye, now sliding toward his cheekbones, and it seemed to me that if he so desired, he could fold them over his nose like hands. Sometimes with a sigh he would stick out his dark little tongue, as round as a pestle, drawing circles with it to moisten his thick, oily lips. I found this more surprising than amusing, and could not take my eyes off him.

The guests drank tea with rum, which smelled like burnt onions. They also drank grandmother's liqueurs, which were golden, or green, or dark as tar. They ate seasoned *varenets* and honey cakes with poppy seeds. They swelled and sweated and praised my grandmother. When they had had their fill they sat back in their chairs, flushed and bloated, and lazily asked Uncle Yakov to play for them.

He bent over his guitar and strummed it as he sang in his unpleasant voice:

> *Oh, we lived as best we could,*
> *Lots of noise, but little good.*
> *Ca-a-ame the lady from Kazan,*
> *Looking for another man. . . .*

I found this a very sad song, and my grandmother said:

"Sing something else, Yakov—a true kind of song. Remember the songs they used to sing, Motrya?"

"There's a new style in songs these days, my dear," said the laundress with an impressive rustle of her dress.

My uncle stared at my grandmother through half-closed eyes as though she were far away, and continued plucking out his gloomy tune and singing his ugly words.

My grandfather was carrying on a secret conversation with the watchmaker, demonstrating something with his fingers. The latter lifted his brow, glanced in my mother's direction, nodded, and a subtle change spread over his liquid face.

Mother was sitting with the Sergeyevs as usual, speaking to Vasili in a quiet, serious voice.

"Hm-m. Have to think about that," he said with a sigh.

Victor gave a well-fed smile, shuffled his feet, and suddenly began to sing in a thin voice:

"Andrei-papa, Andrei-papa. . . ."

Everyone stopped talking and glanced at him.

"He got that from the theáyter," explained his mother proudly. "They sing that in the theáyter."

There were two or three such evenings, memorable for their insufferable boredom. Then one Sunday the watchmaker put in his appearance at noon, just after late mass. I was sitting in my mother's room helping her unravel an old beaded embroidery when the door was suddenly flung open and grandmother's frightened face appeared just long enough to whisper:

"Varya, he's come!"

My mother did not start or move a muscle. A minute later the door opened again and my grandfather said solemnly:

"Dress yourself and come along, Varvara!"

"Where to?" asked my mother without glancing at him and without getting up.

"Come along, and God bless you. Don't start arguing. He's a steady man, a master at his job, and he'll make a good father for Alexei...."

Grandfather spoke with unwonted importance and kept stroking his thighs with his hands, while his elbows quivered as though his arms wanted to stretch forward and he was struggling to keep them back.

"I have already told you that that would never be," said my mother calmly.

Grandfather strode over to her with his arms ahead of him like a blind man.

"Come along or I'll drag you along—by the hair!" he shouted hoarsely, bristling all over.

"You'll drag me?" said my mother rising. Her face was white and her eyes narrowed menacingly. Quickly she began to take off her skirt and blouse. When she remained in only her petticoat, she said to my grandfather:

"All right, drag me along!"

He bared his teeth and shook his fist.

"Put on your clothes, Varvara!"

My mother pushed him away and went to the door.

"Well, are you coming?" she cried.

"I'll disown you!" hissed my grandfather.

"I'm not afraid. Well?"

She opened the door, but he grabbed the hem of her slip and fell on his knees.

"You'll come to an awful end, Varvara, you she-devil! Don't disgrace me. Mother! Mother!" he wailed.

Grandmother had already barred mother's way and was shooing her back into the room like a chicken.

"You fool of a Varka!" she muttered. "Get back, you shameless wench!"

When she had her back in the room, she put the hook on the door and turned to my grandfather. With one hand she raised him off the floor, while she shook the other at him menacingly.

"O-o-o, you old devil, you senseless creature!"

She sat him down on the couch like a rag doll with his head flopping and his mouth hanging open.

"Get into your clothes, you!" she shouted at my mother.

"I won't go out to him, do you hear?" said my mother as she picked up her clothes.

Grandmother pushed me off the couch.

"Go bring a dipper of water, quick."

She spoke almost in a whisper, but calmly and imperiously. I ran out into the entrance-way, from where I could hear someone walking slowly up and down in the front room.

"Tomorrow I'm leaving!" I heard my mother say.

I went into the kitchen and sat down at the window as in a dream.

My grandfather sniffled and groaned, my grandmother muttered under her breath, then a door slammed and all was quiet and terrifying. Suddenly remembering what I had been sent for, I dipped up some water and went out into the entranceway. From the front of the house appeared the watchmaker with drooping head, stroking his fur cap and making hoarse sounds. He was followed by my grandmother with her hands crossed on her stomach, bowing and saying quietly:

"You yourself can understand—no forcing a person to like you."

He stumbled through the door and out into the yard, while grandmother crossed herself and stood there trembling all over, laughing or crying—I couldn't make out which.

"What's the matter?" I asked, running over to her.

She snatched the dipper out of my hands, wetting my feet and crying:

"How far did you go to fetch this water? Lock the door!"

She went back into my mother's room, and I into the kitchen, from where I could hear them groaning and sighing and muttering, as though they were pushing a weight beyond their strength from one place to another.

It was a fine day with long rays of winter sun coming through the frosted panes of the two windows. The table was laid for dinner, and shone with pewter dishes as well as with the decanters containing golden kvass and grandfather's vodka, green from the wort and cowslip added for flavour. Through a thawed circle of windowpane I caught a glimpse of the dazzling snow on the roofs and the sparkling silver caps offence posts and bird-houses. My captured birds played in sun-flooded cages hanging from the window frames: the tame chaffinches chirped merrily, the bullfinches chattered, while the goldfinch trilled a song. But the music and brightness of this silvery day brought me no joy. The day was unwanted. Everything was unwanted. I would have set the birds free, but just as I was taking down the cages my grandmother came bustling into the kitchen, slapping herself on the thighs and crying as she ran to the stove:

"Curses on all of you, devil take you! Ah, what an old fool you are, Akulina!"

She took the *pirog* out of the oven, struck the burnt crust with her fingers, and spat in vexation.

"Burnt to a cinder! There's warming it up for you! Phooh, demons, the whole bunch of you—may you blow up and float away! What you sitting there goggling at, you owl! I'd like to smash the lot of you like cracked jugs?"

She began to cry, turning the *pirog* from side to side, tapping the dry crust, watering it with enormous tears.

My mother and grandfather came into the kitchen, and she flung the ruin on the table, causing the dishes to rattle.

"Just see what's happened, all on account of you, devil take you!"

My mother, now in a calm and merry mood, embraced her and coaxed her to forget it. Grandfather looked tired and wrinkled as he took his place at the table, tied his napkin around his neck, squinted his swollen eyes in the sun, and muttered:

"All right, forget it! We've tasted *pirog* before. The Lord's a bit of a miser—pays for years in minutes and doesn't believe in interest. Sit down, Varya . . . forget it!"

It was as though his mind had been touched. All during the dinner he talked about God and the impious Ahab and the trials and tribulations of being a father. Grandmother angrily interrupted him.

"Go ahead and eat and don't talk so much," she said.

Mother laughed, her clear eyes shining.

"Well, were you frightened a while ago?" she asked as she gave me a nudge.

I had not been very much frightened, but now I felt uneasy and could not understand what had happened.

They ate much and long, as was usual on Sundays. It was difficult to believe that these were the same people who half an hour ago had been shouting at each other on the verge of a fight, sobbing and seething with anger. Nor could I believe that all this had been serious or had cost them any effort. I had become used to their crying and shouting and the scenes which flared up so often and died down so quickly. I no longer took them to heart as I had at first.

Long afterwards I came to understand that Russians, as a result of the poverty and dullness of their lives, sought diversion in grief, playing it up like children, and rarely feeling ashamed of their misfortunes.

When life is monotonous, even grief is a welcome event, even a fire is diversion.

A wart is adornment to a vacuous face.

XI

After this incident, my mother became strong and erect and the head of the household, while my grandfather became quiet and unobtrusive, not at all like himself.

He almost never left the house, sitting alone in the attic reading a mysterious book called "Notes Written by My Father." He kept this book in his strongbox under lock and key, and I had often observed that before taking it out, he always washed his hands. The book was small and thick and bound in tan leather. On the bluish title page was the following inscription in faded ink:

"To the honourable Vasili Kashirin with the fondest regards and gratitude."

It was signed by a strange name ending in a flourish representing a bird in flight. My grandfather would carefully open the heavy leather cover, put on his silver-framed spectacles, and gaze for long at this inscription as he twitched his nose to adjust his glasses. More than once I asked him what the book was, but he always answered impressively:

"That is not for you to know. Just wait a bit—when I die I'll leave it to you, and my racoon coat too."

He began to speak less often and more gently to my mother, and when she spoke he would listen attentively, muttering and making little gestures with his hand and blinking his eyes like Uncle Pyotr.

His trunks were full of many extraordinary costumes: brocaded skirts, satin vests, cloth-of-gold, *sarafani, kiki* and *kokoshniki** ornamented with pearls, bright kerchiefs and scarfs, heavy Mordovian necklaces and beads of varicoloured stones. He brought all this into my mother's room and spread it over the table and chairs. When my mother admired the finery, he said:

---

* *Sarafani*—long, sleeveless dresses; kiki and kokoshniki—headdresses.—*Trans.*

"In my day, people dressed ever so much richer and finer than nowadays! The clothes were richer, but people lived simpler and more friendly. But I suppose there's no going back! Try them on— dress yourself up. . . ."

One day mother went into the next room and returned wearing a dark blue sarafan embroidered in gold, and a pearl headdress.

"Does it please your grace?" she said, bowing low to my grandfather.

Grandfather gasped, beamed all over, and walked around her waving his arms and muttering indistinctly, as in a dream:

"Ah, Varvara, if only you were rich and there were decent people around!"

My mother had taken up her quarters in the two rooms at the front of the house, and she often entertained guests. Most frequent were the Maximov brothers: Pyotr, a huge, handsome officer with a large blond beard and blue eyes—the same in whose presence grandfather had given me a beating that time for spitting on the old gentleman's head; Yevgeni, who was also tall, and pale and long-legged, with a pointed little black beard. He had eyes like sloes and always wore a green uniform with gold buttons and gold insignia on his narrow shoulders. He had the habit of tossing back his long, wavy hair from his high forehead and smiling condescendingly. He was forever telling something in a husky voice, crawling up on whatever he had to say with the inevitable phrase:

"You see, the way I look at it. . . ."

My mother would listen to him with half-closed eyes, often interrupting him with a laugh:

"You're still a child, Yevgeni Vasilyevich, if you'll forgive my saying so. . . ."

"That's what—a child!" the large officer would corroborate, with a slap on the knee for emphasis.

The Christmas holidays passed in noisy merriment. Almost every evening my mother and her friends dressed up in fancy costumes and went visiting. Mother's costume was always the finest.

Every time the gay company went out the gate, the house seemed to sink into the earth; everything became dull and alarmingly quiet. Grandmother moved through the rooms like an old goose tidying up, while grandfather stood warming his back at the tile stove and muttering to himself:

"Well, all right, let her have her own way. . . .We'll see what'll come of it. . . ."

After the Christmas holidays mother took me and Sasha, Uncle Mikhail's son, to school. Sasha's father had married a second time, and his stepmother had taken an immediate dislike to him. She beat him so often that grandmother insisted on grandfather's taking him to live with us. We attended school for about a month. Of all I was taught during that time I can remember only one thing—that when asked what my name was, it was not sufficient to answer:

"Peshkov."

I had to say:

"My name is Peshkov."

Nor could I say to the teacher:

"Don't you go shouting at me, mister. I'm not afraid of you. . . ."

I immediately disliked school. My cousin, on the other hand, liked it from the very start and made many friends. But one day he happened to fall asleep during the lesson and cried out in his sleep:

"No I wo-on't"

When he woke up, he asked permission *to* leave the classroom, for which the other boys teased him mercilessly. The next day, on reaching the gully at Sennaya Square on our way to school, he stopped and said:

"You go on without me. I'm not going to school today. I'd rather go for a walk."

He squatted down, buried his books in the snow, and went away. It was a bright January day with the whole world glittering with sunlight. I envied my cousin, but gritted my teeth and went on for mother's sake. Naturally the books Sasha had buried in the snow were stolen, so that he had real reason for not going to

school on the following day. On the third, my grandfather found
out about his truancy.

Both of us were put on trial: behind the kitchen table sat my
grandfather, my grandmother, and my mother for the cross-
examination. I remember the funny answer Sasha gave to my
grandfather's question:

"How is it you never reached the school-house?"

"I forgot where it was," he said, looking my grandfather
straight in the face with his timid eyes.

"You forgot?"

"Yes. I looked and looked for it. . . ."

"You should have followed Alexei; he remembered."

"I lost sight of him."

"Of Alexei?"

"Yes."

"How could you do that?"

Sasha thought a moment, then answered with a sigh:

"There was a blizzard—I couldn't see anything."

Everybody laughed, because the weather had been clear and
sunny. Sasha also gave a faint smile, but my grandfather bared
his teeth and said sarcastically:

"Couldn't you have held onto his hand or his belt?"

"I did, but the wind tore me loose."

He spoke slowly and hopelessly; I felt uncomfortable
listening to that clumsy, useless lying and could not understand
his stubbornness.

They gave us a licking and hired an old retired fireman with
a twisted arm to escort us to school. He was to see that Sasha did
not wander from the path to knowledge. But all was in vain. When
we reached the gully on the following day, my cousin took off
one of his felt boots and hurled it to the left, he took off the other
and hurled it to the right, and made off across the square in his
stocking feet. The old man gasped and set out after the boots.
When he had found them, he led me home in fright.

All day long my mother and grandmother searched the town
for the runaway, finding him that evening in Chirkov's saloon
near the monastery, entertaining the public by dancing for them.

They brought him home and did not even beat him, so overwhelmed were they by the boy's persistent silence. He lay beside me on the bunk kicking his feet in the air and saying quietly:

"My stepmother doesn't love me, my father doesn't love me, my grandfather doesn't love me. Why should I go on living with them? I'll find out from grandmother where the robbers live and run away to them. Then you'll all be sorry! Let's go together, shall we?"

I could not run away with him. At that time I had another aim in life—to become an officer with a great, blond beard—and so it was necessary to study. When I told my cousin my plan he thought for a moment, then gave his approval.

"That's good too. When you're an officer I'll be chief of the robbers and you'll have to catch me. One of us'll kill the other, or else take him prisoner. I wouldn't kill you for anything."

"Neither would I you."

On that we concluded our discussion.

Grandmother came in, crawled up on the stove and began to talk to us.

"Well, little mice? Ah, my little orphans, my little sprouts!"

In her deep sympathy for us, she began to denounce Sasha's stepmother, fat Aunt Nadezhda, daughter of an innkeeper. This led her to denounce all stepmothers and stepfathers, and this in turn led her to tell us the story of the wise hermit Ion who, while still a lad, brought his stepmother before the judgment seat of God. His father, fisherman on Beloye Lake:

—*Was undone by a vixenish wife.*
With ale she enticed him to drunkenness,
With a potion she drugged him to sleepiness,

Then she placed him, asleep, in an oaken skiff,
In a narrow skiff, like a coffin bed.
She herself took the oars wrought of maple wood,
To the depths of the lake did she row with him,
Where the water ran brooding and lowering,
Awaiting the deed of the shameless one.

There she leaned from the skiff and unbalanced it,
Overturned it, with none to be wise to it.
Like a stone sank her husband in waters deep,
While his wife quickly swam to the forest shore.
  There she fell on the earth, wailing bitterly,
Feigning to grieve for the loss of him,
Him she had murdered so cruelly.

  Hearkened the people and pitied her,
Wept at her plight, at her widow's lot.
  Alas, thou art young to be widowed so,
Bitter and black thy unhappiness,
But the hand of the Lord rules the lives of us,

And 'tis He who doth order the death of us.
It was only her stepson, Ionushka,
Who believed not the tears of his má-chekha*
Softly he whispered rebuke to her,
Holding his hand on the heart of her:
     Oh, thou woman of subtlety,
     Bird-of-the-night, full of treachery;
     Nor believe I thy tears, shed so lavishly;
     The heart in thy breast beats too joyously.
Let us turn to the heavenly judgment seat,
     To the Lord and the powers of holiness,
     And let one of us take up a whetted knife,
     And hurtle it heavenward forcefully:
     If I be to blame—I shall be slain;
     If thou be to blame—thou shall be slain.
Slowly his mdchekha turned to him,
Glanced with a hate-flashing countenance.
Now on her feet standing steadily,
Made she retort to him vengefully:
     Fool that thou art, born ere thy time,
     Belched from the womb of the werewolf!

---

* *Stepmother.— Irons.*

What is this talk, of thy fancy bred?
What are these lies that thy tongue hath spread?
Hearkened the folk who had gathered there,
Heard that the matter was evil-charged,
Silent they glanced, heavy-heartedly,
Softly conferred on the circumstance.
Then out-stepped an elderly fisherman,
Bowed to all sides, to his kindred-men,
Spoke he these words, each with honour weighed:
Bring me, good people, the whetted blade,
Here you shall see me take hold of it,
Into the sky I shall hurtle it,
Him will it kill who has acted ill.
Brought they the knife to the ancient one,
Swung he the blade o 'er his hoary head,
Bird-like it soared in the welkin bright,
Long did they wait for return of it,
Waited and gazed in the crystal heights,
Took off their caps, huddled together,
Stood there in silence, and silent the night.
Then o 'er the lake came the flush of dawn,
Flushed too the machekha gloatingly,
But sudden the knife, like a swallow swift,
Swept from the sky to the heart of her.
Down on their knees dropped the pious folk,
Praying to God in humility:
—Praised be the Lord for His righteousness!
Then to Ion came the fisherman,
Led him away to a hermitage,
Far away on the river called Kerzhenets,
*Near the fabulous city of Kitezh. ... **

On the next day I woke up covered with red spots. This was
the beginning of a siege of smallpox. I was put up in the back

---

* In the town of Kolyupanovka, Tambov gubernia, Borisoglebsk
uyezd, I heard another version, according to which the knife kills the
stepson who slandered his stepmother.—Author's note.

attic, where for a long time I lay blind, my arms and legs tied down with wide strips of bandage, enduring horrible nightmares. As a result of one of them I nearly perished. The only visitor I had was my grandmother, who fed me from a spoon like an infant and told me endless tales and legends. One evening when I was well on the road to recovery, so that my arms and legs were unbound, though I still wore mittens to keep me from scratching my face, my grandmother did not come at the usual time, and this alarmed me. Suddenly I seemed to see her lying face down on the dusty landing of the attic with her arms widespread. Her neck was slashed almost in two, like Uncle Pyotr's, while out of the dusty shadows a large cat crept up on her, greedily rolling its huge green eyes.

I jumped out of bed, smashed the double window with my feet and shoulder, and threw myself into a snowbank under the window. My mother was entertaining that evening, so nobody heard me break the window, and for some time I lay undiscovered in the snow. No bones were broken; I had only dislocated my shoulder and cut myself severely on the glass, but the shock Caused me to lose the use of my legs. For some three months I was unable to walk and lay in my room listening to the growing animation in the house, the frequent slamming of doors and the constant coming and going of people.

Blizzards swept over the roof; the wind raged beyond the attic door, wailing funereally in the chimney and rattling the shutters. During the day I listened to the cawing of the crows, while

on quiet nights I could hear the dismal howling of wolves in distant fields. To the accompaniment of this music, my soul matured. Then shyly and quietly, but more insistently with every day, the spring came glancing through the window with radiant eyes. Cats began to scream and howl on the fence, and little spring sounds penetrated the walls: the snapping of icicles, the sliding of snow off the roofs, the ringing of the bells, whose chiming assumed a solidity it had lacked in winter.

My grandmother came to see me. Of late her words had become more often and more strongly scented with vodka. She even began to bring a large white teapot with her which she would hide under my bed, admonishing me with a wink:

"Don't you go telling your goblin of a grandfather, pigeon-widgeon!"

"Why do you drink?"

"Shhh! Whom you grow up you'll find out."

Then she would take a swallow from the spout of the teapot, wipe her mouth on her sleeve, and turn to me with a blissful smile.

"Well, my fine gentleman, what was it I was telling you about yesterday?"

"About my father."

"And where did I leave off?"

When I had told her, her rhythmic speech would flow on for hours.

She herself had begun to tell me about my father one day when she was tired and sober and unhappy.

"I dreamed about your father last night—whistling he was, as he walked through the fields with a beech staff in his hand and a spotted dog running after him with its tongue a-lolling. For some reason Maxim Savvate-yevich's been visiting me often in my dreams of late—looks like his soul must be wandering about restless-like. . . ."

For several evenings running she told me about my father, stories as interesting as all her others. My father was the son of a soldier who had been promoted to the rank of officer and then exiled to Siberia for cruelty to his subordinates. Somewhere there in Siberia my father was born. He had a hard life, and when he was still a child began making attempts to run away from home. One day his father took a hound and searched the woods for him as though he were a rabbit. Another time after finding him he began to beat him so mercilessly that the neighbours rescued him and hid him away.

"Do they always beat children?" I asked.

"Always," replied my grandmother calmly.

His mother died when he was very young, and when he was nine years old, his father also died. He was adopted by his godfather, a carpenter, who made him a member of the carpenter's guild in the town of Perm. But my father ran away. At first he led the blind about the markets, but when he was sixteen he came to Nizhni-Novgorod and began to work for a carpenter on the steamboats belonging to Kolchin. By the age of twenty he was already a qualified cabinetmaker and upholsterer. The shop where he worked was next door to my grandfather's house on Kovalikha Street.

"A low fence, and nimble legs," laughed my grandmother. "So there we were, Varya and me, picking raspberries in the garden, and all of a sudden I looked up and—ffwwtt!—there's your father Over the fence and me scared out of my wits. He came walking toward us through the apple trees, a giant of a fellow in a white shirt and plush trousers, barefoot and hatless, with a strap holding back his long hair. And what do you think he had come for? To ask for your mother's hand! I'd seen him before a few times walking past the window. And whenever I saw him I thought to myself, 'There's a fine fellow for you!' So when he comes up to me I says, 'How's that you don't know the right road, my hearty?' Down on his knees he goes.' Akulina Ivanovna,' he says. 'Here I am, the whole soul of me at your feet. And there's Varya; help us hold a wedding, for the love of Christ.' Now that was something, I tell you! Stunned I was, and speechless. I looked up and there's that vixen of a mother of yours hiding behind an apple tree, red as a raspberry, and making signs to him, her eyes full of tears. 'Ah, you simpleton,' says I. 'Better to wither away than start a thing like this! Have you gone clean out of your senses, Varvara? And as for you, young man, just think what you're doing! Is it for you to bend a birch this size?' Your grandfather was a rich man those days—nothing parcelled out to his children yet—owned four houses and money a-plenty, and honoured by his fellows. Not long before that they had presented him with a uniform and hat all fancied up with galloon for his being nine years head of the workshop. Ah, but a proud one he was those days! So I says what I has to say, trembling with fear the while and my heart like to burst a-pitying of them, so downhearted they was. Then your father up and says, 'I know Vasili Vasilyevich will never be giving me Varya of his own free will, so it's up to me to steal her away, and it's here we're wanting your help! My help, think you! I shoo him away, but he don't budge. 'You can stone me if you like, but help me you must,' says he. 'I'll not give in!' Here Varvara comes up to him and puts her hand on his shoulder and says, 'We've been husband and wife for long already—since the month of May. Only we're in need of a wedding.' I collapsed like they had struck me!"

Grandmother's whole body shook with laughter. Then she took a pinch of snuff, wiped the tears from her eyes, and continued with a happy sigh:

"You're too young yet to know the difference between being man and wife and holding a wedding. But it's a dreadful thing when a girl gives birth to a child out of wedlock. You just remember that when you grow up and never lure a maid into such trouble. That'd be a great sin on your soul, leaving the maid in misery and the babe without the law. See you don't forget, now! You must show pity for a woman and love her with all your heart, and not just for the pleasure of it. This is a good thing I am telling you."

She fell into a moment's meditation before she pulled herself together and went on with her story.

"So what was to be done about it? I struck Maxim over the head and yanked Varvara by the braids, but then he says a sensible thing: 'Beating us won't undo anything,' he says, and she puts in, 'Better to think up a way out and then beat us.' So I says to him, 'Got any money?' 'I had some,' he answered, 'but I spent it all on a ring for Varya.' 'All of three rubles?' 'No,' says he, 'nearly a hundred.' And in those days things were cheap and money was worth a lot. I looked at your mother and father standing there— such children they were! Such little fools! 'I hid the ring under a floor board so's you wouldn't see it,' says your mother. 'We can sell it.' Just like children, weren't they though? Well, however it was, we decided to hold the wedding within the week, and I myself was to fix it up with the priest. But oh, how I wept, and my heart shivering and shuddering for fear of your grandfather, and Varvara all a-tremble. Well, we fixed everything up.

"Only an enemy there was of your father—one of the master-workmen—a spiteful man. For long he had been keeping his eye on them and guessed everything. Well, I dressed up my only daughter in the best I had, led her out the gate, and there around the corner stood a troika waiting. She climbed in, Maxim gave a whistle, and off they went. Back home I came with the tears flowing, and who should meet me but this fellow, the scoundrel! Tm goodhearted,' says he, 'and don't aim to break up their happiness. Only I should ask you to let me have just fifty rubles, Akulina Ivanovna.' I had no money, account I never liked it nor saved it, and fool that I be I up and says, 'I have no money, and so I can't be giving you any!' Then give me your promise,' says he. 'My promise? And where shall I be getting the money once I promise?' 'Is it so hard to steal from a rich husband?' says he. It's me, the ninny, should have kept him there talking for a time, but I spat in his face and went on my way. He ran ahead of me into the yard and—what a row he raised!"

She closed her eyes and a faint smile flitted across her face.

"To this day it's a fearful thing to remember the recklessness that followed. Your grandfather lets out a roar like the beastiest beast—a sorry blow it was to him! Used to be he'd look at Varvara and boast how he'd marry her off to a nobleman, to a *barin*. There's your nobleman for you—there's your *barin*! But the Holy Virgin knows better nor us how the mating's to be done. Your grandfather rushed about the yard like he was a-fire. He calls Yakov and Mikhail, Klim the coachman, and that freckle-faced master-workman; I see him take up a cudgel and a weight fastened to a strap, while Mikhail takes a gun. Ours were good, spirited horses and our buggy a light one. 'He'll catch them sure,' thinks I to myself. But here Varvara's guardian angel sends me an enlightenment. I take a knife and cut the harness at the shaft, thinking it will snap on the road. And so it did. The shaft swung loose, nearly killing your grandfather and Mikhail and Klim. And it held them up, so when they reached the church Varya and Maxim were standing at the altar married already, thank the Lord!

"Well, so our men threw themselves at Maxim, but he was a hefty fellow, Maxim—not many's given the strength he had. He hurls Mikhail off the altar, damaging his arm, and knocks out Klim, so your grandfather and Yakov and that master-workman fear to come near him.

"But Maxim keeps his head, spite his fury. 'Put down that cudgel there,' he says to your grandfather. 'I'm a peace-loving fellow and what I've taken, it's by the grace of God and no man's got the right to take it away from me. And that's all I'll be asking of you!' Our men fell back, and grandfather sits in the buggy and shouts, 'Farewell, Varvara! You're no longer a daughter of mine, and I never want to see you again! It's all the same to me whether you're alive or dead!' He came home—gave me a beating, gave me a cussing, but I just grunted and said nothing: I knew it'd all blow over, and what had to be, would be. After that he says to me, 'Look here, Akulina, don't you forget that your daughter's gone for good—you have no more daughter here nor anywheres else, understand?' And I keeps thinking to myself, 'Go on lying, you redhead! Your temper's fast, but it won't last.' "

I listened with bated breath. I was surprised by certain parts of her story—grandfather had described my mother's wedding quite differently. He had been opposed to the wedding and had not allowed my mother into his house afterwards, but according to his account, the wedding had not been secret and he himself had been present. I hesitated to ask grandmother which version was correct because I preferred hers, which was more romantic. She rocked back and forth as she spoke, increasing her movement when she came to sad or dreadful parts, and raising one arm as though warding off a blow. Often she would close her eyes, her heavy brows trembling and a warm smile playing in the wrinkles of her cheeks. Sometimes I was touched by the blind way in which she forgave everything, but at other times I wanted to hear her cry out harsh words of protest.

"Well, for the first two weeks or so I had no idea where they were, Varya and Maxim, but then they sent a little boy to tell me. The next Saturday I set out like I was going to vespers, but instead I went to see them. They were living far away in the wing of a home on Suyetinsky Street. All kinds of workmen were living in the yard—dirty it was, and noisy, but they paid no attention, just went on purring and playing together like a pair of happy kittens. I brought them some presents—tea and sugar and cereals and jam and flour and dried mushrooms and some money— don't remember how much—whatever I could steal from your grandfather—no harm in stealing long's it's not for yourself! But your father would have none of it. 'Is it beggars we are?' he asked, hurt-like. And Varya takes up the tune: 'Now why did you have to bring all that stuff, ma?' I gave it to them all right! 'It's a God-given mother I am to you, you simp,' I says to him, 'and a blood mother to you, you little fool! Where's it written you can insult your own mother? Once you insult your mother here below, you cause God's mother to weep up above!' So then Maxim grabs me up in his arms and carries me around the room—even does a jig with me—-strong as a bear he was! And Varya struts around proud as a peacock of that husband of hers, and starts talking grandly about their 'home' like an honest-to-goodness housewife—split your sides to listen! And the *vatrushki* she served with tea! Break the teeth of a wolf. And the cottage cheese! Like so much gravel.

"So that's how it goes on for a long time. You were about to put in your appearance, and still grandfather keeps mum—stubborn creature he is, the old goblin! I kept on sneaking off to them and he knew it, but made believe not to. Nobody in our house was allowed to mention Varvara's name, and no one did, nor me either, but all the time I knew a father's heart couldn't hold out for long. And sure enough the time came—one night when a blizzard was raging and the wind tearing at the window like a pack of wolves, the chimneys screaming, and all Hell's devils turned loose. Your grandfather and me were lying there side by side unable to sleep and I up and says to him, 'A dreadful night for the poor,' I says, 'and still worse for them as has trouble on their mind.' Suddenly grandfather says, 'How they getting along?' 'Right enough,' I says. 'Not bad at all.' 'And who do you think I'm asking about?' he asks. 'Our daughter Varvara and our son-in-law Maxim.' 'How did you guess it was about them?' 'Enough of this comedy, father; says I. 'Time to quit the game—who's it making happy?' He gives a big sigh. 'Ah, you devils, you! You little red devils!' he says. Then he asks, 'But what about that gawking fool'—meaning your father—'is he sure enough such a fool?' 'A fool,' says I, 'is him as does no work and lives at other people's expense. If you'd have a look at your Yakov and Mikhail, now—aren't they the ones to be called fools? Who does the work and brings in the money in our house? You. And a lot of help you get from them!' Here he starts cursing me out, calling me a fool and a bitch, and a harpy and a beldam, and goodness knows what all! But I say nothing. 'How you ever could be taken in by a fellow as nobody knows where he came from or what he's like!' he says. Still I keep mum until he's worn out, then I says, 'You might go have a look how they're getting along. They're living together fine,' I says. 'Why should I do them such honour?' says he. 'Let them come here.' Well, when he says that, I just break down and cry with joy, and he starts unbraiding my hair— loved to play with my hair, he did. 'Well, don't go bawling, old woman,' he mutters. 'Think I haven't got a heart at all?' He used to be a good soul, your grandfather, afore he got the idea he was smarter than anybody else—after that he became mean and stupid.

"So they came to see us—your mother and father—on Absolution Sunday. So big they both was, so clean and handsome! Maxim stands up there next to your grandfather, and your grandfather comes just up to his shoulder. 'Don't think, Vasili Vasilyevich,' says Maxim, 'that I've come to get a dowry. No indeed. I've only come to pay my respects to my wife's father.' That pleased your grandfather, and he laughed and says, 'Aha! So that's the kind of a rascal you are! Well, enough of this nonsense. Time you came to live with me.' Maxim frowned. 'That's Up to Varya,' he says. 'Whatever she wants—makes no difference to me.' Then they started arguing again—and no stopping them. I kept winking at that father of yours and kicking his foot under the table, but he would have his own way! Fine eyes he had—clear and bright, and dark brows over them. Sometimes he'd pull his brows down over his eyes and his face'd become hard as stone and then he wouldn't listen to a soul but me. I loved him ever so much more than my own sons and he knew that, and loved me too. Used to hug me up or take me in his

arms and carry me around the room saying, 'You're the only real
mother I've got—like Mother Earth,' he'd say. 'I love you more
than I do Varvara!' Your mother was a lively little vixen those
days. She'd rush at him and shout, 'How dare you say such a
thing, you son of a turnip, you cabbage ears!' And the three of
us'd go chasing each other round the room, having a grand time!
Happy days they were, pigeon-widgeon! He could dance like
nobody else too, and knew so many fine songs—learned them
from blind beggars, and nobody can sing like the blind.

"Well, so they moved into the wing facing the garden; that's
where you were born—just at noon. Your father comes home to
lunch, and there you are to greet him. He all but went off his
head with happiness, and as for your mother—he squeezed her
up like it was the hardest job in the world to go having a baby!
He sets me up on his shoulder and carries me through the yard to
report to your grandfather the arrival of another grandson. Even
grand-father took to laughing. 'What a devil you are Maxim!' he
says.

"But your uncles didn't like him—he didn't drink, was sharp
with his tongue and clever at thinking up all kinds of tricks. It's
those tricks were his undoing! Once during Lent a high wind
sprang up, and suddenly there was such a frightful whistling and
howling through the house that everybody was scared out of their
wits. Your grandfather goes running around yelling to light all
the icon lamps and start praying. Then all of a sudden everything
became dead quiet, and that was more fearful than ever. Your
Uncle Yakov guessed the truth: 'That,' he says, 'will be Maxim's
doing!' And sure enough, Maxim himself told us later how he
lined up different bottles on the attic window so's the wind would
go howling through. 'You better watch your step, Maxim!' warned
your grandfather, 'or you'll be getting sent back to Siberia with
those tricks of yours!'

"Came a winter so cold the wolves crept in from the steppes.
One day there's a dog missing, the next a horse gets a fright, or a
drunken sentry is found chewed to death. A lot of trouble they
made, those wolves! Your father would take his gun, put on some
skis, and be off in the night. He always came back with a wolf or

two. He'd skin them and stuff them and put in glass in their eyes so's you couldn't tell them from live ones. One night your Uncle Mikhail goes out to the privy, and all of a sudden he comes running back with his eyes popping, his hair standing on end, his tongue hanging out so's he can't even speak. He gets all twisted up in his pants and falls down, gasping, 'A wolf!' Everybody grabs up the first thing comes to hand and runs to the privy. Sure enough, there's the head of a wolf sticking out of the hole. They shoot it and beat it, but the wolf stays right where it is. So they creeps up on it—nothing but an empty hide with a stuffed head and the front legs nailed to the toilet seat! Your grandfather was mighty mad at Maxim that time—powerful mad he was! Soon Yakov starts joining your father in his tricks. Maxim would make a head out of cardboard, paint in the eyes, and nose, and mouth, and stick on some oakum for hair. Then he and Yakov'd go down the street and poke this scarecrow in people's windows. Naturally the neighbours got scared and raised a row. Other times they'd dress themselves up in sheets. Once they scared the priest; he ran to the sentry, the sentry also got scared and gave the alarm. They were forever pranking it like this and no talking them out of it. I told them to quit it and so did Varya, but they wouldn't listen. Maxim would just laugh and say what fun it was to see people lose their heads and start running account of some idiotic trifle. Just try to make him see sense. . . .

"Well, so this mischief nearly finished him. Your Uncle Mikhail's like his father—mean and always harbouring a grudge, and he set his aim on getting rid of your father. One day, the beginning of winter, they were returning from a visit—four of them—Maxim, your uncles, and the deacon (he lost his place later for beating a coachman to death). They came down Yamskaya Street and got your father to go with them to Dukov Pond—like as if they wanted to go sliding there. But once they reached the pond, they pushed him through a hole in the ice— seems I told you about that already. . . ."

"What makes my uncles so wicked?"

"It's not they're wicked," replied my grandmother calmly as she took a pinch of snuff. "They're just stupid. Mishka's sly and

stupid; while Yakov's just one of your milksops. . . . Well, so
they push him in, and when he comes up and grabs onto the edge
of the ice, they stamp on his fingers with their boots. Lucky he
was sober and they were drunk. Somehow, with God's help he
managed to stay in the middle of the hole and breathe while they
threw ice at his head, but hit him they couldn't and soon they
went away, figuring he'd drown without their help. But he crawled
out and ran straight to the police—the headquarters is right there
on the square, you know. The sergeant knew him and all our
family, so he asked how it happened."

Grandmother crossed herself and murmured gratefully:

"May the Lord give peace to his soul, the soul of Maxim
Sawateyevich, righteous man, and well deserving! Never a word
did he tell the police as to what happened. All my fault, he says—
went to the pond drunk and fell through the hole. But the sergeant
says he's lying—he never drinks. They rub him down with vodka
there in the station house, dress him in dry clothes, wrap him in a
fur coat and bring him home—the sergeant and two others. Yakov
and Mikhail aren't home yet—doing the saloons to the glory of
their parents. Your mother and me can hardly recognize Maxim—
all blue, and his fingers smashed, and the blood running down,
and something like snow on his temples, only it don't melt and
turns out to be his hair gone white.

"Varvara screams, 'What have they done to you, Maxim?'
The sergeant goes nosing around, asking questions, and I feel in
my heart things are bad. I hook Varvara up with the sergeant
while I try to get the truth out of Maxim. 'Go find Mikhail and
Yakov,' he whispers. 'Tell them to say we parted company on
Yamskaya Street—they went along Pokrovka and I turned down
Pryadilny. Don't let them mix things up or we'll be in a bad fix
with the police.' I go to grandfather. 'Keep the sergeant company,'
I says, 'while I go wait for our sons at the gate.' And I told him
the evil thing as happened. He pulls on his clothes, a-trembling
and a-muttering: 'I knew it, I expected something like this would
happen!' But that was a lie—he didn't know a thing. Well, I greet
my beloved sons with a good box on the ears. Mishka straightaway
comes sober from fright, but Yakov's too soaked. 'I don't know

a thing!' he garbles. 'It's all Mishka's doings—he's older than
me!' We got the sergeant calmed down somehow—he was a good
soul! 'Watch out,' he says. 'If anything happens now I'll be sure
to know who's to blame!' And off he goes. Then your grandfather
walks over to Maxim and says, 'Thank you, son. Another one'd
have acted different in your place, I know that well enough. And
thank you, daughter, for bringing such a good man into our house.'
When he wanted, your grandfather could talk fine like that—it
was only afterwards he got stupid and started locking up his heart.
So there we were alone, the three of us, and Maxim starts crying
and his mind sort of wandering: 'Why should they do such a
thing to me?' he cries. 'What have I ever done to them? Why
should they do it, mama?' He always called me mama stead of
mother—like a little child, and there was much in his nature that
was childlike. 'Why, mama?' And all I can do is sit there and cry
along of him. After all, they're my sons and I can't help pitying
them. Your mother pulled all the buttons off her blouse and sat
there mussed up like as if she'd been in a fight. 'Let's go away,
Maxim,' she cried. 'My brothers are our enemies and I'm afraid
of them. Let's go away!' I gave it to her for that. 'Don't throw
straw on the fire,' I says. 'Enough smoke in the house without
that!' Here your grandfather sends those two idiots in to ask
forgiveness and she gives Mishka a slap in the face. 'There's
your forgiveness for you!' she says. And your father keeps asking,
'How could you do such a thing, brothers? You could have
crippled me for life. What kind of a workman would I be without
my fingers, eh?' They made it up somehow. Your father was sick
the next seven weeks or so, and he'd keep saying as he lay there,
'Let's go to some other town, mama—I'm sick of it here!' Soon
after that he was sent to Astrakhan. They were expecting the tsar
there on a visit, and your father was asked to build the triumphal
arch. They sailed off on the first steamboat that left in the spring—
like parting with half my soul, it was. He was sad too, and kept
talking me into going with them. But Varvara was glad as glad
could be and didn't even try to hide it, the shameless beasty! So
that's how they left. . . . and that's all.. .."

She took a swallow of vodka, a pinch of snuff, and said
musingly, as she looked out the window:

"Your father and me, we had no kindred blood, but kindred we were in spirit. ..."

Sometimes during her tale grandfather would enter, lift his little chipmunk face, sniff the air, glance suspiciously at grandmother, listen a moment, and then mutter:

"Lies, lies, nothing but lies. . . ."

Once he asked unexpectedly:

"Alexei, she been drinking here?"

"No."

"You're lying—I can see by your eyes."

He left unconvinced. Grandmother winked at his departing figure and quoted the saying:

" 'Beat it, Kish, you'll scare the fish!' "

One day he stood in the middle of the room with his eyes fixed on the floor and said:

"Mother   "

"Eh?"

"See what's happening?"

"I see."

"What you think of it?"

"Fate, father. Remember what you used to say about that fine gentleman?"

"Hm-m."

"Well, seems you were right."

"A pauper."

"That's her business."

Grandfather went out. Sensing some disaster, I said to grandmother:

"What were you talking about?"

"Have to know everything, don't you?" she grumbled as she rubbed my legs. "If you know everything when you're little, won't be anything left to find out when you're old." She laughed and shook her head.

"Ah, grandfather, grandfather! You're a very unsizable speck in the eye of God! Don't you say anything, Alexei, but the fact is your grandfather's lost everything—to the last kopek. Lent a gentleman big money, up in the thousands, and the gentleman goes bankroopt. . . ."

She became lost in thought, sitting silent for a long time, and the smile on her face was replaced by a, darkening sadness.

"What are you thinking about?"

"Thinking about what to tell you," she replied, pulling herself together. "Well, how about the story of Yevstignei? It was like this:

> *Once there lived Yevstignei the deacon,*
> *Thinks to himself he's as bright as a beacon,*
> *Brighter than even the priest or the tsar,*
> *And as for the merchant—brighter by far!*
> *Struts like a peacock, foolish fowl,*
> *His eyes popping out like a wise old owl.*
> *Teaches the neighbours from morning to night.*
> *And nothing for him is ever right.*
> *Looks at a steeple—much too low!*
> *Rides in a buggy—much too slow!*
> *Bites an apple—isn't sweet!*
> *Sits in the sun—too much heat!*
> *Says about everything he sees:"*

Grandmother rolled her eyes and puffed out her cheeks and her kind face assumed an amusing look of stupidity, while she drawled:

> *"I could have made it, if you please,*
> *Infinitely better, but as you know,*
> *My time cannot be wasted so. "*

She paused for a moment, then continued in a low voice:

> *Some devils came to him one night:*
> *"You find things here are not all right?*
> *Suppose you visit us in Hell—*
> *The fires burn there surpassing well!"*
> *Scarce had the deacon donned his hat,*
> *Than two of the devils on him sat,*

While others grabbed him in their paws,
Pinched and tickled him with their claws,
And pushed him in the raging flame:
"Well, Yevstignei, are you glad you came?"
As the deacon roasted, he rolled his eyes,
But kept on looking very wise,
And his lip curled scornfully as he spoke:
"The fires of Hell make too much smoke!"

She finished the tale in a deep drawl, then laughed and turned to me with a change of expression.

"He didn't give in, that Yevstignei—a great one for having his own way, like your grandfather! Well, now, time to go to sleep. . . ."

My mother rarely came up to the attic to see me, and when she did, it was only to say a few hasty words and hurry away. She had become handsomer and dressed better, but I sensed the same secretiveness about her I had noticed in grandmother. I felt that she, as well as grandmother, was hiding something from me, and I tried to guess what it was.

I became less interested in the tales grandmother told me— even the stories about my father could not dispel the vague alarms which grew with every day.

"What makes my father's spirit so restless?" I asked grandmother one day.

"How should I know?" she answered, placing a hand over her eyes. "That's the concern of heaven—God's business, not for us to understand. . . ."

During sleepless nights as I lay watching the slow procession of the stars across the dark blue heaven, I thought up sad stories of which my father was the hero. He was always alone, with a staff in his hand and a shaggy dog at his heels. . . .

XII

One evening I woke up after a brief nap and felt that my legs had also awakened. I let them down over the edge of the bed, and once more they became numb and lifeless. Nevertheless, the confidence was born that my legs were whole and I would be able to walk. I experienced such poignant joy that I cried out and placed my feet on the floor. I fell, but crawled to the door and down the stairs, imagining what a shock everyone would receive on seeing me.

I cannot remember how I found myself on grandmother's lap in mother's room, but there I was, surrounded by strange people among whom was a thin, greenish old woman.

"Give him some raspberry jam in hot tea and wrap him in a blanket. . . ." said the green woman in a solemn voice, which drowned out all other sounds.

Everything about her was green—her dress and her hat and her face and the wart under her left eye. Even the hair sprouting from the wart was like grass. She dropped her lower lip and raised her upper one, staring at me with green teeth and shading her eyes with a hand encased in a black mit.

"Who is that?" I asked falteringly.

"That'll be another grandmother for you." answered my grandfather in an unpleasant voice.

Mother laughed and pushed Yevgeni Maximov toward me, saying:

"And here's your future father."

She added some quick, unintelligible words, while Maximov narrowed his eyes, bent over me and said:

"I'll buy you some paints."

It was very bright in the room. On a table in the corner stood silver candelabras with five candles in each. Between them was grandfather's favourite icon, "Weep not, oh mother!" The pearls ornamenting the frame gleamed and melted in the candle light, which brought flashes of fire from the rubies set in golden wreaths.

Round pancake faces peered through the dark windows, flattened noses were pressed against the panes; everything about me began to swim, and the green woman leaned over to feel behind my ears with her cold fingers, muttering:

"By all means, by all means. . . ."

"He's fainted," said my grandmother, and carried me to the door.

But I had not fainted. I had merely closed my eyes, and as she carried me up the stairs I said:

"Why didn't you tell me?"

"All right, all right, no talking now, hear?"

"Fooling me like that, all of you. . . ."

When she had placed me on the bed, she buried her head in the pillow and broke into tears. Her body heaved and rocked with her sobs, and she kept saying to me:

"Go ahead and cry, cry it out!"

But 1 had no desire to cry. It was dark and cold in the attic. The bed shook and squeaked with my trembling, and the green woman would not vanish from before my eyes. I pretended to fall asleep and my grandmother left me alone.

The next few days passed in dull monotony. After announcing her engagement, mother went away, and an Oppressive silence fell upon the house.

One morning my grandfather appeared with a chisel in his hand and began to dig the putty from around the storm window. Then grandmother came with a basin of water and some rags.

"Well, old lady?" asked my grandfather quietly.

"Well what?"

"Are you glad?"

She answered him as she had answered me on the stairs:

"All right, all right, no talking now, hear?"

These words had a special significance—they concealed something big and unpleasant which everybody recognized but nobody wished to mention.

Grandfather carefully removed the storm window and carried it away. Grandmother threw open the window—a starling and some sparrows chirped out in the garden; the intoxicating odour of thawing earth filled the room; the blue tiles of the stove paled with frustration—it made me shiver to look at them. I crawled out of bed.

"Don't walk around barefoot," warned my grandmother.

"I'm going into the garden."

"Wait til the dampness is gone."

I did not wish to obey her. It was unpleasant for me to see the grownups now.

Pale green needles of young grass had already pushed their way through the earth, the buds were swelling on the apple trees, lovely green moss carpeted the roof of Petrovna's house, and birds were everywhere. My head swam from the fragrant, murmurous air. Brown weeds, felled by the snow, fringed the pit where Uncle Pyotr had cut his throat. It was unpleasant to look at them—neither they nor the charred beams sticking up so desolately had anything in common with the spring, and in general the pit was irritatingly out of place. I had an angry impulse to pull up the weeds, remove the beams and bricks, clear away everything that cluttered this part of the yard, and make myself a tidy corner where I could spend the summer alone, without any grownups. I immediately undertook this task, and it helped me forget recent events in our house. To be sure, the hurt remained, but with every day it became less acute.

"What are you pouting about?" my grandmother and mother would ask me. Such a question was upsetting—I was not angry with them; it was just that everything connected with the house had become unpleasant. Often the green woman would join us for dinner or tea or supper, sitting there like a rotten post in an old fence. Her eyes were sewn to her face with invisible threads. They rolled easily about in their bony sockets, seeing everything, scrutinizing everything, rising to the ceiling when she spoke of God, dropping to the floor when she spoke of mundane things. Her eyebrows seemed to be made of bran pasted on in some mysterious way. Her wide, bare teeth noiselessly ground up everything that she stuck into her mouth. She held her fork in a funny, crooked way with her little finger sticking out. Little balls of gristle rolled around in front of her ears. Her ears moved, and the green hairs of her wart stirred as it shifted on her wrinkled, yellow, disgustingly clean skin. She and her son were so immaculate that I dared not approach them. During the first few days of our acquaintance she made several attempts to make me kiss her wizened hand, which smelled of laundry soap and incense. I always ran away.

"That boy needs very careful training, understand, Yevgeni?" she kept repeating to her son.

He would only bow his head obediently, frown, and say nothing. Everybody frowned in that green presence.

I hated the old woman—and her son as well—with a concentrated hatred that cost me many a licking. One day when we were having dinner, she rolled up her eyes and said:

"My dear Alexei, why do you eat in such a hurry, and with such big mouthfuls? You will choke on your food."

I removed the piece from my mouth, stuck my fork into it and held it out to her.

"Here, take it if you want it so bad," I said.

Mother yanked me away from the table and I was ignominiously banished to the attic.

Later grandmother joined me and roared with laughter, holding her hand over her mouth.

"Oh Lord, oh Lord! What a little rascal you are, devil take you!"

I disliked the way she held her hand over her mouth, so I ran away from her and climbed out on the roof, sitting there behind the chimney for a long time. I had an irresistible impulse to make mischief and to say impudent things to them all. It was very difficult for me to combat this impulse, but I was forced to. One day I spread cherry paste on the chairs of my future stepfather and grandmother. They both stuck fast in a most comical way, but after my grandfather had given me a beating, my mother came up to me in the attic, drew me toward her, held me tightly between her knees, and said:

"Why should you be so naughty? If you only knew how hard you make it for me!"

Her eyes filled with bright tears and she held my head against her cheek. How much easier it would have been if she had struck me! I swore never to injure the Maximovs again if only she would stop crying.

"That's right," she said softly. "You mustn't be naughty. Soon we shall get married and take a trip to Moscow, and when we return you will live with me. Yevgeni Vasilyevich is a very kind and clever man; I know you will like him. You will go to the Gymnasium and then become a student like he is now, and after that you will be a doctor or anything else you like. A learned person can do whatever he wants. Well, run along and play now...."

These "thens" and "after thats" seemed to form a descending staircase leading me far away from her, into the darkness and loneliness. The future she pictured promised me no happiness. I wanted to say to my mother:

"Don't get married. I shall work and provide for you."

But I did not say it. My mother always inspired tender and solicitous feelings, but I never had the courage to express them.

My work in the garden progressed from day to day. I pulled up and hacked off the weeds and propped the sliding edges of the pit with bricks. With other bricks I built a seat wide enough to lie on, and I gathered bits of coloured glass and broken dishes which I set in clay between the bricks. When the sun shone on them they glinted and sparkled like the icons in church.

"Smart of you to think of that," said my grandfather one day as he surveyed my work. "Only the weeds'll come up again— you left the roots. Here, bring me the spade and I'll dig them up for you."

When I had brought it, he spit on his hands and pushed the spade deep into the earth with a grunt.

"Throw away the roots and I'll plant sunflowers and hollyhocks for you. It'll be fine—fine. . . ."

Suddenly he leaned motionless on the spade and said nothing. I glanced at him and saw tears streaming from his eyes, that were small and intelligent, like those of a dog.

"What's the matter?"

He shook himself, wiped his face with his hand, and glanced at me.

"Hm, I'm sweating already. Just look all the worms there are!"

Once more he began to dig. Suddenly he said:

"No sense in doing all this. No sense at all. I'll be selling the house soon. Probably in the fall. Need money for your mother's dowry. Hm. At least *she* should live decent. . . ."

He threw down the spade with a wave of his hand and went behind the bath-house to a corner of the garden where he had some hot beds. I began to dig, and immediately cut my toe with the spade.

This injury prevented me from attending my mother's wedding. I could only go outside the gate and watch her walk down the street with Maximov holding her arm, her head bent, her feet picking a careful way among the young grass springing between the cracks of the brick pavement as though she were walking on nails.

It was a quiet wedding. And there was nothing cheerful about the tea which followed the ceremony. My mother immediately went into her bedroom and began packing her trunks. My stepfather sat down next to me and said:

"I promised to make you a present of some paints, but there are no good paints here and I can't give you mine. I shall send you some from Moscow."

"What shall I do with them?"

"Don't you like to draw?"

"I don't know how."

"Then I'll send you something else."

My mother came in.

"We'll be returning soon," she said. "As soon as your father passes his examination and finishes his studies we shall come back."

It was pleasant to have them speaking to me as though I were a grownup, but it was strange that a man with a beard should still be studying.

"What are you studying?" I asked.

"Surveying."

I was too lazy to ask what that was. The house was filled with an oppressive silence, a woolly rustle; I was anxious for night to come. Grandfather stood with his back to the stove staring out the window with half-closed eyes. The green woman helped mother pack, sighing and grumbling the while. Grandmother, who had been drunk since noon, was locked in the attic to keep her from disgracing the family.

Mother left early the following morning. She embraced me in parting, easily lifting me off the ground and gazing into my eyes with a look I had never seen before.

"Well, good-bye," she said as she kissed *me.*

"Tell him to obey me," said my grandfather sullenly, gazing into the sky, which was still rosy.

"You must obey your grandfather," she admonished, crossing me. I had expected her to say something else, and was angry with my grandfather for interrupting.

They got into the droshky. Mother's skirt caught on something and she fussed irritably for a long time setting it free.

"Help her, can't you see?" my grandfather said to me, but I was too deep in the throes of despair to help.

Maximov carefully drew in his long legs encased in tight navy blue trousers, while grandmother handed him some packages which he piled on his knees, holding them with his chin.

"Enough!" he drawled as he nervously wrinkled his pale brow.

The green woman and her elder son, an officer, got into another droshky. She sat stiff as a wax figure, while he rubbed his beard with the hilt of his sword and kept yawning.

"So you're off to the war?" asked grandfather.

"I am indeed!"

"That's fine. Have to lick those Turks."

They were off. Mother turned around several times and waved her handkerchief. Grandmother leaned weeping against the wall of the house and also waved, while grandfather stood squeezing tears from his eyes.

"Nothing good—will come—of this," he mumbled.

I sat on a stool watching the droshky bounce over the ruts— there they went around the corner—something inside of me slammed shut. . . . tight . . . .

It was still early in the morning. The streets were empty and the shutters of the windows still closed. Never before had I seen such utter emptiness. From somewhere in the distance came the long-drawn wail of a shepherd's pipe.

"Come have breakfast," said my grandfather, taking me by the shoulder. "Looks like you're fated to go on living with me—scratching up against me like a match on a brick."

From morning to night he and I silently worked in the garden. He dug the soil, tied up the raspberry bushes, scraped the lichen off the apple trees, and squashed caterpillars, while I kept improving my corner. Grandfather chopped off the ends of the charred beams, and stuck poles into the ground on which I hung my bird cages. I wove awnings of dried weeds to protect my house from sun and dew. The corner became delightful.

"It's fine for you to be learning how to fix things up for yourself," said my grandfather.

I highly prized his observations on life. Sometimes he would lie down on the seat I had covered with turf and speak to me unhurriedly, seeming to pull each word out of his mouth with great deliberation.

"Now you're a piece hacked away from your mother. She'll be having other children, dearer to her than you. Your grandmother, as you see, has taken to drink."

He would fall into a long silence, as though listening to something, then continue dropping his heavy words:

"This is the second time she's taken to drink—the first was when Mikhail was to be called up for army service. She talked me into buying him a recruit certificate, fool that she was. Maybe he'd have been different if he'd served in the army. Ah me! And I'll be dying soon. That means you'll be left all alone, understand?—all alone to shift for yourself. Hm. Learn, to wait on yourself, and never let others make you wait on them. Behave yourself calm and quiet-like, but stick to your chosen path. Listen to everybody, but do what you yourself think best. . . ."

Except 'for rainy days, I spent the entire summer in the garden, even sleeping out there on warm nights—grandmother had given me a piece of felt for a bed. She herself would often spend the night with me, bringing out an armful of straw which she would spread next to my couch, and lie down beside me, telling me stories which were interrupted by sudden exclamations like:

"Look—a falling star! That's somebody's soul as felt a longing for mother earth. A good man's been born somewhere."

Or:

"A new star's come up—look! What a jewel! The sky, the sky, how far it is—garment of God, all gem-bedecked!"

"Catch your deaths, you idiots," grumbled grandfather. "Get the lumbago, or else robbers' ll come and cut your throats. . . ."

The sun would go down, flooding the sky with rivers of fire, which, in expiring, scattered red-gold ashes over the green velvet of the gardens. Then the world would noticeably darken, swelling and expanding as it absorbed the warm twilight. The sun-sated leaves would droop on the branches and the grass would bend its head to the earth. Everything became richer and softer, emanating a perfume as soft as music. And music would come floating from the army camps in distant fields. The night brought a feeling as strong and refreshing as mother love; and like a mother's caress was the silence, stroking the heart with a warm, furry paw, soothing away all that should be forgotten—all the fine, caustic dust accumulated during the day. It was delightful to lie gazing up at the sky, watching the stars come out, each one opening up new depths to the heavens. These receding depths seemed to lift you lightly off the earth, and you could not tell whether the earth had shrunken to your size, or whether you had marvellously expanded until you were one with all that surrounded you. The silence increased, the darkness thickened, but invisible strings vibrated with little sounds, each of which— the singing of a bird in sleep, the rustle of a passing porcupine, the sound of a human voice—had a special quality distinguishing it from daytime sounds and lovingly stressed by the sensitive silence.

The playing of an accordion, a woman's laughter, a spur striking against the bricks of the pavement, the yelping of a dog— all these were last leaves falling from the dying day.

Sometimes there would be a sudden brawling of drunken voices out in the street or on an open lot, and the patter of running feet. Such sounds were too ordinary to deserve attention.

Grandmother would lie awake for hours on end, her arm under her head, recounting something with quiet emotion, apparently indifferent to whether I was listening or not. She never failed to select a legend which added significance and beauty to the night.

I would fall asleep to the sound of her rhythmic speech, waking up with the sun in my face and the singing of birds in my ears. The morning air stirred gently as it warmed in the sun, the leaves of the apple trees shook off the dew, the grass was vividly green and assumed a crystal transparency in the veils of mist which hovered above it. Rays of sun fanned across the sky, transforming it from lavender to blue. The song of a lark came from some invisible height, and all the sounds and colours of the newborn day seeped like dew into my soul, filling me with quiet happiness and the desire to be up and about, and to live in harmony with all creatures.

That was the most calm and contemplative period of my whole life. It was that summer which nurtured in me a sense of my own strength. I came to avoid people. When I heard the voices and cries of the Ovsyannikov children I was no longer filled with a longing to join them, and instead of being glad when they came to see me, I only feared they might spoil something in my garden— the first thing I had made with my own hands.

My grandfather's harangues also ceased to interest me. They became ever more crisp and complaining. He began to have frequent quarrels with my grandmother and to put her out of the house, at which times she would go either to Uncle Yakov's or to Uncle Mikhail's. Sometimes she would remain away for several days, and then my grandfather would cook for us himself, howling and cursing, burning his fingers, breaking the dishes, and becoming more cantankerous with every day.

When he came to visit me in my corner of the garden, he would seat himself comfortably on the turf and watch me for a long time without speaking. Then suddenly he would ask:

"Why don't you say something?"

"I don't know."

"We're not the quality, you know," he would begin in an instructive tone. "Nobody's going to teach us anything—got to learn it all ourselves. Books have been written for others, schools have been built for them—but not for us. We got to get everything ourselves. . . ."

He would go off into a brown study—mute and motionless—dreadful to look at.

That autumn he sold the house. At the breakfast table one morning preceding the sale, he announced to grandmother in a sad, resolute voice:

"Well, mother, I've been feeding you for a good long time already, but now it's over—have to shift for yourself from now on."

Grandmother remained utterly unmoved, as though she had long expected him to say just this. She unhurriedly took out her snuffbox, stuffed her spongy nose, and replied:

"Well, nothing to do about it. Have to make the best of it."

Grandfather rented two dark rooms in the cellar of an old house in a blind alley. During the moving, grandmother took an old bast shoe with long laces and thrust it under the stove. Squatting down, she began to call the hearth goblin:

"Come, goblin, come, goblin, climb inside and take a ride to bring us luck in the other house. . . ."

Grandfather, who was out in the yard, glanced through the window.

"Taking it along, are you? I'll show you, you heretic! Disgracing me like this!"

"Oh, watch out, father! It'll mean bad luck for sure!" she warned, but grandfather flew into a rage and forbade her taking the goblin along.

For three days he sold our furniture and other things to Tatar secondhand men, cursing and bargaining furiously. Grandmother watched them from the window, sometimes laughing, sometimes crying, and calling softly:

"Go ahead and take it—take everything—break every-thing. . . ."

I was also ready to cry at the thought of leaving my playhouse in the garden.

Two carts came to move us, and the one I rode in shook as though trying to toss me off the pile of goods and chattels.

And it was with this sensation of being constantly shaken off that I lived for the next two years—until the death of my mother.

Mother came to see us soon after grandfather moved into the basement. She was pale and thin, with enormous eyes burning with a kind of hurt astonishment. She studied everything intently, as though she were seeing her mother and father and me for the first time. She looked at us and said nothing, while my stepfather kept walking up and down the room, whistling under his breath, clearing his throat, and twiddling his thumbs behind his back.

"Good heavens, how big you've grown!" said my mother, taking my cheeks in her hot palms. She was wearing a wide, ugly brown dress, bulging over her stomach.

"Hello," said my stepfather, holding out his hand to me. "How you getting along?"

He sniffed the air.

"Damp here."

Both of them looked worn and dishevelled, as though they had been running and wanted nothing so much as to lie down and have a good rest.

We had a dreary tea, during which grandfather watched the rain running down the windowpane and asked:

"So you lost everything in the fire?"

"Everything," said my stepfather in a resolute tone. "We hardly managed to escape ourselves."

"Hm. A fire's no joke."

Mother pressed up against grandmother and whispered something in her ear that made grandmother narrow her eyes as though struck by a bright light. The atmosphere became even more dreary.

Suddenly grandfather said spitefully, in a loud, calm voice:

"I've heard rumours, Yevgeni Vasilyevich, as how there wasn't no fire at all, but you just lost everything at cards."

A deathly silence ensued, broken only by the tapping of the
rain on the window and the steaming of the samovar.

"Father. . . ." said my mother at last.

" 'Father'!" roared my grandfather. "Well, what next? Didn't
I tell you it was crazy for thirty to marry twenty? Well, here you
are—fine specimen, isn't he? Made you a gentle woman, eh?
Well, how do you like it, daughter?"

Then all four of them began shouting, my stepfather loudest
of all. I went out into the entranceway, and sat down on a pile of
wood, stunned. This could not be my mother—she was entirely
different. I had sensed this vaguely there in the room, but now
that I was seated out here in the darkness I could vividly recall
what she had been like.

Then, in some forgotten way I found myself in Sormovo, in
a new house with unpapered log walls. The chinks between the
logs were stuffed with hemp and inhabited by innumerable
roaches. Mother and my stepfather lived in two rooms facing the
street, while my grandmother and I lived in the kitchen, which
had one window overlooking the roof. Beyond the roof, black
factory chimneys were silhouetted against the sky, pouring out
thick, curly smoke which the winter wind scattered over the
district. Our unheated rooms were always filled with the greasy
odour of this smoke, and early in the morning the factory whistle
howled like a wolf:

"Oo-oo-aw! Oo-oo-aw!"

By standing up on a bench and looking through the top
windowpane, I could get a glimpse of the lighted factory gates,
open like the toothless mouth of an old beggar devouring a horde
of little people. At noon there came another whistle. The black
lips of the gates opened up, revealing a deep hole through which
the factory vomited forth these same little people, now well
masticated. They flowed in black streams down the streets, driven
into the houses by a rough white wind. The sky could rarely be
seen. Above the roofs and sooty snowbanks of the district, hung
another roof—flat and grey, stunting the imagination and blinding
the eyes with its cheerless monotony.

In the evenings, a dull red glow hovered above the factory. It lighted the tips of the chimneys and created the impression that instead of rising from the earth, they were projected from out that lurid cloud, thrusting down to feed on fire, belching and howling with satiety. It was insufferable to gaze on that scene day after day, and my heart became filled with aching malevolence. Grandmother did all the housework. From morning to night she was busy preparing food, scrubbing the floor, chopping wood, and hauling water. When evening came she grunted and sighed with exhaustion. Sometimes after she had prepared the dinner, she would put on a short quilted jacket, tuck up her skirt, and set out for town.

"Go have a look how the old man's getting along," she would say.

"Take me with you!"

"You'll freeze to death. Just look what a wind!"

She would walk seven versts to town over roads lost in snow fields. My mother, yellow and swollen with pregnancy, would sit huddled in a ragged grey shawl bordered with long fringe. I hated that shawl, which distorted her large, handsome body; I hated the tattered fringe, and would tear it off. I hated the house, and the factory, and the whole district, Mother went about in worn felt boots, coughing so that her enormous belly shook; her grey-blue eyes flashed with hard, dry anger or stared dully at the bare walls, as though glued fast to them. Sometimes she would gaze out into the street for a whole hour. The street was like a jaw in which some of the teeth had become blackened and distorted with age, while others had fallen out altogether and been replaced by clumsy new ones, too big for the jaw.

"Why do we live here?" I asked.

"Ah, don't ask," she replied.

She spoke little with me these days, limiting her communications to orders and requests:

"Bring me this, take that, run to the store. . . ."

She rarely let me go out to play, for I always came home badly beaten by my fellows. Fights were my only pleasure, and I gave myself up to them with all the zest of my impassioned nature.

Mother gave me strappings for this, but the punishment only irritated me, so that the next time I fought even more furiously— and my mother punished me even more severely. Once I warned her that if she continued beating me I would bite her hand and run away to freeze out in the fields. She pushed me away in consternation and began to pace the floor.

"You little beast!" she said, gasping with exhaustion.

The living, vibrant rainbow of feelings called love gradually faded in my heart, giving way to blue flashes of resentment against everyone and everything and to a smouldering discontent and sense of loneliness in this dull, nonsensical world.

My stepfather was stern with me and laconic with my mother. He was forever whistling and coughing and standing in front of a mirror picking his crooked teeth. Ever more frequently he quarrelled with my mother, addressing her in cold, distant terms which I desperately resented. During their quarrels he would close the door into the kitchen, evident by unwilling that I should hear what he said, but I made a point of listening to his gruff bass voice.

Once he stamped his foot and shouted:

"I can't invite anybody to the house on account of your damn belly, you old cow!"

Overwhelmed with surprise and fury, I jumped up on the bunk and struck my head against the ceiling with such force that I bit through my tongue.

On Saturdays dozens of workers came to my stepfather to sell the food coupons enabling them to buy products in the company store. These were issued by the factory instead of wages. My stepfather bought them for half their value. He would receive the workers in the kitchen, sitting at the table looking very important and frowning over every coupon.

"Ruble and a half."

"Yevgeni Vasilyevich, for the love of Christ. . . ."

"Ruble and a half."

This muddled, dark life did not last very long. Just before mother was to give birth I was taken to live with my grandfather. He now had quarters in a two-storied house on Peschanaya Street in Kunavino, above the cemetery of Napolnaya Church. The tiny room he occupied contained a large Russian stove and two windows facing the yard.

"Well!" he laughed with a little squeak as he met me. "According to the saying, your best friend's your mother, but in this case it turns out to be your old devil of a grandfather! Phooh, what people!"

Scarcely had I become acquainted with my new home when mother and grandmother came with the baby. My stepfather had lost his job at the factory for cheating the workers, but he had appealed to friends and immediately received a job as cashier at the railway station.

Much empty time flowed by until I was again sent to live with my mother in the cellar of a stone house. Mother immediately sent me to school; from the very first day I disliked school.

I put in my appearance dressed in a pair of mother's shoes, a coat made out of grandmother's blouse, a yellow shirt, and long trousers. This immediately aroused ridicule, and the yellow shirt won me the nickname of "the ace of diamonds." I easily put things straight with the boys, but the priest and the teacher took a disliking to me.

The teacher was a bald, yellow-faced man who was subject to nosebleeds. He would enter the classroom with bits of cotton stuffed up his nostrils, take his place at the desk, ask us questions in a nasal voice, and stop in the middle of a word to pull out the cotton and examine it with a shake of his head. He had a flat, brassy, sour face with a kind of green mould filling the wrinkles. The most hideous feature of his face was the tiny eyes which seemed to have no place in the general ensemble, and kept plastering themselves to my face, making me want to wipe my cheek with my hand.

For the first few days I sat on the front bench, directly under the teacher's nose. This was unbearable. He seemed to see no one but me, and kept saying through his nose:

"Pesko-o-v, change your shirt! Pesko-o-v, stop shuffling! Pesko-o-v, again your shoes have left a puddle on the floor!"

I repaid him by thinking up the most extravagant tricks. One day I got hold of half a frozen watermelon. I scooped it out and hung it on a pulley to the door in the dark entrance-way. When the door was opened, the watermelon rose in the air, but when the teacher closed the door, it descended like a cap on his bald head. The night watchman escorted me home with a note from the teacher, and I took a hiding for my mischief.

Another time I sprinkled snuff in the drawer of his desk. He had such a fit of sneezing that he was forced to leave the classroom, sending his son-in-law, an officer, to substitute for him. The officer made us sing "God save the tsar" and "Ah my freedom, blessed freedom" over and over again; if anyone got out of tune he would tap him over the head with a ruler in a manner that made a lot of noise and was funny, but did not hurt.

The teacher of religion was a young and handsome priest with a lot of fluffy hair. He disliked me because I had no copy of "Sacred Stories from the Old and New Testaments," and because I imitated his manner of speaking.

As soon as he would come into the classroom he would say:

"Peshkov, have you brought the book or not? Yes, the book."

"No, I haven't. Yes."

"What do you mean, 'yes'?"

"No."

"Get along home with you! Yes, home. I have no intention of teaching you. Yes, not the slightest intention."

I had no objection to being sent home. I would wander about the dirty streets of the district until school was over, observing the noisy life about me.

The priest had a fine, Christ-like face with affectionate, feminine eyes. He had small hands which seemed to caress everything they touched, whether it was a book, a ruler, or a pen. It was as though he loved every object and looked upon it as a live thing that might be injured by careless handling. He was less affectionate with the children, but they were fond of him nevertheless.

In spite of the fact that I received satisfactory marks in my studies, I was soon informed that I would be expelled for my conduct. That upset me. Unquestionably the consequences would be severe: my mother was becoming more irritable every day, and had taken to beating me very often.

But I was saved from this disaster. Quite unexpectedly Bishop Chrisanth,* a hunchback as I remember, visited our school.

An unfamiliar atmosphere of warmth and good cheer filled the classroom when this little man in flowing black robes entered and took his place at the desk.

"Well, let's have a little chat, my children," he said, taking his hands out of his voluminous sleeves.

My turn to be called up to the desk came towards the end of the list.

"How old are you?" he asked me. "Really? My, what a tall fellow for your age! Must have done a lot of standing out in the rain!"

He placed one thin hand with its long, pointed nails on the desk, and took hold of his scanty beard with the other, while he gazed at me kindly.

"Well, tell me any story from sacred history that you like."

When I replied that I had no book and therefore could not study sacred history, he adjusted his cowl and said:

"How's that? You have to learn these things, you know. But maybe you know something without the book—heard the stories somewhere? Do you know the Psalter? Good! And the prayers? Now, then you see? And maybe the lives of some of the saints? Even in verse? Well, it turns out you're quite a learned one!"

Our priest came in, all red and puffing. When the bishop had blessed him, he began to tell him about me.

"Just a minute!" said the bishop, stopping him with a gesture. Then he turned to me again. "All right, supposing you tell us about Alexei, Man-of-God. . . ."

---

* Bishop Chrisanth was the author of the three-volume work "Religions of the Ancient World" and the articles "Egyptian Metampsychosis" and "Woman and Marriage". The latter article, read in my youth, made a great impression on me. It seems that I have distorted the title—it was published in some religious magazine in the seventies.— *Author's note.*

"Wonderful verse, isn't it, son?" he said when I stopped because I had forgotten a line. "Maybe you know something else—about King David? Fine. Only too glad to listen!"

I could see that he really enjoyed listening, that he was fond of the verse. He let me go on for a long time before he interrupted me.

"Did you learn your letters from the Psalter? Who taught you? Your good grandfather?

Your bad grandfather! Well now, you can't mean that. But they tell me you're always up to some kind of mischief."

I blushed, but confessed my guilt. At some length the teacher and the priest confirmed the fact. The bishop listened with downcast eyes.

"Hear what they say about you?" he said at last with a sigh. "Come here!"

He placed a hand smelling of Cyprus on my head and said:

"What makes you so mischievous?"

"School's a bore."

"A bore? There's something wrong here, son. If you found school a bore, you would be a bad student, but your marks show that that isn't so. There must be something else the trouble."

He took a little book out of his robe and wrote:

"Peshkov, Alexei. Hm. It'd be better if you stopped your mischief, son. A little bit's all right, but people can't stand too much, you know. Am I right, boys?"

"You're right!" came a gay chorus of voices.

"And what about you yourselves—I suppose you do very little mischief, eh?"

"Oh no, a lot!" laughed the boys.

The bishop drew me to him and leaned back in his chair, saying with an air of surprise that made even the teacher and the priest laugh:

"Just think—I was a mischief-maker myself at your age! What do you suppose makes us like that?"

The boys laughed and he asked them questions, cleverly entangling them in their own words so that the atmosphere became more and more merry. Finally he got up and said:

"A pity to leave you rascals, but it's time for me to be on my way!"

He raised his arm, tossing back his wide sleeve, and made the sign of the cross above the class.

"May you live and do good in the name of the Father, and of the Son, and of the Holy Ghost. Farewell."

"Farewell, your holiness! Come back soon!" shouted the boys.

"I'll come, I'll come all right," he replied, shaking his cowl. "I'll bring you some books." Then he turned to the teacher. "Let them go home now."

Out in the entranceway he stopped me and said in a low voice:

"Promise me you won't make so much trouble in the future, all right? Oh, I understand why you do it, of course. Well, goodbye."

I was very much moved by this. A peculiar emotion seethed in my breast, so that even when the teacher kept me after class and began to tell me that from now on I must behave like a lamb, I listened attentively and willingly.

As the priest was putting on his coat he said affectionately:

"From now on you must attend my lessons. Yes, that you must do. But sit quiet! Yes, quiet!"

Things became better at school, but a nasty thing happened at home. I stole a ruble from my mother. This crime was not premeditated. One evening mother went out somewhere, leaving me alone with the baby. For want of anything better to do, I took out one of my stepfather's books—"Notes of a Physician," by Dumas the Elder. Among the pages I found a one-ruble bill and a ten-ruble bill. The book was too difficult for me, but on closing it I was struck with the idea that for a ruble I could buy not only the "Sacred History," but "Robinson Crusoe" as well. I had learned about the existence of such a book a short time before. During recess one cold day I had been telling the boys a fairy tale. Suddenly one of them said scornfully:

"Fairy tales are no good! 'Robinson Crusoe' now, that's a real story!"

A few of the other boys had also read "Robinson Crusoe," and they all praised the book. I was hurt that they should have scorned grandmother's tale, and resolved to get hold of "Robinson Crusoe" so that, having read it, I could say that *it* was no good! The next day I came to school with the "Sacred History," two dog-eared volumes of Andersen's fairy tales, three pounds of white bread and a pound of sausage. In the dark little bookshop at the corner next to Vladimir Church I had found a copy of "Robinson Crusoe"—a skinny little book in a yellow binding. On the title page was the picture of a bearded man with a fur cap on his head and a tiger skin over his shoulder. This did not attract me, while I found even the worn bindings of the fairy tales fascinating.

During the long recess I shared my bread and sausage with the boys and we began reading "The Nightingale," a wonderful tale which gripped the heart from the very first page.

"In China, all the people are Chinese, and even the Emperor is a Chinaman." I can still remember how this sentence delighted me with its simple humour, its smiling music, and something else that was wonderfully good.

I had no time to finish reading "The Nightingale" at school, and when I came home my mother asked me in a strained voice, as she stood frying some eggs:

"Did you take a ruble?"

"Yes. Here are the books. . . ."

She gave me a vigorous tanning with the frying pan and took away the fairy tales, hiding them for all time. This punishment was infinitely more painful than the licking.

I did not return to school for several days. Apparently my stepfather told the people at work what I had done and they in their turn related it to their children. The boys carried the tale to school, and when I returned I was greeted with a new nickname— the thief. Brief and clear—but unfair. I had not attempted to hide the fact that I had taken the ruble, but when I tried to explain this, nobody believed me. So I came home and announced to my mother that I would never go back to school again.

Pregnant once more, she was sitting at the window feeding my brother Sasha. She turned her grey face and stared at me with crazed, tortured eyes, opening her mouth like a fish.

"You're lying," she said softly. "Nobody could have heard about your taking the ruble."

"Go ask them."

"You must have told them yourself. Tell me the truth—didn't you tell them? But don't lie—tomorrow I'm going to school to find out for myself who told!"

I named the student. Her face became drawn and melted in tears.

I went into the kitchen and lay down on the bed behind the stove which had been made for me out of some old wooden boxes. I could hear my mother sobbing in the next room:

"Oh Lord, oh Lord   "

The smell of warm, greasy rags became intolerable, and I went out into the yard.

"Where are you going?" called my mother. "Come here to me!"

We sat together on the floor with Sasha on my mother's knees pulling at the buttons of her dress, bowing to them and saying: "Bubbons," which meant buttons.

I snuggled up to my mother, and she put her arm around me.

"We're very poor," she said. "Every kopek—every single kopek.. .."

She squeezed me with her hot hands and seemed unable to finish what she wanted to say.

"Oh, what a beast, what a beast!" she suddenly burst out, repeating a word I had heard her use once before.

"Beat," mimicked Sasha.

He was a strange baby—clumsy and large-headed, with wonderful blue eyes which looked smilingly about as though expecting something. He began to speak at an unusually early age and never cried, living in a constant state of quiet joy. He was so weak that he could hardly crawl, but he always rejoiced on seeing me, stretching out his little arms and playing with my ears with his soft little fingers which for some reason smelled of violets. He died quite unexpectedly, without having been ill at all. In the morning he was quietly happy as usual; in the evening, when the church bell was tolling for vespers, he was already laid out on the table. This occurred soon after the birth of the second baby, Nikolai.

Mother had carried out her promise to clear up things at school, and once more I was studying normally. But again I had to go live with my grandfather, for the following reason.

One day at tea time, as I was entering the kitchen from the yard, I heard my mother crying desperately:

"Yevgeni, Yevgeni, don't go, I beg of you!"

"Nonsense," replied my stepfather.

"But I know you go to her!"

"Well, what of it?"

Both of them were silent for a few minutes, then my mother said between fits of coughing:

"What a mean and worthless beast you are!"

I heard him strike her. I ran into the room and saw her on her knees, bracing herself against a chair with her back and elbows, her head thrown back, her eyes shining unnaturally, while he stood in front of her, spick and span in a new suit, kicking her in the breast with a long leg. I picked up a silver-handled bread knife— the only one of my father's things left to my mother—and aimed it at my stepfather's side with all my force.

Fortunately my mother had time to push him away, so that the knife only ripped his coat and grazed his flesh. He let out a groan and ran out of the room, holding his side. With a shriek my mother grabbed me up and hurled me onto the floor. My stepfather tore me away from her when he returned from the yard.

Late that evening, when he had gone out in spite of everything, mother came to me where I lay behind the stove, gently embraced me and kissed me.

"Forgive me, dear. I have wronged you. But how could you have done such a thing? A knife!"

With a perfect understanding of the full import of my words, I swore that I would kill my stepfather and myself as well. And I think I would have done it—at least attempted it. Even now I can see that loathsome foot with the bright braid down the trouser leg swinging in the air and landing on a woman's breast.

Sometimes when I recall the abominations of that barbarous Russian life I question whether they are worth dwelling on. But on further consideration I am convinced that they demand being exposed, for they are the vicious, tenacious truth, which has not been exterminated to this very day. They represent a truth which must be exposed to its roots and torn out of our grim and shameful life—torn out of the very soul and memory of man.

But there is another, more positive reason impelling me to describe such horrors. In spite of their repulsiveness and the way in which they mutilate what would otherwise be fine natures, the Russian is sufficiently young and wholesome in spirit to abolish such things and he will surely do so.

Our life is amazing not only for the vigorous scum of bestiality with which it is overgrown, but also for the bright and wholesome creative forces gleaming beneath. And the influence of good is growing, giving promise that our people will at last awaken to a life full of beauty and bright humanity.

XIII

Once more I was living with my grandfather.

"Well, you rascal," was his greeting as he rapped nervously on the table. "I'll not be feeding you any more. It's up to your grandmother now."

"I'll manage," she said. "As though that was such a job!"

"Well, go ahead," he shouted, but then he explained to me more calmly: "Everything's separate with us now—each for himself."

Grandmother sat at the window making lace. Her bobbins clicked cheerfully above the pillow bristling with brass pins that glistened in the spring sun like a golden porcupine. Grandmother herself seemed cast of bronze, and had not changed in the least. But grandfather had become leaner and more wrinkled. His hair was thinner and the calm pompousness of his movements had been substituted by an impetuous fussiness. His green eyes looked at everything suspiciously. With a laugh, grandmother told about the division of property which had taken place between her and grandfather. He had given her all the pots and crocks and dishes and had said:

"That's all yours, and don't be asking me for anything else!"

Then he took all her old dresses and belongings, including a fox cape, and sold them for seven hundred rubles, which he lent at interest to his godson, a converted Jew who traded in fruit. He had become sick with greed—shamelessly greedy. He began to visit old acquaintances—rich merchants and artisans with whom he had formerly worked—and ask them to give him money, saying that his sons had ruined him. Out of respect for his former position they made him generous gifts. He would come home and wave a sizable banknote under my grandmother's nose, gloating like a schoolboy:

"See this, you old fool? Nobody'll give you a tenth as much!"

My grandfather lent this money at interest to a new acquaintance—a tall, bald-headed furrier who was nicknamed "The Whip," and his sister, a fat, red-cheeked, dark-eyed storekeeper, as sweet and sticky as molasses.

Everything in the house was divided: today grandmother prepared dinner from products bought with her money, tomorrow grandfather bought the bread and food. The dinner was always worse on his days. Grandmother bought good meat, while he bought lungs and tripe. Each kept his own store of tea and sugar, but tea was brewed in the same teapot, and grandfather would ask in alarm:

"Wait—let me see—how much did you put in?"

He would sprinkle the tea leaves into his hand and carefully count them.

"Your tea's finer than mine—mine's thicker, makes a better brew, so you got to put in more."

He watched to see that grandmother poured him tea that was just the same strength as hers, and that they both drank the same number of cups.

"Have a last?" grandmother would ask just before pouring out the final brew.

"Suppose we may as well have a last," agreed grandfather after a glance into the teapot.

Even the oil for the icon lamp was bought by each in turn—and this after fifty years of labouring side by side!

I found these tricks of my grandfather amusing and disgusting—grandmother found them only amusing.

"Forget it!" she would say to me. "What of it? He's old, is the old man, and he's gone queer. Four score already—just think the number of years! Let him be queer—don't hurt anybody. As for me and you—be sure I'll always earn a crust of bread for us!"

I also began to earn money. Early Sunday mornings I would take a sack and go through the streets and yards collecting old bones, rags, nails, and paper. The junkman would pay us twenty kopeks a pood for rags or paper or metal, and eight or ten kopeks a pood for bones. I collected junk after school during the week as well, and every Saturday I earned from thirty to fifty kopeks (or even more if it had been a particularly successful week). Grandmother took my money and hurriedly deposited it in the pocket of her skirt, lowering her eyes as she rewarded me with words of praise:

"Thanks, pigeon-widgeon! You and me won't go hungry, will we, now? Just to think!"

One day I caught her gazing at one of my five-kopek pieces and weeping softly, one bright tear hanging from the end of her spongy nose.

But I found that the profits from junk dealing were less than those from stealing boards from the lumberyards on the bank of the Oka River or on The Sands, an island where they traded in metal during the annual fair, putting up makeshift booths for this purpose. When the fair was over, the booths were taken apart and the lumber stacked on The Sands, where it remained until the rising of the river in the spring. House owners would pay us ten kopeks for a good board, and we could steal two or three in the course of the day. However, it was necessary to carry on operations on foggy or rainy days, when the watchmen were indoors.

It was a friendly band of youngsters with whom I worked: there was Sanka Vyakhir, the Dove, ten-year-old son of a Mordovian beggar-woman—an affectionate child who was always quiet and good-natured; there was the waif Kostroma, skinny and impetuous, with enormous black eyes—later, when he was thirteen, he hung himself in a home for juvenile delinquents to which he had been sent for stealing a pair of pigeons; there was the Tatar Khabi, a twelve-year-old Samson, who combined extraordinary strength with a simple, generous nature; there was the pugnosed Yaz, eight-year-old son of a gravedigger and cemetery watchman, silent as a fish and afflicted with the "black sickness"; and finally there was the oldest of our band,

Grishka Churka, son of a widowed seamstress, a very just and
reasonable person, and an expert at fist fighting. All of us lived
on the same street.

Stealing was not considered a crime in our district. It was
the usual, and almost exclusive means of getting a living for most
of the half-starved petty tradesmen. The month and a half of the
annual fair could not keep them alive throughout the year, and
many respected householders "made extra money on the river,"
that is, they fished out boards and logs washed away by the tide,
and hauled light baggage on makeshift rafts; but for the most
part they went in for stealing—"monkeying" along the banks
of the Volga and the Oka, robbing the wharfs and barges and
riverbanks of anything they could lay their hands on. On Sundays
the grownups would boast of their luck, and the children would
listen and learn.

In the spring, during the busy weeks of preparation for the
fair, drunken artisans and other workmen would fill the streets
after their day's labour. Then the children of the district would
ply their trade of pickpocketing, an occupation which was
accepted as quite legitimate and was fearlessly carried on with
the grownups as witnesses.

They stole hammers from carpenters, monkey wrenches
from fitters, axle bolts from carters. Our band did not go in for
such things.

"I won't go stealing—mom won't let me," Churka
announced one day.

"And I'm scared to," put in Khabi.

Kostroma always shied from thieves and pronounced the
word "thief with a peculiar emphasis, and if he found boys
robbing a drunkard, he would chase them and give them a
merciless beating. This sullen, large-eyed boy was always posing
as a grownup. He walked with a rolling swing like the stevedores
and tried to make his voice deep and gruff. Altogether there was
something tight and old and unnatural about him. The Dove was
convinced that stealing was a sin.

But the snatching of boards and poles from The Sands fell into quite a different category. None of us was afraid to do it, and we worked out a technique that greatly simplified the task. In the evening when it was already dark, or on foggy days, the Dove and Yaz would set out over the bulging, slushy ice to The Sands. They would go openly, trying to attract the attention of the watchmen, while the four of us would creep up unnoticeably from different sides. While the watchmen were busy keeping an eye on Yaz and the Dove, we would gather at the appointed place and select our boards; then while our fleet comrades teased the watchmen and fled from them, we set out on the return trip. Each of us had a rope with a bent nail at the end which we fastened to the board in order to haul it over the snow and ice. The watchmen rarely saw us, and if they did they were unable to catch us. On selling the boards we divided the spoils into six equal parts. Usually it came out to five or seven kopeks apiece.

This was enough to eat as much as we liked for one day, but the Dove's mother would beat him if he did not bring her vodka; Kostroma saved his money to go in for the pigeon hunting he dreamed of; Churka's mother was ill, so he needed all he could get for her; Khabi was also saving money in order to return to the town from which he had been brought by an uncle who was drowned shortly after arriving at Nizhni-Novgorod. Khabi had forgotten the name of the town, remembering only that it was on the Kama River near the Volga.

For some reason we found the idea of this town very funny, and kept teasing the slant-eyed Tatar about it:

> *There's a town very fair,*
> *But he doesn't know where—*
> *Here or there*
> *Or in the air!*

At first Khabi became angry with us, but once the Dove said to him in a cooing voice which well justified his nickname:

"Come off now, Who ever heard of pals getting angry?"

The Tatar was ashamed. He accepted the rebuff and thereafter he himself used to sing the song about the town on the Kama.

But still we preferred collecting junk to stealing boards. It became particularly interesting in the spring, when the snow had melted and the rains came to wash the cobbles at the empty fair grounds. It was always possible to find nails and bits of metal in the gutters of the fair grounds. Often we found copper and silver coins, but in order to keep the watchmen from chasing us and taking our sacks away, we had to give them two-kopek pieces or lick their boots. In general, it was not easy to make money, but we became the best of friends in the effort. Occasionally there would be quarrels among us, but I cannot remember our ever having had a fight.

The Dove was our pacifier. He was always able to find just the right words to calm our passions—simple words, but ones which had the effect of surprising us and making us ashamed of ourselves. He himself seemed surprised when he spoke them. He never took offence at the mean tricks Yaz would play, calmly dismissing everything bad as stupid and useless.

"Now why would you do such a thing?" he would ask, and it became clear to everyone that there was actually no sense in it.

He referred to his mother as "this Mordovian of mine," and none of us found it funny.

"Last night this Mordovian of mine came home soaked to the gills," he laughed, his little round eyes glinting with gold. "Flopped down on the doorstep and there she lays singing her head off, the old hen!"

"What'd she sing?" asked Churka seriously.

The Dove slapped his knees in time to the music as he sang his mother's song in a high little voice:

Tap- a- tap- tap!
The young shepherd's rap
At my window pane—
I am off with my swain!
The sunset glows,
The shepherd blows
Upon his pipe, so sweet and clear,
And all the village stops to hear.

He knew many such gay songs, and sang them with zest.

"Yes," he went on, "and she falls asleep there in the doorway, letting all the cold air in, and me shivering my pants off and unable to haul the bulk of her away. This morning I says to her, 'What you want to get so drunk for?' 'It's all right,' she answers. 'Try to bear it a little longer, I'll be dying soon!' '

"Sure, you can see it won't be long, all bloated up the way she is," confirmed Churka impressively.

"Will you be sorry?" I asked.

"Of course," answered the Dove with some surprise. "She's been a good one to me."

And in spite of the fact that we all knew that the Mordovian beat the Dove, we were convinced that she was a good soul; on days when our gains were slight, Churka would say.

"Let's each throw in a kopek to buy the Dove's mother some vodka, else she'll lick him."

Churka and I were the only ones who knew how to read and write. The Dove envied us this.

"When this Mordovian of mine dies," he would coo, pulling at his pointed, mouse-like ear, "I'm going to school too. I'll kiss the teacher's feet to make him take me. Then when I finish I'll be gardener to the archbishop, or maybe to the tsar."

That spring the Mordovian, accompanied by a bottle of vodka and an old man who collected donations for the building of a new church, was killed when a stack of logs collapsed on her. The woman was taken to the hospital and Churka said to the Dove:

"Come live with me. Mom'll teach you your letters."
One day soon after, the Dove stopped in front of a store:
"Gorcery Store," he read, his head lifted proudly.
"Grocery Store, you scarecrow!" corrected Churka.
"I know, but the sybalels get mixed up."
"Syllables!"
"The letters jump around—they're so happy to get read!"
The extent of his love for trees and grass amazed and amused us.

Our district was sandy, so there was little foliage; only here and there in the yards could be found sickly willows, twisted elderberry bushes, or some dry grass hiding under the fences. If one of us sat down on this grass, the Dove would reprimand us angrily:

"What you have to spoil the grass for? Can't you sit on the sand? It's all the same to you."

In his presence we hesitated to break off a bit of flowering elderberry or cut a willow wand on the bank of the Oka.

"What you always spoiling things for, you devils?" he would say, shrugging his shoulders in amazement.

And this amazement made us ashamed.

All week long we collected old bast sandals in preparation for the sport we had on Saturdays. On Saturday evening when the Tatar stevedores were leaving the Siberian wharf, we would hide behind some street corner and throw sandals at them. At first they became angry, and cursed and chased us, but soon they themselves were drawn into the game. In expectation of the coming battle, they would also arm themselves with bast sandals— more than once they even stole our ammunition, having noted where we hid our supply. But we objected.

"That's no game," we said.

So they would divide up the stolen goods and launch the fight. Usually they took up their position in an open place while we yelled and danced about them as we hurled our missiles. They also yelled, and they would roar with laughter every time one of us buried his nose in the sand, tripped up by a well-aimed sandal.

Sometimes the game went on until dark. Petty tradesmen would watch us from the shelter of some corner, remonstrating for decency's sake. But the sandals kept flying through the air like dusty, grey birds. Sometimes one of us took a staggering blow, but the pleasure of the contest outweighed all pain and injury.

The Tatars became as excited as we did. When the battle was over, we would occasionally go home with them, there to be treated to horse meat accompanied by a peculiar dish of vegetables, after which we were served a strong brew of pressed tea and nut cake. We were extremely fond of these huge men, each one of whom seemed stronger than the other. There was something simple and childlike in their natures. I was particularly impressed by the fact that they never took offence, and were always kind and considerate to each other.

All the Tatars laughed irresistibly—laughed until the tears rolled down their cheeks. One of them (a muzhik from Kasimov with a broken nose and fabulous strength—one day he carried a church bell weighing twenty-seven poods off a barge and well up onto the riverbank) would howl when he laughed and keep crying:

"Oooo! Oooo! A word's a bird; heard the word—caught the bird; a golden bird!"

One day he sat the Dove on the palm of his hand and lifted him up into the air.

"Go on live up the sky," he said.

On rainy days we would gather at the little house in the cemetery where Yaz lived with his father. His father was a crooked, bedraggled creature with long arms and sprouts of grimy hair on his head and face. His head was like a withered turnip on the skinny stalk of his neck. He would blissfully narrow his yellow eyes and mutter quickly:

"Lord preserve us from sleepless nights! Oo!"

We bought a bit of tea, some sugar and bread, and a little vodka for Yaz's father.

"Put up the samovar, you rotten muzhik?" Churka would order.

And the muzhik would laugh and obey orders. While waiting for the water to boil, we would talk about our affairs, and he would give us advice.

"Look sharp—the day after tomorrow there's to be a funeral feast at the Trusovs'—ought to be a lot of bones left!"

"The Trusovs' cook collects bones herself," said the omniscient Churka.

"Soon the weather'll be nice enough to go to the woods," mused the Dove as he glanced out of the window into the cemetery.

Yaz rarely spoke, and would silently watch us with his melancholy eyes as he demonstrated the toys he had found in garbage cans: a wooden soldier, a legless horse, buttons, and bits of brass.

His father set the table with odd cups and brought in the samovar. Kostroma poured the tea, while the old man drank his vodka and climbed up on the stove, gazing down on us with owl-like eyes and muttering:

"Curses on the bunch of you—is it humans you are or what? Phooh! A bunch of thieves— Lord preserve us from sleepless nights!"

"But we aren't thieves," said the Dove.

"Little thieves then."

When Yaz's father got on our nerves, Churka would bawl at him:

"Shut up, you rotten muzhik!"

The Dove, Churka and I could not stand hearing him enumerate all the sick people in the district and conjecture as to which of them would die first. He seemed to smack his lips with anticipation and showed not the slightest pity. When he saw that we were loath to listen, he would purposely tease us:

"Aha! Afraid, are you, you little warts! There's one big fat fellow scheduled to kick off soon. Won't it take him a long time to rot though!"

We stopped him, but he was not to be squelched.

"And your turn'll be coming soon! Can't expect to last long living off garbage heaps!"

"All right, we'll die—and they'll promote us to angels," said the Dove.

"You? Angels?" marvelled Yaz's father and broke out laughing. Then he continued torturing us with loathsome tales about corpses.

But sometimes he began saying strange things in a low, buzzing voice:

"Listen, fellows, the day before yesterday they buried a lady with a queer history. I found out all about it, and what do you think? .. ."

He often spoke about women, and always in a filthy manner, but there was something plaintive and inquiring about his stories, as though he were appealing to us to help him think it through. We listened attentively. He spoke haltingly, often interrupting his speech to ask questions, but what he said always left irritating splinters and fragments in our memory.

" 'Who started the fire?' they ask her. 'I did,' she says. 'How's that, you fool? You was in the hospital that night!' 'I did!' she repeats. Now what would she say a thing like that for? Lord preserve us from sleepless nights!"

He knew the life history of almost every one he had dug into the earth of that bare, dismal cemetery. And when he spoke, it was as though he opened the doors of the surrounding houses to us and we entered and observed the lives of the inhabitants, sensing something solemn and important in the act. He seemed capable of talking the night through, but as soon as darkness drew about the windows, Churka would get up from the table and say:

"I'm going home—mom'll be worrying. Who's coming along?"

We all went with him. Yaz walked as far as the fence with us, locked the gate, and pressed his dark, bony face to the bars as he said good-bye.

We called to him, feeling uncomfortable about leaving him there in the cemetery. One evening Kostroma looked back and said:

"One fine morning we'll wake up and find him dead."

Churka often claimed that Yaz lived even worse than the rest of us, but the Dove objected.

"We don't live bad at all," he claimed.

And I agreed with him. I enjoyed the independent life of the streets, and I was fond of my comrades. Our companionship filled me with a great new feeling, inspiring me with the desire ever to help and benefit them.

Again I was encountering difficulties at school. The boys began to call me a tramp and a junkman, and after one of our quarrels they announced to the teacher that I smelled so strongly of garbage that it was impossible to sit next to me. I remember how deeply this hurt me and how difficult it was to return to school after that. The complaint was a mean invention: I always washed myself carefully each morning and never attended school in the same clothes I wore while collecting junk.

At last I passed the examinations for the third class. As a reward for good work I was presented with a Certificate of Honour, a Bible, a volume of Krylov's fables, and another book, unbound, bearing the enigmatic title of "Fata Morgana." When I brought these present's home my grandfather was deeply touched and overjoyed. He announced that we must carefully preserve the books, and for that reason he would put them away in his strongbox. For several days grandmother had been ill and had no money. Grandfather groaned and wailed:

"You'll be the ruin of me—you're eating me out of house and home. . . ."

So I took the books to a bookstall and sold them for fifty-five kopeks, which I gave to grandmother. I spoiled the Certificate of Honour by scribbling on it and then handed it over to my grandfather. He carefully put it away without noticing the scribbles.

When school was over I returned to the life of the streets, which with the arrival of spring became even more fascinating. We made more money now, and on Sundays the whole group of us would go out to the fields and forests, returning home late in the evening pleasantly worn out and bound even closer to each other.

But this life did not last long. My stepfather lost his job and again went away somewhere, and my mother and little brother Nikolai came to stay with grandfather. Since my grandmother had gone to live in the home of a wealthy merchant for whom she was embroidering a coverlet for the Body of Christ, I had to act as nursemaid.

My silent, wasted mother scarcely had the strength to lift her feet. My brother had scrofulous ulcers on his ankles and was so weak that he could not even cry. If he was hungry, he would moan horribly, and if he was not hungry he would drowse and give great sighs, purring the while like a kitten.

"What he needs is good food, but where can I get enough to feed you all?" said my grandfather one day, after a careful examination of the baby.

"He doesn't need much," replied my mother with a raucous sigh.

"This one a little—that one a little—and altogether a lot..."

He gave a disgusted wave of his hand and turned to me:

"Nikolai needs to be out in the sun, in the sand...."

I brought a sack of clean, dry sand and dumped it in a sunny spot beneath the window. Then I buried my brother in it up to his neck, as grandfather had ordered. The baby seemed to like it. He would sit there squinting blissfully and gazing at me with amazing eyes, consisting, it seemed, of only blue irises encircled by a ring of lighter blue.

I became very fond of my brother. It seemed to me that he understood all my thoughts, and I would lie beside him for hours, under the window through which came my grandfather's squeaky voice:

"It don't take much brains to die. If you were only smart enough to know how to live, now. . . ."

This was usually followed by a prolonged fit of coughing from my mother.

Nikolai would free his little arms and lift them toward me with a nod of his pale head. His hair was thin and silvery; his face was old and wise.

If a cat or a chicken would come close, Nikolai would watch it intently, then turn to me with a faint smile. This smile disturbed me—could it be that my brother realized how bored I was sitting there beside him; was he aware of the fact that I wanted to leave him and join my friends in the street?

The yard was small and filled with all sorts of rubbish. A straggling of sheds and other structures extended from the gate to the bath-house at the back of the yard. The roofs were piled high with boards, logs, bits of damp wood and the wreckage of boats— trophies fished out of the Oka when the ice broke and the river was swollen with spring.

The entire yard was cluttered with river-soaked wood which, when heated by the sun, exuded an odour of decay.

Next door to us was a small slaughterhouse. Almost every morning we could hear the moaning of calves and the bleating of sheep, and the smell of blood was so strong that it seemed to me it hung in the dusty air like a fine red net.

When the cries of the animals were silenced by an axe blow between the horns, Nikolai would frown and purse his lips, as though trying to imitate the animal sounds, but he succeeded only in producing a puffing little "phooh, phooh."

At noon grandfather would poke his head through the window and call: "Dinner!"

He himself would hold the baby on his knee and feed it by chewing up bread and potatoes, which he would then poke between the baby's tiny lips, smearing its mouth and sharp little chin. When he had administered a little of such food, he would lift the child's shirt, poke its bloated stomach, and say:

"Wonder if that's enough—maybe a little more?"

"Can't you see he's reaching for the bread?" my mother would say from the dark corner where she was lying.

"A baby can't tell when it's had enough."

But he would push another ball of mush into its mouth. I suffered from the shame of this feeding. Something rose in my throat, choking me and making me want to throw up.

"All right," said my grandfather at last. "Take him to his mother."

When I took Nikolai in my arms, he would moan and reach towards the table. My mother, so emaciated that she resembled a stripped pine, would lift herself to meet me, stretching out her long, fleshless arms.

She rarely spoke any more, and the few words she uttered were wrung raspingly from her seething chest. All day long she lay silently dying in the corner. I sensed that she was dying, and my grandfather made it clear by speaking too often and too insistently of death, especially in the evenings when the air was filled with the heavy odour of decay.

Grandfather's bed stood in the corner almost under the icons. He slept with his head toward the window, and before falling asleep he would keep muttering to himself:

"Well, the time's come to die. A fine sight we'll present to our Maker! What we going to say? As if I hadn't been working all my life—always doing something. And look what it, comes to!"

I slept on the floor between the stove and the window. The space was too short for me and I had to stick my feet under the stove, where the roaches kept tickling my toes. But my observations from this vantage point often gave me a malicious satisfaction. In doing the cooking, grandfather was forever breaking the glass in the window with the other end of the poker or the pole with which he pulled the pots out of the oven. It was strange and ridiculous that anyone as clever as he was should not have thought of cutting off the end of the pole.

One day when something was boiling over in the oven, he gave the pole such a yank that he upset and broke the clay pot and smashed the cross piece of the window and both panes of glass. This was so great a misfortune that the old man sat down on the floor and wept.

"Oh Lord, oh Lord," he wailed.

When he left the house, I took the bread knife and hacked off the end of the pole.

"Curses and damnation!" cried grandfather when he returned and saw what I had done. "Should have sawed it off—do you hear?"—SAWED it off! Could have made some rolling pins out of the piece and sold them! Devil of a family I've got!"

"Better keep your hands off everything," said my mother when he had run out into the entranceway.

She died at noon on a Sunday in August. My stepfather had recently returned from his trip and again had a job. Grandmother and Nikolai had already moved with him into a clean little apartment next to the station where they were to have taken my mother within the next few days.

On the morning of the day she died she said to me in a voice which was faint, but clearer than usual:

"Go tell Yevgeni Vasilyevich I want to see him." She sat up, leaning against the wall for support.

"Run quick!" she added, sinking back on the pillow.

It seemed to me that she was smiling, and a new light gleamed in her eyes. My stepfather was at mass and grandmother sent me to the Jewess for some snuff. She had none ready, and so I had to wait while she pulverized the tobacco.

When I finally returned to my grandfather's house, I found mother sitting at the table dressed in a clean lavender dress, her hair carefully combed, as proud and haughty as she had formerly been.

"Feeling better?" I asked, with unaccountable shyness.

"Come here," she said, giving me a fearful look. "Where have you been gallivanting?"

Before I had time to answer she seized me by the hair, grabbed a long flexible knife off the table and struck me with the flat blade until it fell out of her hands.

"Pick it up! Give it here!"

I picked up the knife and placed it on the table. Mother gave me a push and I sat down on the edge of the stove, from where I watched her with frightened eyes.

Rising from the chair, she slowly made her way to the corner, lay down on the bed and began to wipe her perspiring face. Her hand moved uncertainly, twice falling weakly on the pillow, with the handkerchief twitching in her fingers.

"Some water. . .."

I dipped a cupful of water from the pail. Raising her head with difficulty, she took a swallow, pushed me away with a cold hand, and gave a deep sigh. She looked at the icons in the corner, then at me, moved her lips as if in a smile, and slowly lowered her long lashes over her eyes. Her elbows were pressed close to her sides, while her hands rose to her breast, to her throat. A shadow stole over her face, then receded, leaving her yellow skin tight, her nose sharp. Her mouth opened in surprise, but no breath came.

I stood there for countless ages with the cup in my hand, watching my mother's face stiffen and turn grey.

My grandfather entered.

"Mother is dead," I said.

"What you lying for?" he replied with a glance at the bed.

Then he went to the oven and with a horrible clangour of pan and pole began to remove the *pirog*. I watched him with the knowledge that my mother was dead, waiting for him to realize it.

My stepfather came in, all dressed up in a white linen coat and cap. He quietly picked up a chair and carried it to my mother's bedside. Suddenly he dropped the chair and bellowed like a brass horn:

"She's dead! Look!"

With the pole in his hand and his eyes starting out of his head, my grandfather staggered over to the bed.

When they began shovelling the dry sand down onto my mother's coffin, grandmother wandered off among the other graves. She stumbled blindly over one of the crosses and injured her face. Yaz's father took her to his house, and while she washed the wound he quietly whispered words of consolation in my ear:

"Lord preserve us from sleepless nights! What's the matter with you? Mustn't mind a thing like this, am I right, grandmother? The poor and the rich, all go in the ditch—am I right, grandmother?"

He glanced through the window and suddenly ran out of the house, returning with beaming face and the Dove in tow.

"Look at this," said the old man, holding out a broken spur. "Just look what a find! The Dove and me are making you a present of it. See that little wheel, eh? You can be sure it dropped off some Cossack's boot! I was going to buy it from the Dove— offered him two kopeks. . . ."

"What you lying for?" muttered the Dove angrily, while Yaz's father kept hopping in front of me and winking.

"How's that for a Dove, eh? Can't get away with nothing with him! Well, it's not me but him is making you a present of it, he. . . ."

When grandmother had finished washing, she wrapped a kerchief around her blue, swollen face and called me to go home with her, but I refused. I knew there would, be drinking and probably quarrelling at the feast following the funeral. While we were still in the church I had heard Uncle Mikhail say to Uncle Yakov:

"Well, we'll have a good drink today, eh?"

The Dove tried to cheer me up by hanging the spur on his chin and trying to reach it with his tongue. Yaz's father laughed with obvious exaggeration, crying:

"Just look what he's doing! Just look!" But when he saw that this failed to amuse me, he became serious.

"Enough, enough! Pull yourself together. Everybody has to die, even the birds. Listen —if you want, I'll put some turf around your mother's grave, how'd you like that? We'll go to the fields now and gather it—you and the Dove and me—and my Yaz too. We'll cut the turf and put it around pretty—won't be another grave to match it!"

I liked this idea, and we all went out into the fields.

A few days after my mother's funeral my grandfather said to me:

"Well, Alexei, can't exactly call you a medal hanging around my neck! No room for you here any more. Time you were getting out in the world. . . ."

So I got out into the world.

□ □ □

NOTE

LIST OF TITLES WITH ISBN NO.

ISBN	TITLE
9788194914129	1984
9789390575220	1984 & Animal Farm (2In1)
9789390575572	1984 & Animal Farm (2In1): The International Best-Selling Classics
9789390575848	35 Sonnets
9789390575329	A Clergyman's Daughter
9789390575923	A Study In Scarlet
9789390896097	A Tale Of Two Cities
9789390896837	Abide in Christ
9789390896202	Abraham Lincoln
9789390896912	Absolute Surrender
9789390896608	African American Classic Collection
9789390575305	Aldous Huxley: The Collected Works
9789390896141	An Autobiography of M. K. Gandhi
9789390575886	Animal Farm
9789390575619	Animal Farm & The Great Gatsby (2In1)
9789390575626	Animal Farm & We
9789390896158	Anna Karenina
9789390575534	Antic Hay
9789390896165	Antony & Cleopatra
9789390896172	As I Lay Dying
9789390896226	As You like it
9789390575671	At Your Command
9789390575350	Awakened Imagination
9789390575114	Be What You Wish
9789390896233	Believe In yourself
9789390896998	Best of Charles Darwin: The Origin of Species & Autobiography
9789390896684	Best Of Horror : Dracula And Frankenstein
9789390575503	Best Of Mark Twain (The Adventures of Tom Sawyer AND The Adventures of Huckleberry Finn)
9789390896769	Black History Collection
9789390575756	Brave New World, Animal Farm & 1984 (3in1)

9789390896240	Brother Karamzov
9789390575053	Bulleh Shah Poetry
9789390575725	Burmese Days
9789390896257	Bushido
9789390896066	Can't Hurt Me
9788194914112	Chanakya Neeti: With The Complete Sutras
9789390896042	Crime and Punishment
9789390575527	Crome Yellow
9789390575046	Down and Out in Paris and London
9789390896844	Dracula
9789390575442	Emersons Essays: The Complete First & Second Series (Self-Reliance & Other Essays)
9789390575749	Emma
9789390575817	Essential Tozer Collection - The Pursuit of God & The Purpose of Man
9789390896578	Fascism What It Is and How to Fight It
9789390575688	Feeling is the Secret
9789390575190	Five Lessons
9789390575954	Frankenstein
9789390575237	Franz Kafka: Collected Works
9789390575282	Franz Kafka: Short Stories
9789390575060	George Orwell Collected Works
9789390575077	George Orwell Essays
9789390575213	George Orwell Poems
9788194914150	Greatest Poetry Ever Written Vol 1
9788194914143	Greatest Poetry Ever Written Vol 1
9789390896301	Gulliver's Travel
9789390575961	Gunaho Ka Devta
9789390575893	H. P. Lovecraft Selected Stories Vol 1
9789390575978	H. P. Lovecraft Selected Stories Vol 2
9789390896059	Hamlet
9789390575022	His Last Bow: Some Reminiscences of Sherlock Holmes
9789390896134	History of Western Philosophy
9789390575121	Homage To Catalonia

9789390896219	How to develop self-confidence and Improve public Speaking
9789390896295	How to enjoy your life and your Job
9789390575633	How to own your own mind
9789390896318	How to read Human Nature
9789390896325	How to sell your way through the life
9789390896370	How to use the laws of mind
9789390896387	How to use the power of prayer
9789390896028	How to win friends & Influence People
9788194824176	How To Win Friends and Influence People
9789390896103	Humility The Beauty of Holiness
9789390896653	Imperialism the Highest Stage of Capitalism
9789390575084	In Our Time
9789390575169	In Our Time & Three Stories and Ten poems
9789390575145	James Allen: The Collected Works
9789390896189	Jesus Himself
9789390575480	Jo's Boys
9789390896394	Julius Caesar
9789390575404	Keep the Aspidistra Flying
9789390896400	Kidnapped
9789390896424	King Lear
9789390575824	Lady Susan
9789390896455	Law of Success
9789390896264	Lincoln The Unknown
9789390575565	Little Men
9789390575640	Little Women
9788194914174	Lost Horizon
9789390896462	Macbeth
9789390896929	Man Eaters of Kumaon
9789390896523	Man The Dwelling Place of God
9789390896349	Man The Dwelling Place of God
9789390575909	Mansfield Park
9788194914136	Manto Ki 25 Sarvshreshth Kahaniya
9789390896509	Marxism, Anarchism, Communism
9789390575664	Mathematical Principles of Natural Philosophy

9788194914198	Meditations
9789390575800	Mein Kampf
9789390575794	Memory How To Develop, Train, And Use It
9789390896486	Mind Power
9789390896585	Money
9789390575039	Mortal Coils
9789390575770	My Life and Work
9789390896035	Narrative of the Life of Frederick Douglass
9789390575152	Neville Goddard: The Collected Works
9789390575985	Northanger Abbey
9789390896530	Notes From Underground
9789390896547	Oliver Twist
9789390575459	On War
9789390575541	One, None and a Hundred Thousand
9789390896554	Othelo
9789390575435	Out Of This World
9789390575015	Persuasion
9789390575510	Prayer The Art Of Believing
9789390575091	Pride and Prejudice
9789390896561	Psychic Perception
9789390575381	Rabindranath Tagore - 5 Best Short Stories Vol 2
9789390575367	Rabindranath Tagore - Short Stories (Masters Collections Including The Childs Return)
9789390575374	Rabindranath Tagore 5 Best Short Stories Vol 1 (Including The Childs Return
9789390896622	Romeo & Juliet
9789390896127	Sanatana Dharma
9789390575596	Seedtime & Harvest
9789390896639	Selected Stories of Guy De Maupassant
9789390575206	Self-Reliance & Other Essays
9789390575176	Sense and Sensibility
9789390575299	Shyamchi Aai
9789390896738	Socialism Utopian and Scientific
9789390896646	Success Through a Positive Mental Attitude
9789390575428	The Adventures of Huckleberry Finn

9789390575183	The Adventures of Sherlock Holmes
9789390575343	The Adventures of Tom Sawyer
9789390896691	The Alchemy Of Happiness
9789390575862	The Art Of Public Speaking
9789390896288	The Autobiography Of Charles Darwin
9788194914181	The Best of Franz Kafka: The Metamorphosis & The Trial
9789390575008	The Call Of Cthulhu and Other Weird Tales
9789390575107	The Case-Book of Sherlock Holmes
9789390896110	The Castle Of Otranto
9789390896745	The Communist Manifesto
9789390575589	The Complete Fiction of H. P. Lovecraft
9789390575497	The Complete Works of Florence Scovel Shinn
9789390896820	The Conquest of Breard
9789390896813	The Diary of a Young Girl
9789390896332	The Diary of a Young Girl The Definitive Edition of the Worlds Most Famous Diary
9789390575701	The Great Gatsby, Animal Farm & 1984 (3In1)
9789390575312	The Greatest Works Of George Orwell (5 Books) Including 1984 & Non-Fiction
9789390575992	The Hound of Baskervilles
9789390896707	The Idiot
9789390896714	The Invisible Man
9789390575657	The Knowledge of the holy
9789390575558	The Law & the Promise
9789390896721	The Law Of Attraction
9789390896776	The Leader in you
9789390896363	The Life of Christ
9789390896196	The Man-Eating Leopard of Rudraprayag
9789390896783	The Master Key to Riches
9789390575268	The Memoirs Of Sherlock Holmes
9789390896479	The Midsummer Night's Dream
9789390575466	The Mill On The Floss
9789390896790	The Miracles of your mind
9789390896660	The Mutual Aid A Factor in Evolution
9789390896448	The Origin of Species

9789390896905	The Peter Kropotkin Anthology The Conquest of Bread & Mutual Aid A Factor of Evolution
9789390896806	The Picture of Dorian Gray
9789390896271	The Picture of Dorian Gray
9789390575275	The Power Of Awareness
9789390896356	The Power of Concentration
9788194824169	The Power of Positive Thinking
9789390575411	The Power of the Spoken Word
9788194914105	The Power Of Your Subconscious Mind
9789390896899	The Power of Your Subconscious Mind
9789390896417	The Principles of Communism
9789390575787	The Psychology Of Mans Possible Evolution
9789390896615	The Psychology of Salesmanship
9789390575732	The Pursuit of God
9789390575398	The Pursuit of Happiness
9789390896851	The Quick and Easy Way to effective Speaking
9789390575947	The Return Of Sherlock Holmes
9789390575138	The Road To Wigan Pier
9789390896981	The Root of the Righteous
9789390575855	The Science Of Being Well
9788194914167	The Science Of Getting Rich, The Science Of Being Great & The Science Of Being Well (3In1)
9789390896011	The Screwtape Letters
9789390896073	The Screwtape Letters
9789390575336	The Secret Door to Success
9789390575695	The Secret Of Imagining
9789390896868	The Secret Of Success
9789390896431	The Seven Last Words
9789390575930	The Sign of the Four
9789390896004	The Sonnets
9789390896516	The Souls of Black Folk
9789390896875	The Sound and The Fury
9789390575244	The State and Revolution
9789390896882	The Story of My Life
9789390896936	The Story Of Oriental Philosophy

9789390896752	The Strange Case of Dr. Jekyll and Mr. Hyde
9789390896943	The Tempest
9789390575916	The Valley Of Fear
9789390575879	The Wind in the willows
9789390896080	The Wind in the willows
9789390575763	Their eyes were watching gofd
9789390575831	Three Stories
9789390896950	Twelfth Night
9789390896592	Twelve Years a Slave
9789390896677	Up from Slavery
9789390896974	Value Price and Profit
9789390896967	Wake Up and Live
9789390896493	With Christ in the School of Prayer
9789390575602	Your Faith is Your Fortune
9789390575473	Your Infinite Power To Be Rich
9789390575251	Your Word is Your Wand
9789390575718	Youth
9789391316099	A Christmas Carol
9789391316105	A Doll's House
9789391316501	A Passage to India
9789391316709	A Portrait of the Artist as a Young Man
9789391316112	A Tale of Two Cities
9789391316747	A Tear and a Smile
9789391316167	Agnes Gray
9789391316174	Alice's Adventures in Wonderland
9789391316136	Anandamath
9789391316181	Anne Of Green Gables
9789391316754	Anthem
9789391316198	Around The World in 80 Days
9789391316013	As A Man Thinketh
9789391316242	Autobiography of a Yogi
9789391316266	Beyond Good and Evil
9789391316761	Bleak House
9789391316778	Chitra, a Play in One Act
9789391316310	David Copperfield

9789391316075	Demian
9789391316785	Dubliners
9789391316051	Favourite Tales from the Arabian Nights
9789391316235	Gitanjali
9789391316068	Gravity
9789391316150	Great Speeches of Abraham Lincoln
9789391316662	Guerilla Warfare
9789391316839	Kim
9789391316822	Mother
9789391316211	My Childhood
9789391316846	Nationalism
9789391316327	Oliver Twist
9789391316853	Pygmalion
9789391316334	Relativity: The Special and the General Theory
9789391316389	Scientific Healing Affirmation
9789391316341	Sons and Lovers
9789391316587	Tales from India
9789391316372	Tess of The D'Urbervilles
9789391316396	The Awakening and Selected Stories
9789391316402	The Bhagvad Gita
9789391316303	The Book of Enoch
9789391316228	The Canterville Ghost
9789391316907	The Dynamic Laws of Prosperity
9789391316006	The Great Gatsby
9789391316860	The Hungry Stones and Other Stories
9789391316433	The Idiot
9789391316440	The Importance of Being Earnest
9789391316297	The Light of Asia
9789391316914	The Madman His Parables and Poems
9789391316457	The Odyssey
9789391316921	The Picture of Dorian Gray
9789391316464	The Prince
9789391316938	The Prophet
9789391316945	The Republic
9789391316518	The Scarlet Letter

9789391316143	The Seven Laws of Teaching
9789391316525	The Story of My Experiments with Truth
9789391316532	The Tales of the Mother Goose
9789391316549	The Thirty Nine Steps
9789391316594	The Time Machine
9789391316600	The Turn of the Screw
9789391316983	The Upanishads
9789391316617	The Yellow Wallpaper
9789391316426	The Yoga Sutras of Patanjali
9789391316990	Ulysses
9789391316624	Utopia
9789391316679	Vanity Fair
9789391316020	What Is To Be Done
9789391316686	Within A Budding Grove
9789391316693	Women in Love

Ingram Content Group UK Ltd.
Milton Keynes UK
UKHW040629290623
424267UK00004B/149